MW00630385

# Twelve Years Overseas

## An Educator's Journey Across the Globe

By Carol Hoffman

SAND
BEACH
PRESS
Baileys Harbor, Wisconsin

© Copyright 2021 Carol Hoffman

All rights reserved.

This book or any portion thereof may not be reproduced without the express written permission of the publisher.

Sand Beach Press
7672 Stone Ridge Lane
Baileys Harbor, WI 54202

Hoffman, Carol

Twelve Years Overseas: An Educator's Journey Across the Globe/ written by Carol Hoffman

Summary: After 22 years of public school teaching in Wisconsin, the author accepts a series of teaching and supervisory assignments in international locations. The memoir mixes vivid descriptions of people and places, interesting observations of cultural differences, and humorous anecdotes.
1. Autobiography 2. International Travel   3. International Education

ISBN: 978-0-9907888-8-1

Library of Congress Control Number: 2021904170

*"As you float now, where I held you and let go, remember*
*when fear cramps your heart what I told you:*

*Lie gently and wide to the light-year stars,*
*lie back, and the sea will hold you."*

*from First Lesson by Philip Booth*

*This book is dedicated to my grandchildren:*
*Theodore, Jamison, Madeline, Emma, Benjamin*
*and their grandchildren's grandchildren.*

## DISCLAIMER

The opinions expressed in this book are mine and they were derived by my observations and my relationships with other people. Remember that I'm a big picture kind of person and some of my details might be a little off. It's by accident not design. Remember also that my memory has never been close to eidetic and the older I get, the farther away it gets!

I changed the names of all of the children and some of the adults I talked about and haven't included many photos with children in them because I don't feel I can use them without first gaining permission. Funnily enough I don't have the email address of students who were 7 years old when I knew them!

# TABLE OF CONTENTS

# FOREWORD

— ·>> <<· —

I got to live overseas for 12 years. I lived and worked in Turkey, Kuwait, Belarus, Italy, and Armenia. I made these travels with my late husband Stan Ore. Together we explored, tasted, made friends, and learned what it was like to live and work in each of these countries.

This is the story of how that happened.

In 1985, I sat in the darkened auditorium at Appleton High School-West listening to Marti and Jerry Howard describe the year they spent teaching in a Department of Defense School in Stuttgart, West Germany. Could teachers really do this? Take a leave of absence from their positions and teach abroad? From that moment I knew what I wanted to do.

Here I was, a single parent, glued to the ground in the long, colorless winters of sweet, little "a great place to raise kids," Appleton, Wisconsin, with a teaching job I needed and had worked long and hard to secure. I was divorced and had two little girls in school. They came first in my life and I would NOT move them to any other school, city, state or country.

I loved them fiercely, protectively, and unconditionally, and they needed one sure thing in their topsy-turvy lives. I would be the one to provide it.

What I needed was a dream to keep me going in my life of the endless gift and grind of raising children plus teaching high school students with learning disabilities, and doing all of the cooking, shopping, and housework that our little family of three required to stay afloat. Maybe someday I could do what the Howards had done: take a two-year leave of absence from my job, work overseas, and see the world. That vision kept me barreling off to work every day, sorting socks, and stoically going to bed alone.

I had known about Stan Ore from my first day as an Appleton teacher in 1970. He was the wonder boy, high school principal at the other high school in Appleton. When he spoke, people listened. When he entered a room, people noticed. I was assigned to various schools throughout Appleton and ended up with Stan as principal for three years from 1981–1984 where I was teaching English as a Second Language to Appleton's newly arrived Hmong refugees from Laos. Our relationship was strictly professional, and I liked working with him, but I was just one of 100 teachers at the school. Aside from monthly staff meetings, I had very little contact with him.

Meanwhile I was working on my master's degree in special education. After 3 years at Appleton High School-East, I accepted a special education position at another school and left East just after I received the Educator of the Year award. A year later Stan got divorced and we began dating in January 1988. By Christmas of that year we were married.

Early in our relationship I had talked to Stan about teaching overseas and he also liked the idea. In 1998 the time seemed right. Stan had been retired for a few years. His four kids were all living independently. My older daughter, Laura was already working and living on her own. Melissa, my younger daughter, was in her freshman year at university and would be living on her own for the summer. After having been a single parent, I found it difficult to deal with my daughters leaving home. Going overseas seemed to be a way to take action.

We learned about a job fair in Cedar Falls, Iowa for overseas teaching jobs and made plans to attend. We put together the materials needed: resumes, college transcripts, letters of recommendations, teaching licenses, and a standardized test for teachers called Praxis. Stan and I also filled out applications for the Department of Defense Schools. We (OK, I) looked up all of the international schools I could find in Germany, France, Italy, and Spain and dreamed of going to those places. I read about getting jobs in Europe and learned that we were already aged out of the Netherlands as their top age was 45. (We were 50 and 61) *Too bad!* However, I was determined that we would go somewhere in Europe. How fun would that be?

The 25-year-old conference was well organized. I was nervous, but confident. We had our interview suits, our documents, and a strong belief that we could make a great contribution to an educational environment in a European country. As soon as we arrived, we pored through the booklet with the list of job openings and I got my first let down. Not only were there no job openings in schools in Germany or France (or Spain or Belgium or Denmark) for English teachers, almost all of the openings for all teachers were in places like China, South America, and the Middle East.

However, a Dr. Fred Thompson of the American Collegiate Institute (ACI) of Izmir, Turkey wanted to meet with us. That was our only message, our only request for an interview. Dr.

Thompson had openings for a middle school English teacher and a mentorship assistant principal who would work with the Turkish woman who was already the high school principal at ACI, a great fit for Stan with his long success as a HS principal. Dr. Thompson seemed to be a rational person who explained housing, travel, shipping allowances, and what a great country Turkey was. At that time I held the position of Special Education coordinator in Appleton; the job in Turkey would require me to go back to the classroom. In my mind, that was all fine and good, but it wasn't Germany or France! *Thanks, anyway.* I had pretty much written off the job fair as a great experience that wouldn't provide fruit.

Later that day, in conversation with other attendees, we met a woman who knew Dr. Thompson and had nothing but praise for him. She was a music teacher and she really wanted to go to ACI but there wasn't a music opening.

Another woman was ecstatic because she had accepted a position in Abidjan in the Cote d'Ivoire. I had to ask her again if that was the place she wanted to go. She replied that it was her first choice. I was gobsmacked. At that time, it would have been my last choice. I was astounded by the number of people we met who wanted to go to unusual places: Bogota, Colombia; Ekaterina, Russia; the Mariana Islands. What did they know that I didn't?

Toward the end of the day, Dr. Thompson found us, offered us the positions at ACI and gave us letters of intent. Could we let him know by 6 p.m. tomorrow? Since we didn't have any other interviews, we decided to leave the job fair early. We would talk about the job offer in the car and call Dr. Thompson when we got home.

We left Cedar Falls wiser and even more excited about working abroad, but I was not ready to let go of my dream to work in Germany or France. Stan was open-minded about our job offers and I tried to be too, but I was still stuck on that European job.

In the car on the way home:

Carol: "So what do you think?"

Stan: "We've got a decision to make.

Carol: "It's not the decision I wanted to be making."

Stan: "That's true, but this is the one we have. We'd still be going overseas. We'd get our foot in the door. You'd get a year's leave of absence. It's not all bad."

Carol: "Keep talking."

Stan: "What's the worst thing that could happen?"

Carol: "We wouldn't like the jobs and we'd want to come home."

Stan: "We could do anything for a year."

Carol: "True and we wouldn't have to face another Wisconsin winter. Do you want to go to Turkey?"

Stan: "Trust the universe."

I was looking out the window at the browns and grays of a midwest February day. So cloudy, so barren, so colorless.

We passed cornfield after cornfield. One field in the distance looked odd from afar. What were those odd looking black shapes we could see there in the middle of the field of spent corn stalks? Stan and I were both amazed to see wild turkeys feeding in the empty field. I'd never seen a wild turkey before, let alone six of them in one place. Stan said, "Carol, I think the universe is trying to tell us something."

In the next fifteen minutes we decided to say "yes." Stan called Fred when we got home and within a few months we were selling our house, saying our goodbyes, and getting ready to begin this adventure that started with 6 wild turkeys in a cornfield and a partner who stretched my thinking to accept this possibility. Not once since that day in 1998 have I ever been sorry.

TURKEY

# TURKEY

—⊷≫ ≪⊷—

On August 11, 1998 our 14 suitcases surrounded us in the motel where we stayed the night before our departure for Izmir, Turkey. Our house was up for sale and we needed to leave it spotless, so we cleaned it the day before and moved everything either to a storage unit or the motel near the airport. One car had been sold, the other given to my daughter Laura. Despite my exhaustion, I didn't sleep at all in that motel, in fact, to keep my anxiety at bay, I systematically went through each suitcase writing down each item in it while Stan snored peacefully from the bed.

Stan's son Steve came to take us to the airport and see us off. He would be our power of attorney while we were gone, managing our finances. (Later we loved to charge things and say, "Let's let Steve pay for this one.") We checked into the Appleton International Airport for our flights to Cincinnati, New York, Istanbul, and Izmir. My daughter Melissa and my friend Sue came to see us off, too.

Saying goodbye that day was harder than I thought. Having our friends and family was helpful, but when it came time to say goodbye, it finally hit me that we were really going to do this and I couldn't help crying. It was hardest to say goodbye to Melissa. She was living independently on her own terms. Though I knew this experience would also be beneficial to her, I felt a little like I was walking out on her.

On the plane from New York to Istanbul, we had our first real look at some actual Turks. (Believe me, there weren't any in Appleton.) These gregarious people were far from the veiled women in headscarves I had seen in photos. These were exuberantly social, confident men and women who made their way around the airplane like politicians working a room. They ordered whiskeys and played a kind of musical seats in order to keep talking to someone new. The man sitting behind us introduced himself to Stan and gave us his card. We were to fax him our phone number as soon as we knew it and he would contact his friends in Izmir to get in touch with us.

We talked with a young woman sitting across the aisle from us who was also American and traveling to Izmir to begin her two-year deployment there as a dental hygienist in the Air Force. We exchanged contact information and promised to get together after we got settled. (In fact, Janice became a good friend.)

Somewhere above Western Europe the plane started taking dips, dives, and bumps. I can usually handle one of those sudden drops in altitude that occur sometimes in planes, but by the third one I was afraid I would lose my lunch. I never did so, but I just felt inconsolably nauseated.

On this, our flight to our new jobs for the year, my motion sickness made friends with my anxiety, and I didn't care if we were going to Izmir or the Cote D'Ivoire. I just wanted to be on the ground. *Why was I doing this? What was I thinking? What a horrible mistake I had made.* I wanted to gather up all of the 14 suitcases, turn right around and go back to Appleton. But I couldn't do that. There wasn't a house to go to and I'd have to get back on a plane. *Oh, misery.* I looked over at Stan who was calmly reading his crime novel. As usual, nothing was bothering him. He was quietly looking forward to this experience. I tried to close my eyes and force this flight to be over.

By the time we got to Istanbul, I must have looked positively green. Only a person who has experienced motion sickness can know how much I was dreading the last short flight to Izmir. Yes, I could have taken Dramamine, but past experience showed me that if I had, I'd be sound asleep for 24 hours. How could I do that and make a good impression on arrival?

Luckily the flight to Izmir wasn't bumpy. Landing there was such a relief to me that I practically kissed the ground. Seeing each one of our fourteen bags emerge from the baggage area was another comfort. (It took three carts to get them all out of the baggage area.)

Dr. Thompson was there waiting outside the baggage claim area with Joel Tallman, a young man who served as foreign faculty coordinator (as Americans in Turkey, we were considered the foreign faculty!) It was nice to be welcomed so warmly, and we got ourselves onto the school bus, meeting Hale (pronounced Holly) and Bill (fellow teachers) who had been on our plane unbeknownst to us.

The bus ride from the airport to the school was hot, but it was our first glimpse of Izmir. Golden hills/mountains surrounded the city. Some palm trees mixed with a few deciduous trees, but the buildings which seemed to take up every available space dominated the landscape. They all looked similar: about eight stories high with living quarters up and a business or shop on the ground floor. The streets and these apartments meandered up and down the hills and looked like whitewashed adobe. The traffic was steady and busy, but not like the craziness that the books I read had described. We even saw a donkey and cart.

That I could board a few flights and deplane in a wholly different culture is something I will never quite be able to understand no matter how many times I do it. Plucked from little ordinary Appleton, here we were now, driving through Izmir, Turkey in a hot school bus. I felt like I was *watching* this odd scene instead of taking up space within it.

Our faculty housing was an apartment building called the lojman (lojh MAHN) in a residential neighborhood right next to the school. My stomach was feeling better when we got there. Awaiting us were five strong Turkish workmen whose job it was to carry our 14 bags up to our third floor apartment. I could have kissed them!

The apartment was hot and stuffy when we first walked in, and even though someone told us to open the windows, I didn't see how that would help as the outside temperature wasn't much different. Because I had made that list of the contents of each bag, I knew just where my shorts and flip flops were. Strangely, opening the windows really did help as we were on the northeast corner of the building which generated a somewhat cool cross breeze. We figured the little oblong flat to be about 1,000 square feet and completely functional: one large room, a small bedroom, and a small bath. The bedroom had a queen sized bed, a wardrobe, and dresser. The bathroom had a very modern looking pedestal sink, a shower, and a toilet. A small shelf over the sink was large enough for two toothbrushes and a box of kleenex. A built-in shelving unit in the large room right next to the bathroom had a mirror and lots of shelves. A sleeper sofa (sturdy but butt-numbingly hard), two wing-back chairs, a round, wooden dining table, two pretty beat-up bookshelves and neighbors who were American or Canadian were the feathers in this little nest.

The kitchen, which took up about six feet of one wall with two windows over it, had to be the most dysfunctional space ever. Even that day I decided I wouldn't be cooking there. The hinges on any cabinets that didn't contain a propane gas tank or other piping didn't open wide enough for an adult to reach into them without cursing the mad carpenter who created them. The stove had four gas burners on top, but the oven was electric. No wonder I couldn't find the place to light it.

The refrigerator was pretty large for Europe, but would be considered small in the U.S. at about five feet tall. A lonely ice cube tray, empty, lay in the freezer. In the various cabinets and drawers we found two sets of brand new towels (bigger than we were used to — and which we still own) a set of sheets, two pillows, two rolls of toilet paper, two rolls of paper towels, dishes, pots and pans, a box of matches and a two potted tea pot (tea in the small top part and hot water in the bottom). In the fridge were a box of milk (surprisingly good tasting on the cereal I had brought from home), a block of butter, a package of black olives, a jar of honey, a jar of very soupy strawberry jam, a two-liter bottle of water, and a box of apricot juice (nectar of the gods!)

The floor was wooden except for the terrazzo tile in the entry and bathroom. Another small closet close to the front door housed a water heater and had space for a washing machine. (Anyone who travels knows that clothes dryers are almost unheard of in every country except the U.S., and in a dry country like Turkey, the dryer consisted of an extremely handy rack.) A 5x10 foot patio extended off the large room. Seven windows let in light and air making the large room feel light and airy. Walls, cabinets, and fixtures were all white. Intricately painted ceramic tiles covered the wall above the kitchen and in the bathroom. All in all, it was a lovely place.

Dr. Thompson had told us at the airport that we were to be dressed and ready for dinner at 6:30. *OK, I thought, but what about sleeping?* I guess we would do that later. *After you've been awake for a week, what's another 4 hours?*

Stan left to meet with Dr. Thompson and I started unpacking. I could hear the sounds of children playing in the quiet street below, mothers in the neighboring apartments calling their children home, and people chatting on the street. *Well, Izmir wasn't so different from any other place in the world.* I also noticed how small that pile of our stuff looked in this big new world.

In addition to the street noises, in the distance I could hear a loudspeaker with a harsh voice saying something. It seemed to be repeating the same message and it was coming my way. Militant and demanding, the voice got closer and closer. I kept looking outside but couldn't see anything. If the neighbors were worried, the ones on the street were still calmly walking. No one was running out of their apartment screaming. Was it the police coming by in a cruiser to warn people of a gas leak and to leave their homes immediately? Finally the slow moving vehicle came down our street. The voice became more militant, more insistent. *Good lord, what could be wrong?* As the rickety old truck chugged slowly up the street, I finally smiled when I saw the back end of his little putt-putt. It was full of tomatoes. He was selling them! It's what they do in Izmir! "Come out and buy my tomatoes." The little truck stopped and I could see a woman from the fifth floor across the street lower a basket. The man took the money out of the basket, put tomatoes into it, and the purchaser slowly raised the basket.

At 6:30, 20 newly arrived teachers and 7 veteran teachers met at the lower gate of the school to take taxis to the Ascenseur Restaurant which was located at the top of a cliff. We had to take an elevator to reach this restaurant, hence the name.

From the open terrace at the Ascenseur, we got to experience Izmir at night for the first time. We could see the whole bay and the surrounding foothills all lit up. Soft romantic light, warm breezes, white linen tablecloths and napkins were the backdrop for this perfect evening. Despite my jet lag, I was awed. *Okay*, I thought, *maybe this could be my dream.* We sat at tables arranged in a square and began our first Turkish dining experience.

Luckily the meal had been ordered for us: mezes (appetizers) (pronounced like messes only with a z) were small servings of a kind of potato salad with peas and carrots, a red cheesy stuff with red peppers in it that looked like we should spread it on a cracker, and white yogurt with shredded carrots. Next came two little bread-type things that slightly resembled crescent rolls with some salty meat baked inside. Then, eggplant, roasted red peppers, green beans soaked in olive oil and lemon, a cream cheese sort of dip or cheese spread, a little sausage type of meat, and something they called American salad, loosely resembling potato salad with little cubes of potatoes and carrots and peas drowning in a mayonnaise/yogurt sauce. All of these items were very rich, a fact which took me several months to appreciate, later enjoy, and finally crave! Then there were three battered, deep-fried mushrooms and finally the main course of three kinds of meat and rice, which was a bit of a let-down after all of those exotic appetizers. Dessert was small pieces of watermelon, apple, and some other light green type of melon (best I've ever eaten) with sweet ice cream on top.

By this time a live band was softly playing. The singer, quite handsome, definitely Turkish, was doing some world class mimics of Tony Bennett, "I Left My Heart in San Francisco", Frank Sinatra, "My Way," and Elvis Presley, "Can't Help Falling in Love with You." These songs were odd for our motley crew who could have heard this music in any U.S. bar! We might have expected native Turkish music and dancing, but we got American oldies!

The open air and space saved us from sounding like a flock of seagulls, so excited to meet each other, so talkative about our experiences so far, and so sleep deprived. I saw a few cats meandering amongst our legs and at one point one of them made its way over my foot caressing my leg the way our cat used to do. I was surprised at its brazenness!

About 10:30 the Turkish coffee was next, but most of us opted out and made our way with the experienced taxi riders back to our new little abodes. It must have been 11:30 when we arrived home. Counting the night before we left Appleton when I was too excited and stressed to sleep and all of the hours en route I think I had been up, well, with my math skills, let's just say two weeks.

## SCHOOL TOUR

The morning after the Ascensur Restaurant, I awoke at 6:00 and for the first time in our 10-year marriage, I got up and Stan was still snoring like a coffee pot. This was a new world! The weather was unexpectedly cool and I was glad I knew where to find my sweatshirt in the luggage.

We met at school for our tour of the facility, lunch in the neighborhood, and a trip to the market. The school sat in a four acre garden on the edge of the hill overlooking the bay, three blocks away. The school's grounds were clearly the prettiest place on the south side of Izmir. The campus had a high school building, a middle school building, a library, an administration building (Greene Main Office), Hill Science Center, Shephard Sports Hall which was being built, a lunchroom, an outdoor amphitheater, and a new elementary school. The elementary school had just been added that year (1998), hence the larger than usual number of new staff. A large cadre of groundskeepers kept the garden-like atmosphere of the school. For such a dry summer, the campus was particularly green and flowery: hibiscus, oleander and lots of other flora I couldn't name. Morning glories grew up the side of the admin building. Many olive trees grew between the buildings. We saw our desks in our respective teacher workrooms but knew settling in there would occur a different day. Walking from one building to another rarely involved level ground. I was glad that I had done all those years of aerobics. We climbed to Greene Main Office, a real heavy breather, a place where I would sometimes go to make copies I didn't really need just to look at the morning glories.

## ACI

ACI, or American Collegiate Institute was founded in 1878 and moved to its current site in Goztepe, (GAUZE teh peh) a neighborhood of Izmir in 1913. The school was founded as an American/Christian missionary school for Turkish girls to serve as a cross cultural link between Turkey and the United States. It started accepting boys in 1986. Its school motto was something I appreciated: *Enter to learn, depart to serve.*

After our morning tour where we had been given a feel for the facilities/classrooms and grounds, we walked down on the main street below the school and went to a small restaurant for lunch. We learned the Turkish word for water (su [SUE]) and ate baked spaghetti. Once again Hale, a native Turk, was an indispensable resource with the menu, Turkish foods, drinks and culture.

Books should be written about Turkish outdoor markets. The complex aesthetics of produce arranging must be inborn in every Turk as each market could have been an impressionist painting. Bins of olives, perfectly stacked red-orange tomatoes next to pale green zucchinis, stacked above yellow sweet peppers, then plastic trinkets, electrical equipment, underwear, screwdrivers, and pots and pans. Renoir couldn't have done better.

Over the next few days we began to get acclimated to our surroundings and the country. We slowly explored our neighborhood, the first time with our appointed faculty coordinator, Joel, and later on our own. Goztepe was hot and the sidewalks were crowded with Turks. The main street bubbled with unorganized traffic doing lots of honking. Young women in high heels and tight long pants talked authoritatively on cell phones while navigating the piecemeal sidewalks. Men, older women, and children talked to each other while navigating the sidewalks. For us, walking and trying to take in all of these sounds, sights and smells was a challenge.

## IZMIR BAY

Sadly the Gulf of Izmir was polluted and not the clear aquamarine of the Aegean at Cesme, a small resort about 40 miles west of Izmir, where we swam and my friend Canan (JAH Naan) had a house. We heard that raw sewage was dumped into the Gulf of Izmir and that was why it was brown and smelly. I crossed the gulf by boat one time to reach Canan's Izmir house on the other side praying fervently the whole way that the boat wouldn't sink during its ten minute ride. It didn't sink, but I took the bus back. We understand now that the bay has been cleaned up since we left, and the water is beautiful.

## ISTANBUL

Three days after our arrival in Izmir, we flew back to Istanbul for our week-long orientation to ACI. The association has three schools in Turkey: Izmir, Tarsus, and Uskudar (right outside Istanbul). All the new people from all three schools came to the orientation sessions where we got a crash course in Turkish language, history, geography, culture, politics, and teaching in an ACI school.

We also got an orientation to the educational philosophy of ACI's teaching of English which was about as far on the pendulum swing away from rote learning as it could go (hence its great popularity among local Turks). Meaningful assignments, activities, literature, and drama were ACI's preferred learning tools, and with over 50 years of experience, it was clearly successful. An interesting practice required by the Turkish education ministry was that all students in the same grade at the same school had to have the same curriculum and were tested with the same test and graded on the same writing assignments. The teachers graded the tests jointly and for example, if a teacher was assigned to grade essay question one for the 7th grade test, he or she had to grade all of the 7th grade tests on question one. All the tests were all administered on the same day. This practice required a great deal of cooperation between teachers and offered consistency in lesson delivery and fairness in grading. After we returned the tests to the students, they were re-collected, put together in a bundle and saved for the Ministry of Education visit/inspection that happened sometime in the summer. A full-personality English woman who was married to a Turk and was the English department head determined what the writing assignments would be. These had been pretty consistent over the years, were time-tested, improved over time and some of the best I've ever seen. I never thought I would be comfortable using someone else's writing assignments, but I have to admit it was a huge relief not to have to create our own assignments with so many other demands and lovely distractions on our time.

In the afternoons of the orientation week, we went with Joel to various tourist destinations in and around Istanbul. We ate at a different restaurant every night and sampled as much Turkish food as we wanted. Dr. Thompson had told us in our interview that the school "wined and dined you in the beginning and then worked you like crazy," which was true. Later we *did* work like crazy, but that week was one of the best tourist experiences I've ever had.

### OBSERVATIONS OF TURKEY — WOMEN

Tolerance, both religious and cultural, seemed to dominate the role of women in Turkey in 1998. We saw about four styles of dress. As they walked down the street talking on their cell phones, young women mostly had up-to-date hairdos and wore skin-tight capri pants, funky, high-heeled sandals, and tight tank tops over their push up bras. Their overall look was dressed up and snazzy, not punk looking or green haired like American teens. We never saw any Turkish women in shorts despite the heat: long pants, skin tight, dominated. Older women were dressed in more sensible shoes with skirts and blouses, but always classy looking. A small minority (say 1 in 25) wore longish skirts and loose blouses with a headscarf.

Occasionally there would be a woman in a headscarf and floor length, dull-colored coat. None of these ever appeared in our neighborhood, but we saw some in downtown Izmir. The most extreme group dressed in all black. They were covered head to foot with only their eyes showing. They even wore black gloves and black socks. We saw only a few of these in Izmir, but quite a few in Istanbul. The first woman I saw dressed like this had an odd impact on me. I felt a mix of shock, pity, and the sense of something being terribly wrong.

To us it appeared that all of these women mixed with others of different dress. It seemed that whenever we saw a woman in covered dress, she would have children with her who were dressed in the most up to date, colorful clothing, including shorts, sleeveless tops and colorful little hair bows and barrettes. The dullness of the women's clothes seemed to be compensated for in their children's appearances. I'm not sure what the Turkish women say about dress, but some of the Americans in Turkey told us that dress for women is not a matter of religion, but rather a political statement. The more restrictive the clothing, the more conservative the political/religious view.

The Turkish Daily News, an English language newspaper is published in Istanbul, but we could get it in Izmir. From what we read in the beginning, some right wing groups were trying to get a foothold in the political structure. Apparently, a woman had recently tried to enroll in an Istanbul university wearing a headscarf and they wouldn't enroll her because of the headscarf. Unlike now, headscarves were not allowed at that time. She complained that if she enrolled in an American university this type of thing would be readily accepted and considered a right.

Of course, Ataturk, Turkey's adored leader from the 1920s to 40s, forbade the wearing of veils back in the 30s in order to modernize the country. He also banned the fez for men. Collared shirts, pants, and leather shoes were the norm for almost all men in Turkey.

In my American way of thinking, I felt sorry for the women who dressed in those long coat-like garments as well as the ones all in black. The heat surely made their garb miserable. One extremely hot afternoon (high 90s) while we were in Istanbul, a bunch of us were taking a dip in the hotel pool before our evening out. A darling little girl was having a delightful time, like us, in the pool. Mom, covered head to foot, sat in a pool chair watching. She looked so hot. I'm glad I haven't had to make this type of sacrifice for my political or religious beliefs.

## TEACHER ORIENTATION

Teacher orientation for our school began on August 24 with a general meeting for foreign staff and English speaking local staff in learning styles (how to work with the various kinds of learners: visual, audio, global, sequential), a pretty ho hum subject for me as a special educator, but new for Stan who had been a high school principal for 27 years. We got to experience our first school lunch on the day of the general meeting: three ground meat patties, three slices of fresh tomato and some couscous with ayran to drink and watermelon for dessert.

This, 1998, was the first year that ACI would have an elementary school due to a change in the law. The government was trying to eliminate the fundamentalist religious schools and the law was having an impact on how private schools could operate.

The faculty meeting agenda was pretty similar to all other schools we've worked in: a welcome back, an introduction of the new staff, a review of the process for evaluating staff, a list of graduates and where they were attending university, how many kids were on scholarship, and the testing schedule for the new students. The atypical thing was that everything said in English had to be translated to Turkish and vice versa. It was slow-going. Luckily the building was one of the three on campus that had air conditioning.

When the meeting was over, there was a reception with hors d'oeuvres, soda, wine, coke, and raki (RAH kuh) (the Turkish liquor of choice) all under a large white awning. White table cloths on card-table sized tables scattered all over the yard, and waiters in white shirts and black pants delivered appetizers (small bread rolls topped with cheeses or olives or was that watermelon?) We sat under a tree and some of our new colleagues joined us. The table had a large bowl of nuts on it as well as some chips that look like Doritos but were infinitely better. A few of the Turkish teachers came by to welcome us. What a relaxing end of the first two days of this new job. Soon we headed home and ate cheese sandwiches for dinner. This set a pattern that we would eat a hot meal for lunch and a sandwich for dinner. In the whole time we lived in Izmir, I don't think I cooked more than five meals in that dysfunctional kitchen.

We had been told that the first-day-of-school opening ceremony would occur at 9:00 sharp on the first day in the big outdoor amphitheater. Parents, local dignitaries, kids in freshly pressed white blouses and plaid pleated skirts for girls and gray slacks with white shirts and ties for the boys made the ceremony standing room only. There were more flowers than I had ever seen at a funeral. Bouquets, standing wreaths and sprays of peach, yellow, red, flowers with shiny, glittered ribbon popped out in the morning sun. At least 20 people came to the microphone to wish the kids and us a great school year. I think one of the people who spoke was the mayor of Goztepe. Others were nearby business owners and other

Izmir bigshots. It was jaw-dropping to watch the hoopla over the first day of school. I couldn't help thinking that we should do this in America: *Show the kids that they are supported. Let the teachers know the whole community is behind them. Okay*, I thought at that point: ***THIS IS WHY I CAME HERE.***

However, I wouldn't recommend that we adopt what came after for the elementary students. Because this was the first year of the elementary school, all of the younger kids were new, nervous, and as unwilling to let their mothers go as the mothers were to let them go. The elementary staff later commented that the mothers stood outside their children's classrooms all morning and the kids were crying because they wanted to go to them. The kids could see their mothers out the window. Within a few days, though, the mothers dwindled away and the kids, as kids do, got along fine without them.

## CLASSES

I really liked the 40 minute classes at ACI as opposed to the 50 minutes I'd always done in Appleton. Finally a school recognized that kids can't sit that long. I quickly learned the names of the 60 kids I would be working with. Natural exuberance combined with the hormonal craziness of 11–13 year olds made for some really wonderful kids and unforgettable teaching experiences.

Meltem was a teacher pleaser. She wrote in her journal how much she liked me. On every page! Tarkan stayed after class every time to talk with me, asking questions like "Ms. Hoffman, what do you think it looks like on Mars?" "Ms. Hoffman, did you watch the football match last night? My father watched it." Orhan was another story. He was a really intelligent young man but he, like so many other middle schoolers anywhere in the world, found entertaining his classmates much more fun than school work. I tried all of my regular and special education strategies for improving his behavior. I stood near him when he misbehaved (he would say things in Turkish the minute I walked elsewhere), changed his seat (no effect at all), talked quietly to him in the hall (yes, he would behave for 30 seconds), or walked to him and paid him a whispered compliment (no effect at all).

I met the 60 kids in various sections all week: reading, writing, drama. For example, on Monday I would have 7th grade reading, then 8th grade writing, 7th grade writing, 8th grade drama, 7th grade reading again for a total of five classes per day. It was like the schedule for an American middle school teacher in that each week, I taught about 25–30 classes. On Tuesday mornings I had no classes until after lunch. Each week there was a supervisory duty and an after school co-curricular.

Preparing for those classes was just as much of a challenge as in an American school, but since all testing and all assignments were the same, in some ways it was easier. It was time consuming, however because all of the 7th grade teachers had to literally be on the same page. We would all be reading the same short story on Monday, and on Tuesday we'd all be working at the same writing assignment. Patrice and Liane were my fellow teachers of 7th graders and we often collaborated to see how we would each approach the next short story or the next writing assignment. The two 8th grade teachers had been around longer. They told me what they were doing, and I adapted.

The best writing assignment was the last one of the eighth grade year. Students were to write a three part autobiographical essay. Each part had five paragraphs. In the first part they wrote about their favorite toy. What did it look like, where did they get it, what did they do with it and where was it now? I still remember Deniz writing that his favorite toy was a plate. He "drove" that plate all over the house, using it as his steering wheel. He was one of those eighth graders who was as tall as a six-year-old and had the smile of the happiest child on earth. Ece, who was a scholarship student, wrote about the soccer ball that fell off of a truck that was driving down his street. When the truck didn't turn around to pick it up, he happily took the ball home. He played constantly with that ball for weeks until his father, seeing that soccer had become more important than school, punched the ball with a pair of scissors. Reading his story, I felt those scissors punch into my heart.

In the second part of the writing assignment, the students had to write about the person who had had the most influence on their life so far. Who was the person, what relationship did they have with this person, where was this person now? Aydin wrote about his grandfather who had been such an important part of his life until his death one year before. His grandfather's death changed him. Aydin was as tall and lanky as Deniz had been short and muscular. Another student, Irmak, had a best friend who helped her through her elementary years. The kids who wrote about their mothers were the sweetest ones to read. "My mother doesn't tell me that she loves me, but I know she does."

Writing about an event that changed their lives was the final part. *What was the event,* we asked them, *what did you learn from it, and how has it changed you?* As in Aydin's case, the person and the event morphed together. He suffered through his grandfather's death and grew emotionally because he now knew that a person has no control over the lifespan of someone he loves.

In drama the kids practiced short plays for the first part of the term and then had to collectively write a script for a play they would perform at the end of the term. Getting the kids to work together was the hardest part of this task. Were they only children with no brothers or sisters to deal with? First borns who were used to getting their way? Nobody wanted to cooperate.

For six weeks, one group tried to hammer out a script and even at the dress rehearsal at the end of the year, they were still fighting and their efforts hadn't produced anything other than a lot of peacock prancing around the stage. The ones who weren't on stage were running around the periphery of the stage and peeking their heads through the curtains. Their group deserved and got a low grade. Because of the way report cards were handled, unfortunately I had to grade them for the semester based on their dress rehearsal.

At the actual performance, their play was the funniest, most cleverly screwball segment of the whole program. (Clearly they had finally realized that their play was terrible and they would need to get together outside of school to work on it.) The final version was a melodrama in which a very skinny man (a 5'10" 13-year-old who weighed about 100 pounds) is cuckolded by his girlfriend. He gets so mad at his girlfriend's new boyfriend that he comes to a meeting with him and pulls an enormous rifle out of his pants and "shoots" the boyfriend. Saturday Night Live couldn't have done it any better.

## BEST FRIENDS

In all of my years of teaching and working in schools, I almost always managed to find a best friend in each school. In Turkey, that was easy because of Liane (Lee Ann). In her first year of teaching, she was young enough to be my daughter, easy to be around and a kind of gorgeous, who-is-she, head-snapping beauty. She had very little teaching experience, but she bonded with her students from the first moment. They loved her, wanted to know everything about her, and she loved them.

She and I were the two new teachers in the English office so we stuck together from the first day. We were on a team of three teachers and our other team member, Patrice, had been in the school for several years. She was a dedicated teacher who spent most of the weekend planning her lessons. Liane and I (and Stan) would often get together on weekends to go around Izmir and try to keep our school work for weeknights.

An interesting thing happened to Liane. She lived in an apartment with another new teacher who had been hired to teach in the elementary school. They did things together and got along well (it would have been impossible not to get along with Liane,) but they weren't ever going to be best friends. When we first arrived, the school collected all of our passports to get the proper stamps and visas. Stan and I didn't care about this. We weren't going to be taking any trips out of Turkey for a long time, and having or not having our passports wasn't important to us. Thinking about this years later, I can say that the hardest thing about overseas teaching is getting the proper visas and permits. Each country has its own process and it usually takes months, but of course, I didn't know that then. Anyway, our passports traveled with Brian, the librarian, Kristine's husband, (a retired professor who came to Turkey to do research) to Chios, Greece for some kind of stamp and again to another location for some other official hocus pocus.

We all got our passports back sometime in October, properly stamped, well-traveled and all ready for their next adventures. The next morning Liane's roommate was gone and there was an envelope sitting on their kitchen table with Dr. Thompson's name printed on it. Apparently Liane's roommate missed her boyfriend from back home too much and didn't like Turkey. She had waited all of those weeks to make her escape. Liane (and the rest of us) were shocked, mostly because she hadn't confided in anyone and disappeared in the middle of the night.

After a few weeks, a new teacher showed up and moved in with Liane. While Liane would never have said it, anyone could tell that this new roommate was a better fit for Liane and they spent their free time exploring Izmir and its environs venturing out without surrogate Mom and Pop — Carol and Stan.

Liane stayed in Turkey for two years. From Turkey, she got a job in Tanzania where she worked for two years before coming to Kuwait where I was.

She's a darling and I wish we were still in touch.

## SUBSTITUTE HOURS

The school didn't hire outside substitutes. Instead, substitute hours were built-in to each teacher's schedule. For example, I was designated to substitute on Mondays third period, Tuesdays second and third periods and Fridays seventh period. If no one was out sick, these were prep hours. If anyone was out sick, I took whatever class they had at that time. The burden of these sub hours helped most of us to try to stay healthy no matter what! One teacher was out for two weeks and the rest of us covered her classes. We didn't hear until later why she was out, but the routine got old fast. She had lesson plans, but they were incomplete (third period Tuesday — discuss "If" by Rudyard Kipling) so we all had to spend time in preparation. Luckily we didn't find out until after she left for the year that she had gone somewhere to get her lips "done." She might not have left with them still intact if we had known!

## OVERSEAS STAFF

Overseas teachers seem to fall into three categories: adventurers, outliers, and income seekers.

Adventurers — those who wanted the experience of living in a foreign country/culture and the opportunities for travel that this lifestyle afforded. Stan and I put ourselves into this category.

Outliers — those who wouldn't have made it in a traditional school setting. Tom was a little like that. He was likable but not a joiner, had social skills not quite up to the bar, loved long distance cycling, running, journeying with a backpack, but he combined all this with heavy alcohol ab/use. One of the women was an aging hippie complete with gray-streaked long hair. Simon and Garfunkel music constantly flowed from her window. She quickly "went native" identifying with the local country/culture and forgetting that she was American, proclaiming the Turkish cleaning lady her best friend and seeking out other Turkish friends instead of hanging out with the ex-pat crowd.

Income seekers — those (especially couples) who had figured out that two teachers who lived a bit frugally in a foreign country with only food and telephone for expenses could amass a sum of money much greater than they could teaching stateside.

On a side note, although Stan and I were not in this category, we were unsure of our finances going in. Our ridiculously low salaries ($19,500 each-not even as much as a beginning teacher in Appleton at the time) didn't seem like much until we realized that the only costs we would have would be TV cable, phone, cleaning lady (about $5/week), food for breakfasts and dinners as school provided lunch on work days, and any other things we chose to do.

In general most of these three types of people can get along, work together, and do right by the kids. We were all overseas; we lived in the same building; we had the same holidays off, and we had many other shared interests. We are still friends with many of the colleagues we met that year.

## How Did I Become a Teacher?

While I was growing up in the 1950s and 1960s there were very few career options for women. Based on what I understood, nurse, secretary, or teacher seemed to be my choices. I knew I could never be a nurse as I could barely keep my lunch down on a normal day. Once I threw up on the bathroom floor before we were to get a TB test and couldn't even look at my own scraped knees without feeling woozy. I took typing and shorthand in high school, but wasn't much good at either one and didn't see myself sitting at a desk all day typing, answering phones and taking dictation.

During my senior year in high school, I had the opportunity to be a co-op student. That meant that I would go to school in the morning and in the afternoon I would go to a job. My sister who was three years older than I was, worked at Michigan Bell (the telephone company back in the old days) as a sales representative and somehow I got a job there, too. Thank you, Judy, for your outstanding work performance! I was hired to be an information operator. If a customer who had a telephone wanted to know someone's phone number, all they had to do was dial 4-1-1 and someone like me would get a little buzz on my headset and I'd say, "Information." The customer would say they wanted the number of Ron DeHaan on Brookside street and I would look it up in my special, more up-to-date phone book with a daily addendum of newly installed phones, then say the number. In front of me was a poster sized board with the most frequently asked for numbers like Herpolsheimer's Department Store which we were encouraged to memorize in moments when we didn't have a customer on the line. Working at the phone company was considered a great job for someone my age and a respectable career for a woman without an advanced education. There was good pay, benefits, reliable, indoor work, and the opportunity for advancement to information supervisor.

It wasn't long before I had mastered the tasks involved in this work that I came to find it soul-crushingly boring. In addition, we had to remain seated facing forward at all times except for our two 15-minute breaks and 30-minute lunch hour in an 8-hour shift. We also had to work all kinds of weird hours. For example, apparently peak times for people who didn't want to use their own phone books were 11 a.m. to 2 p.m. and 6 to 10 p.m. So when I worked weekends and summers as a full time employee, sometimes I had to work that split shift. That meant goodbye to the entire day! *If this was the best I could do without a college degree, sign me up for college classes right now.*

Even though I was already planning to go to college, this job quickly sealed the deal and kept me studying all four years. I would take no gap year, no breaks, and no dropping out, no matter what. I was not going to work at Michigan Bell.

I had no idea what to study in college and my non-college educated parents and friends didn't seem to either. Most of us were the first in our families to attend college. My depression era mother had always wanted to go to college so I was fulfilling her dream as well as mine.

I ended up majoring in English at Western Michigan University because I liked literature and writing and even hoped to be a writer someday. I got to my junior year and decided that I'd better get a teaching license because I wasn't likely to make any money at writing and wouldn't have had a clue how to do that anyway. A steady paycheck seemed like a good thing. I don't remember getting any career guidance from anyone at the university. Looking back on it, I was probably so naive that I wouldn't have known what to do with any advice they had given me, if they had.

It was the sixties and I was opposed to becoming a sorority sister. I was a bit of a rebellious hippie and enjoyed all of the sit-ins, be-ins, and presidential campaign speeches. George Wallace once came to our campus to campaign for President in 1967. I held a protest sign against him and a very angry Wallace supporter came up to me and grabbed the sign out of my hands, violently ripped it up, and stomped on it. I just quietly backed away, totally cowed by this seething bigot.

Drugs were just then becoming an in thing to do. I went to one party where there were some drug-laced foods to try. I think there were marijuana brownies or cookies. I was just watching, not trying anything, and saw a crazy-haired girl slowly pacing around and around the apartment where the party was. She stared straight ahead zombie-like. She walked like that the entire time I was there and never interacted with anyone. I decided drugs were not for me.

So, thanks to Ma Bell and my hard work, I got my teaching license. I even graduated with money in the bank as opposed to crippling student loans (BTW in that era, if you didn't have enough money for the next semester of college, you dropped out, got a job and worked until you did. I'm just saying.) My supervising teacher for my student teaching experience gave me the highest possible recommendation and I got a job right away. While I liked teaching, I never felt that it was the profession I was meant to do or that I was a particularly gifted teacher. I cared deeply about my students no matter where I was teaching and I worked hard, really hard, always going the extra mile and doing the very best job I could, but I'm still waiting to find out what I was supposed to do with my life.

In my teaching jobs I used mutual respect for classroom management. Sometimes I said it and sometimes I hoped they'd get my message without me saying it: *I care about you, I will work hard for you, and I need you to work hard for me.* I was never a screamer, a sharp-tongued meany, or an insensitive bully. The kids knew I cared about them and wanted them to do well. That technique had served me well until I got to Turkey. Ninety percent of those kids responded beautifully to my methods, but the other 10% needed a firmer sense of what they could and couldn't do. The only other strategy I had was to turn into a sharp-tongued meany for that minority. I didn't like it.

## DISCIPLINE

My first taste of culture shock happened at school. One of my two classes (the 8th grade one, imagine that!) with whom I spent 12 of my 25 weekly teaching hours started to become a major problem. The perfect storm of immature boys made *me* think about buying a plane ticket home sometime in early October. But, of course, that's not who I am.

As individuals, the kids were the nicest you'd ever want to meet, but as a group, they were a challenge. This group was excitable and intense about things that most other 8th graders I've worked with wouldn't have blinked twice at. For example, I had already made arrangements with an 8th grade English teacher in Appleton to do a letter exchange. Each of our students would have a partner in the American class and we would package up their letters and mail them as a group overseas. We had dutifully sent our letters and the day we got their responses was like 100 of those new high speed hand dryers were blowing at the same time in our classroom. I didn't even try to teach a lesson that day. The kids couldn't have been contained no matter what.

As I shared my situation with one of the teachers who had taught this group the previous year, she asked if Orhan was in my class? Well, yes, in fact, he was." No wonder!" she told me. "It wouldn't have mattered where they put him, he can ruin any class." This was a kid who was not mean, but he was excitable and loved to be the center of attention.

After I had exhausted all of my behavior strategies for Orhan, I asked the school secretary to call his parents in for a conference. Only his father came, bearing a huge bouquet of flowers. Apparently his mother was a doctor with no time to spare. Father was so sorry for any trouble Orhan had caused. We developed a strategy for keeping Orhan from disrupting his classmates by speaking Turkish swear words in class. I would keep a tally on my desk of times when his behavior was appropriate which I would report back to Dad. That strategy lasted for about a day. After another week, I called his father in again. This time he brought chocolates and again apologized for any trouble his son had caused. We made a new strategy. This time it was that each class where Orhan behaved appropriately, I would hand him a "ticket" with the date and my signature. Orhan would collect a certain amount of these tickets and his father would buy him some kind of computer equipment. It worked and at last, he behaved himself. I've taught special education, worked with almost all age groups over 25 years; but I had never dealt with a student as difficult as Orhan. I just couldn't reach him. The thrill of being in Turkey was tempered by this situation.

## GETTING TO KNOW IZMIR

When we first toured Izmir, our guide said that people have likely been living in the Izmir area for over 3,000 years. Atop a hill sits the remnants of a castle that Alexander the Great built next to the Roman agora (marketplace) where the columns and aqueducts left from that period still stand on the ground where those people did their daily marketing.

*Izmir Agora.*

Poking our way through the downtown bazaar in 1998 helped relive what those early days might have been like. The downtown bazaar is a happening place that fills one's senses with sounds, smells and colors of vegetables, fruits, spices, grains, legumes, bread, and all manner of other goods that men hawk in the streets. A man would stand with two dozen men's undershirts on his shoulders and shout out what good quality they are and how much they cost. Shoe salesmen popped out of their little shops to shout that the shoes cost *bir milyon, bir milyon, bir milyon,* or one million Turkish lira — about $3.66 at that time. Gold shops with necklaces, rings and bracelets, leather jacket shops, carpet shops, copper shops with hammered plates, Turkish coffee makers and decorative pots, tacky souvenir shops with paper Turkish flags, clothing shops with nightgowns, men's shirts and printed blouses for women, CD and tape shops which blared songs like "Un-Break My Heart." The owners would sit or stand outside trying to drum up business. Most wares are displayed in the area right outside the shop because most shops were about as big as small bathrooms and stuffed to the gills with packaged shirts, boxes, pots and pans or whatever was being sold there.

Determined market vendors tried English, German, then French to get a sale. They didn't leave us alone until we responded in some way. Soon we learned to say that we, dead ringers for Americans, were from Izmir and they left us alone.

## PAVEMENTS

Because we walked almost everywhere (or took the bus), we noticed the sidewalks and pavement on an hourly basis. First of all, there is very little green space in Izmir. Apartment buildings line the bay where the 3 million and some inhabitants live. In the summer it doesn't rain, and the air is basically dust. This dust enemy must be combatted at every turn. Shopkeepers in the bazaar had dishwashing detergent bottles filled with water and they sprayed this water on the pavement in front of their shops like little boys with squirt guns. Blacktop had been used to fill in any spaces between the streets and the buildings, and the asphalt butted right up to the wall.

Second, since everything is paved and the paving doesn't seem to have been conducted by the government (or maybe was!), no surface is uniform. In front of one building the sidewalk might be made of pavers of a certain type neatly, or not, fitted together while the next building has used another type of bricks at a higher or lower level. Some of the paving blocks were loose so that when we stepped on them, it felt like we might lose our balance. In other places, paving blocks were missing so we'd have to step on or over the dirt or step over a puddle in the rainy season. In front of a doner (dough NAIR) shop with its conical shaped meat cooking on a red hot spit, a large boulder stuck out of the sidewalk which had been built around it. People walked around this rock obliviously. In another place we had to watch out for a missing paving block with six large bolts sticking up out of the ground as if they had been holding something in place, but the something was gone.

In general the sidewalks were much higher than the street. Sometimes a handicap ramp would take us from the height of the sidewalk down to the street. Heaven help the wheel chair or runaway stroller that would go down that suicidal 70 degree ramp! To cross a street, we cautiously stepped way down into the street looking in every direction for cars, hurried across, (constantly on guard for a wild car) and stepped way up to the sidewalk on the other side. We learned that it was a good idea to cross with a native.

Walkers also needed to be constantly vigilant for what might be called "garden" shops. These are shops below ground level with five or six stairs leading down to their doors. No sign, fence or guard rail stood between us on the sidewalk and the edge of this low kind of patio. If we weren't looking, we could tumble right on down.

What all this means is that we spent most of our time looking down when we walked anywhere. Gawking at the shop windows could cause a tumble. Apparently Turkish people are meant to be shorter than us because we not only had to look down, we also had to look up. Some of the shop awnings were so low that Dr. Thompson at 6'2" once got a nasty cut on his forehead. I wondered if Turks found the pavements as challenging as I did.

## SIMIT

Another sight on Izmir streets and sidewalks were the men who balanced artfully arranged layers of simits (SIM its) on their heads. Simits are a little like bagels but skinnier and more dense like a circular breadstick about the diameter of a softball and covered with sesame seeds. A simit was a perfect mid-morning snack. I liked them immediately. A man who balanced 6 or 8 rows of these bread snacks on a board on his head walked around our street singing, "Simit." We could hand him the money (less than 50 cents for 1) and he would make change, reach up and hand us one from his board. This was so different from Appleton!

## CANAN (JAH NAHN)

Early in the year, I happened to be in the office when the secretary asked if I would be interested in tutoring the adult woman she had on the phone whose daughter would be marrying an American man. The woman wanted to be able to speak with her future son-in-law and any possible children who might come along. It sounded interesting to me so I said, yes, I would be willing to talk to the person. A day later I got a call from her son who told me that she was a wonderful person who, once she made a friend, would consider that person a friend for life.

Canan and I have been friends since that year (1998.) In fact, I spent the day with her on January 29, 2019. She and I were both born in early May and we share many bonds.

## LAURA AND MELISSA AT OUR FIRST OVERSEAS CHRISTMAS

Part of living overseas had to include a way to be able to see my two daughters, Laura age 23 at the time and Melissa age 20. I had been particularly worried about Melissa, as she had announced right after we had committed to our year in Turkey that she planned to drop out of college. Unbeknownst to us, Melissa had partied her way through her first two years of college. Right before we left, she told us that although her grades were fine, she had decided that since she didn't have a career direction she was going to drop out. I think my brain took a ride down my esophagus and tried to go screaming out through my intestines.

*Why, (why, why) would you do that?* She explained, "I'm not sure what I want to do. I like waitressing (goodbye lunch) and I can't see staying in college and paying all of that money unless I know what I want to do."

One minuscule part of me was wondering how she got so smart, but the rest of me was thinking *no, this can't be happening. How can I make her see what she needs to do?* I was crushed, but she was making sense and was not angry or childish. *OK, I'll support your decision* was my outward verbal response. My inward response was *how can I find a way so that she won't do this?* We had already made the commitment to go to Turkey. We would still go, but, oh, now it was so much harder.

Despite the fact that we would have to work, we bought tickets for my girls to visit during the Christmas holiday. The school vacations were scheduled around Ramadan and Eid (the two major Muslim holidays which in 1999 would occur in February and April) so Christmas was just another school day.

The year we spent Christmas in Turkey, I felt like I'd been chewing garlic cloves instead of gum. Nothing tasted right. Back at home in the States it would have been Aunt Ruth's coffee cake, my mother's spritz cookies, opening presents on Christmas morning, a big brunch with scrambled eggs and bacon, and all of us in our jammies. Instead, our Christmas tree in Turkey was actually a tree in a pot with soil. We strung it with popcorn and the few ornaments we could scare up. There wasn't a ham or turkey for Christmas dinner and we shared a party that day with everyone else in our building. There were dishes from lots of places, but as expansive as I want to be most of the time, on Christmas day, I wanted the comfort of my own family and the traditions we had developed over 23 years. Not to mention, school was in session and I was expected to put on a happy face and be there the next day while my daughters explored the city without me. Since ACI had been at this for a long time, their tradition dictated that the American staff had Christmas day off and the local staff had New Year's Day off. We covered for each other and got one day off.

The day my girls were supposed to arrive, I was a nervous wreck. They were flying together but had to change planes in New York and Istanbul. I was pretty sure they could make it through New York, but Istanbul was another story. *What if... they got on the wrong plane and heaven forbid never made it to Izmir? What if they ended up in downtown Istanbul? It would be impossible for them to find their way.*

We were at the airport early, went to the international terminal and waited impatiently. I paced, smiled at others, and tried to keep my panic at bay. When the prescribed time came, we saw that indeed, their flight from Istanbul had landed. The people had to board buses which brought them to the terminal. We watched many people disembark from the buses. I made "friends" with a woman who was standing next to me as I tried to keep my composure. I practiced my nascent Turkish on her. My kuzum (daughters) were arriving from America. She smiled sympathetically.

Finally, all of the people had been delivered from the flight, but my daughters were not among them. I almost lost it. I found, ok, grabbed, someone and spilled my story. Where were my daughters?

*Well,* I was told, *they were probably at the other terminal, the domestic terminal since this flight was arriving from Istanbul.* Well, where was the domestic terminal? He pointed out the door way across a huge parking lot about a half mile away.

"Hurry up," I yelled frantically, "get in the car"! We tore over there — as much as Stan was capable of "tearing" which wasn't much. We pulled up to the terminal and I sprang out of the car and into the terminal, running past the security guards. At last I saw my two daughters. *Oh thank, God.* Quickly a guard approached me and pointed me toward the security line where I had to put my bag on a conveyor belt and walk through a metal detector.

Finally, I could greet my daughters. After explaining that we'd been waiting at the wrong terminal. Laura said, "We were wondering if you got new kids!"

On the ground floor of our apartment building was a guest room available to whomever signed up for it. So Laura and Melissa stayed there. It was a pleasant little room with a refrigerator, TV and bathroom. It wasn't long before that room looked like their rooms at home: kind of torn from end to end. On the weekend we rented a car and traveled to Bodrum down on the southern coast of Turkey. We had so much fun together that we forgot about how Christmas just didn't feel like Christmas.

## RAMADAN

Most people have a basic idea of Ramadan. In Turkey in the late 1990s Ramazan (as it was called there) was an important religious holiday but only loosely followed in their somewhat updated culture. Ramazan is the most sacred of all months.

Muslims fast from sun-up to sun-down and deny themselves pleasures in order to become closer to God (Allah). As foreigners we were not expected to participate, but it was interesting to observe.

In Izmir each morning of Ramazan just before dawn, a man would walk around the neighborhood playing a drum about one beat per second. The purpose of the drum was to waken all Muslims so that they could arise and take nourishment before the sun came up. This was so foreign to me, but I loved the other-worldliness of the sound. Bong — bong — bong — bong in the cold darkness of that winter. No other sound. Children were exempt from the fasting so they still ate school lunches and as non-Muslims, we American staff would eat lunch too, but many of the local staff didn't go to the lunchroom during Ramazan.

## PRAYER CALLS

In Izmir there was a mosque relatively near our apartment where the muezzin sang out prayer calls five times each day. The mosque was far enough away that we only heard the calls that came in the early morning because the sound didn't have to compete with traffic noise. I loved the haunting chant of the prayer calls and tried imagining what it would be like to grow up in that culture. To make the first thing you did in the morning a ritual prayer to praise God and promise to be a faithful Muslim all day? What would it be like to pray five times a day? Would it change my outlook on life? Would I feel more holy?

Sometime during the winter of that year we learned that a group of feral dogs roamed our neighborhood at night. We heard about this but never saw any dogs. However, word got around school that these dogs would sleep on a nearby hill and howl along with the early morning prayer call. I didn't think much about this amusing possibility until the morning I heard it while I was lying awake very early. I heard the prayer call begin, "Allaaaaahhhhh." Just a few seconds later I began to hear the dogs all howling along with high pitched tones, deep throated howls and whiney mews. Beautiful.

About a week later we heard that the city had poisoned all of the dogs and I never again heard that wonderful sound that made me smile at 5:00 in the morning.

## EATING AND DINING IN TURKEY

### School lunches
While we lived in Turkey, we ate the most healthy lunches either of us had ever put in our tummies. Rice, meat, salad with lemon juice and olive oil. Vegetables and fresh fruit were standard. Yogurt and cucumber soup, which I first hated but over about two months came to crave, would accompany a stew with a little meat and garbanzo beans. My favorite meal was light green zucchinis with seeds removed and stuffed with a rice and meat mixture then a ladle of tomato sauce over it with a dollop of plain yogurt on top. At some point every morning the smell of chopped onions, cucumbers, frying meat or onions gave us some clue about what would be served for lunch. If the whole world could eat those lunches, we might not need doctors.

### Available foods
The grocery stores offered about five kinds of cereals, most of which were sugar coated like sugar smacks or cocoa puffs. They also had corn flakes, bran flakes, and several kinds of muesli. They had raspberries, but only in the summer. I taught the kids how to say raspberries and they said "grass berries." In Turkish it's ahududu, yeah, that's ah-HOO-DOO-doo. I loved that word!

It was hard to find ground decaf, but it was possible even if it came from Germany. (Starbucks, where are you?) I love hazelnut decaf coffee, but American coffee is just not "in" in Turkey not to mention flavored coffee that is decaf. Turkish coffee was widely available, but I'd be bug eyed electrified for three days and three nights if I drank any. Tea, tea, and more tea was the norm. Everywhere we went there was a tea lady whose job it was to provide tea for the employees or customers.

### The First School Dinner

On the third Friday in September the school sponsored a dinner for all staff and their spouses. Dinner was served on the top of the library which is a lovely kind of terrace area. It was supposed to start at 7:00. We and 4 other new teachers arrived promptly at 7:00. Besides the kitchen workers, we were the only ones there! After 30 minutes or so, a few others trickled in. That's when the first drinks were served. The first plates of mezes were served around 8:30. I almost ate the plates, I was so hungry by then. The main course came about 9:30 and fruit and ice cream were not served until 10:30.

In between courses was a lot of dancing (so like Greek dancing, we could have been in Greece instead). By 10:00 there must have been 150 people sitting at tables, dancing and eating. I learned that for any dinner event, it is better to eat dinner at home first and then enjoy the evening. Like so many other cultures, the Turks like to eat late. In fact, our bedroom window was about a car width from our Turkish neighbors' kitchen window. Most nights we went to bed to the sounds of them sitting down to eat dinner.

### Turkish Breakfast

Bread, olives, tomatoes, cheese, tea, and possibly hard and soft boiled eggs is the standard Turkish breakfast. When we were in hotels, that's what I ate. At home, I ate whole grain cereal with milk and fruit just like I did in the States. For me, it's more to do with digestion than local habits. Stan usually ate hard boiled eggs with toast, olives and not being a coffee drinker, tea from the dual teapot. We would head off to school together, the whole five minute walk, and say "Gunaydin" (gun AYE din-Turkish for Good morning) to anyone we met. Often we would meet the same people on the street and they seemed to enjoy greeting us.

## WEATHER

By October Stan and I had both caught Turkish colds which are remarkably indistinguishable from American colds. The nights were cool (around 60) with afternoon highs in the high 80s, with a fast cool down starting about 4:00. The funny part was that the Turkish kids wore winter jackets in the 60 degree mornings! In Wisconsin at 60 degrees, the kids are wearing flip flops with their shorts and the winter jackets have been put away for another year. The coldest it ever got in Izmir that year was one January night when the low was 40 degrees. Since I've experienced -25 degrees in an Appleton winter, I felt like I was playing hooky from winter, too.

## TRAVELING

### The Funniest Thing That Happened in Turkey

Sometime in October Stan and I were feeling confident enough to try our first weekend away with a car rental. Our destination (which had had many recommendations from local and foreign staff) was Aphrodisias, a Greek ruin, which was southeast of Izmir by about 2 hours. We planned to stay in a hotel there that someone had recommended.

We were nervous but excited to be exploring the country by ourselves. We had our trusty map, our rental car and a very few Turkish words to get us through the next 36 hours. We followed the map exactly and it worked! We got to Aphrodisias! We even used a shortcut that the map indicated.

A treasure trove of more Greek and Roman ruins than Greece or Italy, Turkey's historical sites are far more accessible than those in other countries. While the laxity of Turkish control over these culturally rich sites is a bit worrisome for long term survival, what a delight for newbies like us to be able to sit in the amphitheaters, touch statues, and clamber unimpeded over the whole site. The unanswerable question is whether it is better to leave the sites as is or strip them out of their original habitats and cart them off to places like Berlin and look at them under glass like in the Pergamom Museum. The way sidewalks were maintained in Izmir didn't give us much confidence that these historical sites could be protected in place. However, they were still there after hundreds of years.

At Aphrodisias we visited the amphitheater (similar to a small football field) where the acoustics were so good we could hear the private conversation of some people across the field. We saw the archeological dig being conducted by New York University though we didn't see any diggers. I guess they didn't dig on weekends. They may not be in a hurry as they'd been there since 1962! However we did see their set up: the large, carefully controlled grid in which they were digging, completely closed off to the few tourists who visited the site that day.

On Sunday we headed back to Izmir. We saw a yellow road shortcut on the map that looked like it would save an hour or more of driving. Since we had taken a yellow road to get to Aphrodisias the day before, we said, *let's try it.* We drove and drove and drove. We saw nothing. The car was starting to run low on gas. Finally we came upon a little settlement that had a gas station. They would only let us buy one million lira worth of gas (about one gallon). We understood from body language and finger pointing that they were saving their gas for tractors and other farm vehicles. We forged ahead.

The road got smaller. Bumpier. It became less a road and more a rocky river bed. *Should we turn around?* That didn't seem wise, what with all of the distance and nowhere to get gas. We came to a mountain and it looked like the end of the road, so we started to get quite nervous. What would we do, stranded out here? We had no gas, no food, no warm clothes and no way to contact anyone we knew. Even if we could contact someone, how would we describe where we were? What would they do?

The road, still rocky, snaked around the mountain. Still not really looking like a road at all, we followed it, kept going. Frustratingly slowly, the road became more of an actual road. I could unclench my stomach. We could see a settlement up ahead. A little town! We got out of the car in the center of the town where some old men sat on a bench. We looked helpless, and two of them approached. The older man was dressed in a 20s era looking wool suit despite the warm day here in this tiny crossroads.

We kept saying "Izmir?" "Izmir?" as we laid our map on the hood of the car. The older man was talking a blue streak. He barely glanced at our map as if it were the used wrapping of a sandwich. After about ten minutes of non-communication, he opened the back door of the car and got in. He sat, waiting for us to get in.

"OK," we said to each other, "I guess he's going to show us what to do."

We started down the road slowly with our Turkish guy in the back talking a mile a minute. We had no idea what he might be saying. Everybody says the Turkish people are really nice, right? Soon the road came to a T. We had to turn right or left. He didn't point or indicate in any way what we should do even though he was talking excitedly and loudly.

"I guess we'll just turn right." Stan turned right.

"Hayir (High YEAR), hayir, hayir." He shouted.

No other cars were coming so Stan stopped.

"Oh, I know." I told Stan. "Hayir means no. He's saying no. Turn the other way."

We turned around. He calmed down. We went another ten miles. He was relaxed in the back seat, still talking as if he was discussing whether it would rain tomorrow or if a diesel engine was preferable to the traditional kind.

Finally, we came to another T intersection and this time there was a sign that pointed Izmir to the left. We turned left. Oh, he had a fit.

"Hayir, hayir, hayir."

"You'd better stop," I told Stan.

Stan stopped the car and our little old Turkish man opened his door and got out, waving and smiling at us as he walked in the other direction. It wasn't long before we recognized the outskirts of Izmir and found our way back to our apartment. So much relief but so much joy and confidence that we had made it!

Yes, the Turkish people are really nice!

### Turkish Carpets

All of the Turkish cities we visited had carpet shops and many tourist locations would have carpets strung like laundry on street corners. Izmir had many carpet shops, too. A visit to a carpet shop was a kind of social event. We were welcomed in as if we were old friends. "Come in, sit down, would you like a cup of tea?"

Our favorite shop was called Motif, and Adeel (a DEAL) was our friend there. Adeel invited us to sit down on a stack of folded carpets and have tea first. A tea lady came with the tray of hourglass-shaped glasses of apple tea. As Adeel made polite conversation "How is the school? Do you like Turkish food? How is your apartment?" we would sneak looks at the carpets on the walls, the carpets piled four feet high all around, and more carpets folded and stacked behind those. The warehouse-sized room smelled wooleny, and wool dust bunnies floated all around the edges of the carpets. All manner of reds in the carpets, intricate patterns, and lacy fringes drew our eyes to the carpets on the walls and floors, a bombardment of color. Our eyes couldn't concentrate on one carpet without looking at the next one. And, we thought, *How can we find money and a place to put all of these carpets, because we must have them.*

Finally, Adeel would encourage us to look around and point to any carpet that interested us. His helper would take it out, unfold it and hurl it to the floor as if it were a pizza dough. Soon the showroom was covered with our favorite pieces and we were having a hard time deciding which one/s we liked best. Adeel made us feel like he would do this gladly all day long, just for us.

Most carpets are rectangular. Sizes are mostly 1x2 meters and are either large or small prayer rugs, though there are really large ones, too. Kilims (KILL ems) which are woven and not tied cost the least, then wool carpets, and finally the extremely expensive silk carpets, which, to me, sorry, look like Elvis paintings. After we'd chosen our five to six favorites, Adeel's helper folded them all up, found out our address and sent them with a driver to our house where we could keep them for a few days so that we would be able to choose our favorite/s. When we called him after a few days with our decision, Adeel and his helper came back to our house, picked up the carpets we wouldn't be keeping and asked for the cash to pay for the ones that became a part of our lives from that day on.

We own four carpets that we bought from Adeel's shop: a red Bukara with burlap fringe, a mauve, navy and cream colored Isfahan with cream fringe, and two navy and red Herekes with white fringe. I never get tired of looking at them.

*Me, Laura, Janice (whom we met on the plane),*
*Melissa and Stan at a carpet shop.*

## THE CARPET VILLAGE

In the spring, someone in our group organized a bus trip to a carpet village that was having a carpet festival. We rarely said no to opportunities like that and even though we had our surfeit of carpets (all that we could afford or think where to put at home!) we joined the trip. Buses in countries like Turkey are not greyhound coaches that we have in America. The seats are small and no matter how high you crank up the AC, it's hot inside. Sitting leg to leg with someone else doesn't help either, but the scenery: mountain passes, gravel hills and flat, green stretches of land were worth the discomfort.

The carpet village might have been home to 500 people, but that would be stretching it and would include newborns and the aged. Every villager had carpets strung along on top of cars and trucks, ropes strung between houses, or even laid out on the bare gravel ground. We went to someone's home whose living room was a 10x15 foot room where colorful, patterned carpets covered every inch of floor. What a contrast for this American who grew up with wall to wall beige.

I found a carpet I liked, but since we had already maxed out our budget for carpets, we were not ready to pay much for this interesting light blue, very unusual carpet with braided fringes!

This is one of those situations where I lost all sense of being a kind-hearted, caring person because I walked away and told my husband, who in situations like these had ice running through his veins instead of blood, to negotiate for that blue carpet. In fact everyone in our group wanted him to help them negotiate for their carpets. He was that detached. When I walked back to him after a stroll through the neighborhood, the carpet was in the bus. He got it for $60. I still feel guilty about it if I let myself, but it looks beautiful in the Florida house.

*At the Carpet Village Trip.*

## ROMAN TURKEY

We read that there are more Roman ruins in Turkey than in all of Europe. While I'm not sure if that's actually true, we visited lots of those historic sites, some of which are UNESCO World Heritage sites in Turkey. (There are 18 UNESCO sites in Turkey but they are not all Roman ruins.) For many of the Roman sites, we could drive to the site, park in an uncrowded parking lot and make our way to the site unimpeded. Sometimes there was a guy who would come and collect a few lira ($5.00) admission, but from there we could explore the whole site unaccompanied and free. We could sit in the seats of the outdoor parliament, walk on the ruins of residences and sing songs in the amphitheaters.

Our favorite Roman ruin was Priene where we would usually be the only tourists. We could touch everything, walk in what used to be residences and observe the pine trees that were growing inside what used to be the agora.

*The amphitheater in Priene.*

Didyma was another favorite for the same reasons and that one still had those enormous Roman columns. Two of us could stand on either side of one and not encircle it with our arms. One of the main ruins is Ephesus (as in Paul's letter to the Ephesians in the New Testament and one of the Seven Wonders of the Ancient World). It was quite near Izmir but it was far more controlled. There were pathways where visitors had to walk and many things we couldn't touch. Even so, it was impactful. Ephesus was a large city, still being excavated, which lends a feeling of what it might have been like to live in a Roman city in 200 BC. Walking uphill on what was a Roman street, at the top we looked down on the amphitheater and choked at the sight: a magnificent half circle of tan limestone blocks with three sections which can seat 25,000 people. Sting performed a concert there in 1993 (we heard that Sting was the last rock and roll concert there because the noise did some damage to the structure) and Elton John performed a concert there in 2020. The acoustics were better than any electrical speaker in today's technology market.

*Didyma*

Near Ephesus is the home where Mary supposedly lived out her last days. We could still see the black on the wall where she would have had her fire. I couldn't speak. Is it possible that Mary sat here to cook her dinner?

## KAŚ

We returned to Turkey a year after we left there so that we could see more of the tourist sites we had missed especially along the southern coast of the Mediterranean from Marmaris to Antalya. While the entire southern coast of Turkey is fascinating, our hands down favorite was a city called Kaś (KAHSH). My friend Canan told me about it. We will never find a more quintessential Turkish city. The beautiful main street is on a slight slope down to the deep blue of the Mediterranean where we stayed in a sea side hotel. I took a dip in the very deep, very cold, very blue water of the sea for about 5 minutes. Though I'm a pretty good swimmer, I had the feeling I was going to be pulled under, it's so deep. We got that whole

experience for about $20 a night including a seafood dinner served on their patio which was carved out of the rock at the edge of the water, right next to the ladder I had used to climb out of the water earlier. It was impossible to be nonchalant about that experience. Had we climbed aboard a rocket ship and been transported to an undiscovered planet? Tiptoed into a cave made of glass? Departed entirely from the human race and created our own new world? It was magic.

Visiting Ankara was also a thrill. We took the overnight train from Izmir and arrived in Ankara in the morning. While I can't say I slept much on the train, (I kept feeling I would fall out of bed because it was a pretty wobbly ride) we had a guided tour there that hit the highlights of Turkey's capital city. Our favorite was a museum that is said to contain some of the oldest objects in the world. I was fascinated that some of the items are still common today: bracelets, coins, and hair adornments that looked like combs. "Plus ça change, plus c'est la même chose," right? (The more things change, the more they stay the same.)

Pamukkale is the sight seen most often on travel brochures for Turkey, the calcium encrusted thermal pools that look like mini-swimming pools surrounded by cotton (the word for cotton is pamukkale in Turkish). People are allowed to swim in these pools, however, environmentally it's better not to. We visited there and found an indoor hot spring pool that was much more relaxing.

## LEAVING TURKEY
Going to Turkey was wonderful, difficult, fascinating, eye-opening and sometimes overwhelming. Because it was my first experience living overseas, I did have trouble with culture shock and homesickness. I got tired of the uneven sidewalks, the holes that nobody fixed, and the strain of

having to adjust to everything new. But it was also a lesson that helped me in future overseas experiences.

When we left Turkey, I didn't know if we would ever live overseas again, but I reflected that if we had been able to come home for Christmas, I think my attitude would have been much different. Sometimes we just needed to get out of our situation and take a breather. Also, I learned that overseas teachers didn't have to make all of their focus after school hours be about taking advantage of their setting. Sometimes it was just fun to hang out with other Americans in the shelter of our apartments. Another thing I appreciated later was Skype which we didn't have in Turkey (we barely had email) and in later overseas experiences, when we got connected so that we could call our families and they could call us, I felt a calm reassurance that I hadn't felt in Turkey.

Stan said many times in those early months after we accepted the jobs in Turkey that I was like the dog who was always barking at cars and now that the car stopped for me, I didn't quite know what to do. He was right, but what I think now is that without his encouragement and steady keel, I wouldn't have taken this leap. Stan showed me a path where I could step into the wide universe and fly into the star dotted sky. He nudged me toward this first step and held my hand as we explored the light and dark of the strangeness of this new experience together. The gift of these first steps was one of many in our five part adventure.

# KUWAIT

—•>} {<•—

## LET'S TRY RETIREMENT

Toward the end of the year in Turkey, I had to admit to myself that I wasn't enjoying being back in the classroom again after having spent three years in a semi-administrative role in Appleton. The more Stan and I talked about not staying for a second year, the more I knew that's what I wanted to do. Another part of the reason we left Turkey after one year was because we knew that the school was having some financial difficulties. One less salary to pay might help them. I would have to be replaced, but Stan wouldn't. Stan's job was to mentor the high school principal and he felt that she had been an apt pupil who was ready to fly free. Still another reason was that I had been working for other people's kids for so long, I wondered if maybe it was time for me to work for myself. When I made that autobiography writing assignment for our 8th graders, I wondered if I could take the time to write my story, too.

So we would leave. I felt relieved from the first moment we made the decision. After my first job overseas, I felt ready to stop. *Maybe it was time for me to retire too.* I gave up my job in Appleton and jumped into retirement.

We came back to Florida because that's the only home we had at the time. By October, though, I was working as a part time English teacher for adults who were learning English. Apparently, I wasn't at all ready for this lifestyle change. After about 2 weeks, I started looking for a permanent job. Being at home all day with Stan was not at all like I had envisioned retirement. I felt dependent on Stan and his income. Not only that, when a husband and wife are first retired, they learn things about each other that they didn't necessarily want to know. It turned out Stan was completely happy to stay home, go out to lunch occasionally but mostly sit in his comfy chair. I needed much more activity. I tried getting involved in community activities, but I was a good 20 years younger than all of the people I was interacting with in Florida. By January, I had a full-time job in Sarasota as a high school special ed teacher.

With me working, Stan had the house to himself all day and could do whatever he wanted. I had my own income and things to talk about at the dinner table. Life moved along quite smoothly. He cooked dinner for me every night. Though he never said it, I think he was relieved too! I kept that job for a year and a half.

Even though I had been ready to leave Turkey after one year, the seed for overseas adventure had been planted and taken root. During my second year in Sarasota, I took personal time so that Stan and I could go to a job fair in England. Though we enjoyed the trip, and Stan was always ready to travel abroad, it didn't result in a job offer. I fought my own demons over that one. Finally, in June at a job fair in Philadelphia, I accepted a job in Kuwait. Stan was happy to accompany me to Kuwait, but he didn't want to work anymore. I had already resigned my position in Sarasota, breaking my steadfast rule that I would never quit a job until I had signed a contract for the next one, but I couldn't have done that job for another year, especially since I didn't really have to. So we were both excited to travel to the Middle East and see what it had to offer.

In Kuwait I would hold a position at a Center that evaluated students for learning disabilities. I had three responsibilities: administer diagnostic achievement assessments to students with suspected learning disabilities, supervise the teaching of English in the small school (50 Kuwaiti students with learning disabilities) connected with the Center, and in the late afternoon supervise the tutoring of students who came to the Center from other international schools.

Here's a cruel irony that happened. A few weeks after I accepted the job in Kuwait, I received a call from the Department of Defense Schools. Was I interested in teaching English and Humanities in Belgium? Yes, I was, but I couldn't because I had already committed to the position in Kuwait. In the end, though, I'm not sorry. For me, Kuwait was an all-encompassing, otherworld life experience that I cherish to this day. Yes, I could have ditched the Kuwait job, but that's not the person I am. Plus, if I had accepted the other job, my life would have gone another way and I like the way it went.

The Center held a summer seminar at a Massachusetts university that was aligned with the school. An American professor there was the liaison, and she invited me to attend and there I met four of the administrative staff at the Center. We worked together for three days and I got a great opportunity to meet the people with whom I would be working. Mr. Salem (SAAH lem), the school principal was Palestinian, Laila (LAY luh) the school psychologist was Lebanese, Majda, (MAHJ duh) the elementary principal was Kuwaiti, and Mr. Mowafak, (MOO ah fahk — yes, very hard to say) the mathematics diagnostician was from Syria.

Spending time with these people was a great introduction to the job, the culture, the people and the country. I felt like I would be going to a place where I had friends. A month later I left for Kuwait from Green Bay because by then we had another condo in Door County. Stan didn't travel with me because his visa hadn't arrived. He would have to wait at least another week for it.

## ARRIVAL

I left for Kuwait on September 9, 2001. I flew from Wisconsin to New York where Laura and her boyfriend Christopher met me at La Guardia. They visited with me in the airport (when you could still do things like that) until it was time for my flight to leave. Walking away from them, I felt like I left my rib cage behind. Waiting alone in the gate area for my flight, other parts of my physique were missing too. For the first time since I had accepted the job, the bottom of my confidence fell out. My stomach felt like it had dropped out of my body and the rest of me was liquefying and swirling down the same drain. What was I doing? I'd spoken with the person who held the job the previous year, and she had nothing but positive things to say about the school and the country. Where were her encouraging words now? I didn't think of not going, but I felt like a balloon that had popped and become a withered piece of pink latex lying on the floor.

Once on the plane, I had a routine to follow: arrange the pillow, check the TV for possible movies, stow my book, get out one of my crossword puzzles and pen.

On this long flight to Kuwait, my take off routine puffed my little balloon with air and my self confidence started blowing back in.

After 13 punishing hours, I landed in Kuwait in a jet-lagged fog. I noticed that the deplaning passengers who had almost all been in western style dress on take-off were now dressed in long black robes and hijabs (hih JOBS) for the women (at first glance I thought, Nuns?) and white robes with keffiyeh (KEH fih yuh) headdresses for men. I had failed to notice how that change had come about, but I was now a stand out in western dress.

I stumbled through passport control and though I was sleep deprived, I saw a man with a paper that said my name. He guided me to the exit and when the doors opened to the sunshine, the heat took my breath away. It was a giant oven and I was the chicken.

My greeter's name was Ashraf (AAHSH ruf). He took me to my apartment and in his limited English showed me around, how to work things and how to contact Stan with a phone card. Soon he left me there telling me that he would pick me up at 9:30 the next morning.

The apartment was lovely, modern and cool. There were three bedrooms: a queen size bed in the master, another bedroom with twin beds and an office with a desk. The master bath had a bathtub, sink, toilet and bidet; the other a shower. The living room was about 10x20 with marble floors. A sofa across from the television was comfortable and the phone was next to the sofa. Two side chairs were on the same wall as the TV. Later this is where I would have my cup of tea and two cookies every afternoon after lunch (no wonder I gained weight that year). A 10-seater dining room table with 6 chairs was at the other end of the room with a large sideboard on the short wall. The furniture could have been in any living room in America.

The door of another bathroom, which we hardly ever used (toilet, sink and washing machine) opened off that wall. The kitchen faced southwest and was always hotter than the other rooms. A drain in the middle of the floor assisted our Filipina cleaner, Sabastina who would mop the floor and then dump her bucket onto the floor which was surrounded by a one-inch lip that held in the water. How useful to have the entire kitchen floor a kind of shallow kitchen sink! The windows in this room were so high up that I couldn't look out unless I stood on a chair. So there was natural light, but no one was going to be able to look into that room from anywhere. If I took a plate from the cabinets on the outside walls, it was warm.

After I took a really long shower, I unpacked all of those items I had chosen to bring and they made a small pile on the large bed. I haven't had a first day in any country where I've lived without feeling very small after I empty my suitcases. The things I pack so carefully loom large at home and shrink when I arrive in the new apartment. In fact, I learned to carry a tube filled with posters to put on the walls so my new home didn't seem so alien.

Sliced meats, cheese, tomatoes, mango juice (more nectar of the gods), eggs, cereal, milk and bread had been provided, even shower gel. I ate a small dinner, used the phone card to call Stan and climbed into the bed.

On the next morning, September 11, I was awakened early by prayer calls. First I could hear two or three coming from different mosques that were pretty close. Since Muslims are required to pray 5 times a day, a mosque has to be within walking distance of every neighborhood. I didn't get up as it was still dark outside. About 15 minutes later another round of prayer calls rang out "Allaaaaaah." I never tired of hearing that haunting sound and learned later that the reason for

*The view from my apartment*

prayer calls at different times was a result of two branches of Islam, the Shia and the Sunni, which hold different beliefs about the timing of prayer calls. Soon I was up, showering again and getting ready for my first day at The Center.

As scheduled, Ashraf was there at 9:30 sharp and he drove me to work on the Kuwait expressways. I lived in a section of Kuwait called Hawalli (HOW wall ee) a good place to be. Right down the street from me were two other International schools and many expats lived in the vicinity.

It was teacher orientation week and the students would be arriving next week. I met the teachers that first day. Two of the four English teachers in our school were American. Suzanne's husband was a pilot who had worked for TWA before it went under. Now he was employed as a pilot by a local sheik so that the sheik could travel wherever and whenever he wanted on his private jet. I found it strange that Suzanne and her husband had converted to Islam, but we rarely spoke about it. She loosely equated Islam to her strict Catholic upbringing. She wore the long skirts, loose blouses and the type of headscarf that many Arab women wear. Jo was from Texas and had met her Kuwaiti husband when he was there at the university. They now had four daughters in middle school, high school and university. She dressed somewhat conservatively but didn't cover her head. Talal (tuh LAL) and Hind (pronounced like the beginning of the word Hindu) were from Syria. They both had excellent English skills. Talal, his wife and their two babies lived in Kuwait. Hind's Syrian doctor husband and their two daughters were still in Syria. Hind scandalized Suzanne with her tight pants and low cut shirts, and there were definitely no head coverings for Hind.

I met Mrs. Amani, the director of the Center that first morning and gave her the jar of homemade cherry jam which I had so carefully bubble-wrapped and brought in my carry-on. As a person from Door County, a jar of homemade jam is the most generous gift I could give. She said, "Thank you," while looking at it as if it were a pile of grass that she would quietly slide into the garbage after I left the room. I was expecting a different reaction.

The school occupied two buildings on either side of a quiet road at the north end of Kuwait City and were about a football field apart. One building contained 12 small classrooms, a large teacher workroom where each teacher had a desk, an additional special room for the four English teachers, the principal's office, and an enclosed, tiled play area. Since no toys or playground equipment whatsoever were available, the kids basically chased each other around during breaks.

My office was in the other building where the diagnostic work was done. Normally school was in session until 1:00 when the kids went home for the day. Students who came for tutoring were generally from other schools and arrived at 4:00, 5:00 or 6:00. So I was back to the split shifts I hadn't enjoyed as a Michigan Bell employee, but since I knew it wasn't forever,

I adapted. I would go home at 1:00, have some lunch, enjoy my cup of tea and cookies and leave for work again at 3:30. I could have hired others to do the tutoring, as there wasn't too much of it but I had nothing else to do and I quite enjoyed it.

In the mornings I would spend some time at the school, talk to the teachers, and see what was happening. If I had a student to assess, I did that in the morning also, but I never did more than two to three students in a month.

After my first school day, Ashraf took me home and made plans to pick me up the next day again at 9:30. I had learned that there was a taxi company on the ground floor of my building with a great driver named Ali who would take me wherever I wanted to go. As soon as I ate dinner, I went down to see if Ali could take me to the Sultan Center, an American-type shopping mall. At least this first time, I wanted to buy groceries where I might recognize some staples and begin to stock my kitchen.

In the car on the way to the Sultan Center, I learned that Ali was from Bangladesh where he had a wife and 4 children. I told him that I had lived in a Muslim country, Turkey, and that I already liked Kuwait and thought my time here would be very interesting. He dropped me at the mall and promised to return in two hours at 7:00 p.m. Kuwait time to pick me up, exactly right here. It was a leap of faith for me. I had no mobile phone, no way to communicate where I lived, and I had never been to this place before.

The Sultan center grocery store was a delight. Stacks and stacks of fresh green mangoes, other fruits and vegetables stood in colorful piles throughout the large produce department. There were fresh baked breads, canned goods, peanut butter, (they even had Jif) jam, some kinds of cereal like corn flakes and corn puffs. No other country has as much breakfast cereal as America! They also had lamb — lots of it. Eating well would not be a problem here.

I was having a great time exploring the many wonders of this almost Walmart-like store and time was flying by. As I neared the check out, I overheard some Americans talking to each other. One was wearing a military uniform, clearly an officer, and he was talking to another young man in civilian clothes.

"Hey, I just heard that a plane crashed into the World Trade Center."

I was thinking, OK, that seems a little far-fetched, but the World Trade Center has been bombed before, so I wasn't worried. I checked out my groceries and went to wait in the place Ali had directed me to.

Soon Ali was there, right on time to pick me up. He took my groceries and put them in the trunk of his taxi.

"Oh, miss, I so sorry. I see the planes. I see the building go down."

At the stoplight he used his hand as an ersatz plane and his other arm as a tall building and demonstrated how the plane smashed into it.

"I so sorry. I sick."

Ali helped me get to the elevator with my groceries and went up with me to get them into the apartment.

"Madam, I so sorry."

I came inside and immediately called Laura. The message was that all lines were busy. I called Stan. Laura had sent him an email saying that she was OK and was at Christopher's apartment in lower Manhattan. They had been advised not to tie up the phone lines. As I heard this, I was watching the pictures for the first time. I had only three stations on the television and they were all in Arabic, but you don't have to understand the language to know something about what happened. I first thought that the planes had hit and the buildings had gone down immediately. Thank goodness I had Stan to explain that many people were able to escape. Oh, my God. He explained that there was thinking that this had been a terrorist attack. Another plane crashed into the Pentagon and still another had crashed somewhere in Pennsylvania. Oh, I wanted to be in his arms right then. This was too much to bear. I kept holding my head. Maybe if I shook it hard enough this information would fall out and be gone.

"You'll be OK. I love you."

"Love you too."

Crying, I wandered into the outside hallway where I could hear the neighbors' TV. They were getting English on their TV, but not loud enough for me to hear what was being said.

I came back into my apartment and called the only person whose number I had: Laila. It was her home phone and it rang and rang and rang. An hour later I called her again, but I heard only the same ringing and ringing.

I had brought one book to read. After walking around the apartment crying and trying to understand what had happened, I tried to go to bed and read myself to sleep. Ironically, the book was *Executive Orders* by Tom Clancy in which a plane crashes into a joint session of congress and most of the government is wiped out in one event.

So began one of the worst nights of my life. *What am I doing here? Why did this happen? Who are those crazy people who would crash planes into buildings?* I found one book in the apartment: *Anne of Green Gables.* I tried to read it, but after a short time, I just wanted to tell Anne to shut up. If I slept, I was not aware of it.

Next morning Ashraf was on time and very sheepish. He looked at me and said, "Sorry."

At school as I made my entrance into the teachers' room all eyes were on me. I know I didn't look very well. I'm sure they were watching to see what kind of reaction I was having.

Mr. Salem said, "Mrs. Hoffman, this is not Islam. Islam is a religion of peace. I am so sorry. Those were very bad people."

"I know."

When I walked into the English office, I started to cry. Not exactly the way I wanted to start out my new job. Suzanne and Jo greeted me with hugs. We all sobbed silently in each other's embrace. "Oh my God. I can't believe it." "Me neither." We three Americans sat in a little circle inside the English office talking, shedding tears, supporting each other at the outrage of what had happened in our country thousands of miles away. The rest of the teachers who were all Arabic sat sickly at their desks outside as if they'd each just been told they had incurable cancer.

My psyche felt like someone had peeled it with a razor blade. This wasn't my self-confidence taking a vacation, it was far more primal. It seemed that the bottom of the whole world had fallen out and we were all slipping into a black unknown.

I learned later that Mrs. Amani had arranged for someone to go to my apartment that day and outfit me with something that would give me TV channels in English. She later said that she had called Laila and told her to contact me the night before. "Laila, you need to go over and talk to that poor woman." Laila said later that she had called me twice and thought I was sleeping because I didn't answer. I was probably at the Sultan Center when she made those calls.

Was I meant to find out what I was made of that night with no outside help? I guess I was. And I got through it one horrible minute at a time.

The next days were a blur of working, being glued to CNN and Peter Jennings, obsessing about the horror, struggling to learn about what happened, and trying to make sense of the worst events most of us have ever experienced. Did every day get easier? It must have, because I got through it all without collapsing, screaming, or blaming the people I was now working with every day. Luckily, I understood immediately that this event was carried out by bad people and had nothing to do with the people with whom I was having contact every day.

I talked often to Stan. He was clearly shaken by this event. He was in Florida in the middle of a tropical storm where he spent a day without power. Was the universe trying to tell us something? A few days later his visa came through. He would come within the week.

He was one of very few passengers on his flight to Kuwait. Ashraf had taken me to the airport and waited with me. Seeing Stan walk out of the baggage area was probably the most comforting thing I have ever experienced. I hadn't been so happy to see his beautiful bald head in a very long time. We hugged, I sobbed and life was more right. He was fine despite his jet lag. We talked again when we got to the apartment about whether we should stay or go. For now, we would stay and see what happened. We were a unit again, ready to have this experience together.

Somehow, I had gotten connected with a group of guidance counselors from the other international schools in Kuwait where many of Kuwait's children are educated. This group's loose alliance met once a month and I was invited. At the first meeting, we all shared the difficulties we were coping with in our various situations. My school was only 50 students-all Kuwaiti, but all of their schools had 1,000 to 1,500 students containing many ex-pat students and teachers. The guidance counselors for the kids also became the therapists for the teachers who, like me, were largely American and far from home in what could have been considered a hostile land.

However, I never saw Kuwait as a hostile land. The people I met were kind and ready to help in any way. If I asked for anything, a pencil, an eraser, five people jumped to get me what I needed.

The counselors, some of whom had been in Kuwait for years, some of whom were married to Kuwaitis, didn't look like they would be going home or anywhere else anytime soon. One counselor said that in a situation where your current location didn't feel safe, a good plan was to pack a suitcase so that you can grab it and run if necessary. (This is now so common that it is called a "Go Bag," but then it was a new concept.) After I got that idea, I stopped thinking about going home. I didn't actually pack a suitcase, but in my mind, I had a plan of exactly what I would take. I knew I could put it all together in 15 minutes. That seemed to be all I needed.

I established a routine and stumbled my way through. Stan called himself my houseboy and found his way around the neighborhood making friends with an Egyptian guy, Ece, who was the manager at the grocery store where Stan went every day. Ece really enjoyed his relationship with Stan and began to call him his father.

## DRIVING IN KUWAIT

About two weeks into my stay in Kuwait a car for my use was delivered to school and I was able to dispatch Ashraf to his other duties. I had learned the way from home to school from his good driving and I was ready to solo. The car was a red, brand new small car that the Center was leasing.

Kuwait driving was one major freeway and lots of round-abouts. It was easy to get around and hard to get lost, a first for me, but the drivers were maniacs. The old timers believed that the line in the middle of the road meant the middle of your car should be on that line. The teenagers believed they would never die in their Bimmers, Mazeratis, and Mercedes no matter how fast they went. Police patrolled the roads, but the Kuwaitis knew they would never be ticketed because every driver's father "knew someone." If there was a fiery wreck with a fatality, the police would leave the burned up car on the side of the road for weeks as a moral lesson saying: *See, that's what will happen if you go too fast.*

I had heard from everyone that defensive driving was the only way to go in Kuwait and I practiced it every day. The four lane roundabouts were the most stressful because driv-ers would sail in without looking for anyone coming in the roundabout and immediately head for the center. When they were ready to exit, they would shoot across the 4 lanes for traffic to their exit, again without looking. The biggest round-about in Kuwait was near my school and I had to drive in it every day. On my way home at 1:00 it was the busiest and I would wait for an opening and then stay in the outermost lane driving about as fast as a toddler on a Big Wheel. I exited slowly while watching for those cars coming from the middle lane. My attitude was, "Oh, excuse me, I didn't know that was your lane. Please, go ahead."

## NOOR

In Kuwait it seemed that every workplace had an employee whose job it is to clean and bring tea to those who want it when they want it. In Kuwait this was Noor, a Bangladeshi who greeted me every morning with a shining smile and three of the ten English words he knew, "Hello, good moaning." If I needed anything copied, Noor was the one to accomplish this task. I would say, "Noor, may I have three copies, please?" while holding up three fingers. He was extremely efficient at this task and seemed to enjoy bringing tea even though I didn't request it very often. When Laura came to visit me in Kuwait, I brought her to the office to show her where I worked and introduce her to my colleagues. When we met Noor, he looked at Laura, looked at me, pointed to Laura and said with his shining smile, "Copy."

## DUMPSTER DIVING

One busy day I'd stopped at a little restaurant to buy some lunch to eat in the car. I left the empty box on the front seat. When I got home, after locking the car, I threw the box in the big dumpster next to the carport and immediately realized that I had also thrown the only set of car keys I had into the dumpster with the box. Unbeknownst to me, Stan, who had been waiting for me to come home, was upstairs looking out the bedroom window and saw me commit this stupid act.

It's not like he wasn't prepared for me to do something like this. On our first date, way back in 1988, Stan had picked me up in his truck (yes, I went with him anyway). I was excited about this date. He was someone I respected and I was happy to go anywhere with him. *Could this be the beginning of something?* I wore my best cream-colored pants and a cream colored top with a teal scarf. It was the best I had and we left the house happily off to a place he liked called VanAbel's, a (wait for it) bowling alley. Dinner was deep fried fish and a greasy potato dish that Stan highly recommended, fried potatoes buried in cheese and fried onions. I ate some of the potatoes. Pinched face. "Yes, they're delicious." Maybe I could stick my finger down my throat in the bathroom.

On the way home Stan told me, "I'm not looking for a deep relationship." It was something that turned out to be completely untrue, but I wish I had known that then.

I was almost crushed, but thought to myself, *well, your loss, guy.*

When we got to my house and got out of the car, I was hit with a sinking feeling where those greasy potatoes were still perched. Did I have a key to my house? On my person? I searched my purse and came up empty. I never went anywhere that I didn't drive to, so I always used the garage door opener... which was in my car inside the locked garage.

What to do? I knew the window above my bed was slightly open. Would Stan lift me up so that I could go in through the window, land on my bed and open the door for Stan? Yes, he would try. The window was about 5 feet up. We got the screen off and Stan knelt down so I could step on his knee. Well, that didn't work because I couldn't get high enough and he couldn't push me up from a kneeling position. So I stood on both of his knees while he stood. I grasped the bottom of the window and Stan pushed me upward, one hand on each cheek. Yes, those cheeks! I was thinking, well, this is pretty personal for the first date, but I don't know how else to get into the house. Later he told me he was thinking, *Wow, it's only the first date and I already have my hands on her ass!*

When he came around so that I could let him in, we shared our first kiss. He was warm and gentle and when he hugged me, he felt like a giant teddy bear. For many years I teased Stan, asking him to let me know if he thought he was ready yet for a long term relationship. Almost from the day he told me he wasn't ready for a long term relationship, he was a part of my life every single day for the next 29 years until September 2018 when he passed away. When I get to heaven, I'll see if he's made a decision about a long term relationship yet. Of course, maybe he will already have a girlfriend there, but if the food is good, he probably won't.

Back to that afternoon in Kuwait, it was lucky that the dumpster had been emptied that morning so I could see the keys down there on the bottom. I tried to jump myself up to my waist to see if I could reach in and get the keys. At 5'6" I was too short. I had to walk to the door of our apartment building, ring the bell and get buzzed in by Stan. He already knew the whole story and said he would go down and try to help. My hero hooched himself up so that his waist was on the rim of the dumpster and was able to seesaw himself down and reach the keys using a stick. Too bad he wasn't there in Brindisi six years later when I dropped my keys down a storm sewer!

## LIFE IN KUWAIT

Because of the oil money in Kuwait, citizens get cash from the government. No Kuwaiti has to worry about poverty. Plus, some needs like food and gas are subsidized. We paid about $1.25 per gallon for gas, and if we shopped at the local food coop as opposed to the Sultan Center, we could get really cheap groceries, too. The problem, I learned later, is that Kuwait, at that time (2001), had about 70 more years of oil. When the oil is gone, it's gone, and Kuwait hasn't planned ahead well enough to sustain its current level. The citizens are used to these perks and when the end of the oil comes, there is likely to be a crisis. I hope they have been making changes so that they can avert this situation.

Every morning the 50 students at the Center gathered in the open courtyard in front of our little school. Configured by age, the girls wore green and white checked dresses and some with white hijabs (it wasn't required) and the boys wore gray slacks and white button up shirts. The school principal, Mr. Salem, and his assistant, Mr. Mowafak would speak to the kids about various topics. While I couldn't understand anything that was said, I was told that along with school announcements and encouragement, he said *to work hard* and *do well today.*

## MY NON-CONVERSION

Talal, the Syrian English teacher, and I often had short philosophical discussions about religion. I wondered if he was the designated proselytizer to convert Mrs. Carol (or Mrs. Carrot as the kids called me because that was one of their English vocabulary words) to Islam. After all, Jo, the American English teacher who was married to a Kuwaiti, converted and Suzanne, the other American English teacher, had converted completely on her own. Talal spoke so gently and positively about Islam I guessed that he was extolling Islam's virtues to either educate me or change my mind about Christianity. I once asked him how he envisioned peace coming between the Arabs and the Jews. His response was, "On the last day of the world, that's when we'll have peace."

Unless Islam were a religion that could encompass all faiths, that could be open to accepting and loving people the way they are, and that could value men and women equally, my conversion wasn't going to happen (I wasn't that good at being a Christian), but gentle Talal never gave up.

## THE SECOND IRAQ WAR

In the time I was in Kuwait — about 17 months all together — there were only a few incidents that were troubling. One occurred when a group of us expats were seated in the outside patio area of a local restaurant on a weekend evening. A car went by and the people in it shouted something negative to us and threw a soda bottle at the street near where we were sitting. Another time a Canadian man was shot and killed when jogging around in a neighborhood in Kuwait in his shorts and tank top. This was worrying, because until then an activity like that would have generated scorn, not murder. Arabs didn't like to see anyone who wasn't completely dressed and no Arab would ever have run around a neighborhood in shorts.

Another incident happened during my second year just prior to the outbreak of the second Gulf War. Because of Stan's retired military status (USCG Reserves), we often went out to the U.S. army base commissary for groceries like bacon or pork, for church because they had an American minister, or for a comfort food lunch (baked chicken and mashed potatoes) in their mess hall. Sometimes Stan would drive out there while I was at work to buy groceries. The whole military operation there was supported by contractors such as architects, engineers, or food service managers who all had the same kind of vehicle, white Pajero SUVs. One day two American contractors were driving from the army base in Kuwait back into Kuwait City in one of those Pajeros. They were shot to death at an intersection as they waited for a traffic light. Stan had driven through the same intersection just 20 minutes before that happened. This horrible event made me think, *it's time to get out for a while. I didn't sign up for this.*

War seemed inevitable and there was a voluntary evacuation of all Americans from Kuwait. Later the evacuation became mandatory. Additionally, I'd been to the doctor over Christmas break that year with small pains in my right side. The doctor said I had gallstones that needed to be taken out along with my gallbladder. I was thinking of having this surgery the following summer, but along with those troubling incidents, we decided it was time to bug out. It was a weekend just a few weeks before the second Iraq war started when we went to the base and hopped a military Space A flight back to the States. There were so few people on that flight that we were asked to place ourselves around the large cabin so that the weight would be better distributed. We could have each had 5 rows to ourselves! The flight stopped in Aviano, Italy and the Azores (beautiful place!) for refueling and landed in Charleston, SC at about 10 p.m.

We weren't sure how we were going to get to Florida and got in line for a rental car where we met a guy who was going our way. He rented the car and we paid him something and started on an interesting journey. We spent the night at the air force base in Jacksonville, Florida and the next day made our way to Bradenton. We had a car there and the guy dropped us off at our condo and went off to Sarasota which was his home.

I had surgery a few weeks later, recovered, planned and took a trip to Europe with Laura and Melissa because I always said I would take them both to Europe when Melissa turned 25, an age which I had pre-determined would be past the whiny, intractable teenage years. They could both get away from their jobs/schools/boyfriends for two weeks, and we had a great time.

The Iraq-U.S war started when we were in Paris. We heard only one negative comment during that whole trip. A man inside a ticket booth where we were trying to buy a ticket, looked at me, apparently recognizable as an American, and said, "Je protest." I didn't have enough French (or time) to explain to him that I was completely with him. I had even written a letter to George Bush telling him it was a terrible idea to invade Iraq. You see how well he listened to me and how well that whole thing turned out. We and so many others are still paying for those missteps.

Our trip to Europe was exactly as I had hoped. No whining, everybody able to drink wine and beer, and because of the war, so few tourists we could choose any accommodation or restaurant. In Bacharach, Germany, we stayed in a hotel made from one of the four embattlements of the medieval city wall. Our room was in the tower on the top floor. From our window complete with shutters we could see both inside and outside the old city wall.

We took the train around France, Germany, and Switzerland and came home intact as the nuclear family of three we had been during those early years before puberty and the not-completely-welcome installation of Stan into the family unit.

In May when I was back at home in Florida and the war was over, I contacted my school and asked if I could/should come back and finish out my contract. That was okay with Mrs. Amani, and I returned to Kuwait sometime in May and stayed until mid June. Stan didn't return with me.

Our friend Dan was not only a teacher but also a pastor at the "happy clappy" church we had begun attending. He never left Kuwait because of his role as part-time pastor to the many, many Filipino, Indian, Bangladeshi, and Sri Lankan Christians who served as household help for Kuwaitis. Dan knew that even if the Kuwaitis left, many would not provide for their hired help to get out of Kuwait. So Dan stayed.

He reported that he only experienced one situation that was fearful. Dan had an extensive movie collection and one evening he was sitting in his recliner watching a movie. He heard a noise like an arriving jet but he was either too slow or uncomprehending to move out of his chair. Something went roaring past his 14th floor apartment and when it did, both Dan and the chair in which he was sitting lifted off the floor and came back down again. He later learned that a scud missile had gone awry that night and exploded in the desert not far from where he lived.

## MAJDA'S NIECE'S WEDDING

Our elementary principal, Majda, (MAHJ duh) told me and Suzanne that her niece was getting married and asked if we wanted to go to the wedding. She handed us an invitation which we couldn't read, but Majda gave us the details. Well, of course we wanted to go. We were dying to go.

On the prescribed day, Suzanne and I drove together to the site of the wedding at about 5 p.m. It was in a tall, modern-looking hotel. We parked in an open field across the street and walked to the hotel which was at one end of the field. At the opposite end of the field, lights were strung on a cord forming a large square. Low sofas were set around the perimeter of this area. The male guests would celebrate there and the females would celebrate inside the hotel.

The path to the wedding room was deliberately circuitous so that no outsiders (males) could find it. Luckily a woman was there to get us to the elevator and as soon as we reached the 8th floor, we heard the celebration. Rock music screamed through the halls and throbbed through our bodies as we walked into the long room. It was similar to the pounding one gets in the ribs when sitting behind a car with a big bass radio at a red light.

The room was about 100 feet long and 50 feet wide. At the far end of the room was a kind of stage set with chairs and flowers. Little girls wore frilly dresses with patten leather shoes and ruffly anklets and ran around the room just like all kids do. Some of the women wore full abayas and some young women wore the skimpiest of dresses. One I noticed was a dark-haired, jaw-droppingly beautiful woman of about 17 whose dress literally hung on her nipples. To this day, I've never seen a more erotic dress. The whole top of her breast was exposed right to the edge of her nipples. *How did she even hold it up?* Her appearance seemed so contradictory because in this ultra-conservative culture, any male-female contact was strictly forbidden. She might have been ready for "action," but it wasn't going to be happening for her here in this room full of women. It was so puzzling to see all of the older women tolerate the deafening, rib-vibrating music and the undress of a few of the young women. My mother would have been scandalized, but these women sat chatting, as nonchalant as if they were buying mangoes at the Sultan Center.

Adjusting to the music was hard for me. When I can feel the bass in my body, I start to feel nauseated. I think it's related to the reason that I also can't go on boats, drive on winding roads or feel happy when an airplane takes a few dips, but for some inexplicable, wonderful reason, the speaker exactly behind us literally blew up with a loud pop and a little smoke. It didn't burst into flame, it just quit playing. The women noticed this event, but didn't seem to be bothered by it. The smoke diminished and soon my ribs stopped vibrating and the music became tolerable. Eventually a woman employee of the hotel came to look at the speaker, and she figured out that it wasn't going to explode so she walked away without doing anything. *Thank you!* The other six, yes, six speakers in the room were blasting out so much music that perhaps no one but me noticed the loss of that one.

Waiters began to come with glasses of juice (mango, orange and apple) and hors d'oeuvres. Jo told us that while we were in this room, most of the women would take off their abayas, but about half of them didn't. Eventually Majda's niece's entourage arrived at the door. Her mother, his mother, her female relatives and her groom's female relatives entered and slowly walked to the stage area. Once they were seated, Majda's niece appeared at the door. She wore a billowy lemon chiffon gown that complemented her perfect skin. She was gorgeous. She began to slowly glide her way down the center aisle between the tiers of chairs as if she were on a sidewalk belt moving an inch a minute. Is there training for this demonstration? I've never seen anyone move more slowly down an aisle. When she got to the end, she greeted all of the relatives and gracefully sat down. A few of the women in the "bleachers" approached the stage and greeted the wedding party on the stage. While they chatted, more hors d'oeuvres and juices arrived. After about 45 minutes, the whole entourage stood up and floated slowly back out the way they had come in.

Much later Majda's niece once again entered the room. This time she was dressed in a puffy white wedding dress, the kind you would find in any wedding shop in America. It was bouffant, prim, and tasteful. Once again the entourage inched its way to the stage receiving greetings on the way. This time the bride sat behind a curtain on the stage and the rest of the entourage stood or sat in front of the curtain.

What felt like hours later we were told to put on our hijab (not me!) because the men were going to be entering soon. On went the abayas and the few women who were out of their seats returned to them. The music was different now, louder with more vocals. Soon some young men with drums strapped around their bodies came in singing and pounding their drums. Behind them the groom's relatives and friends made their way slowly to the stage. The groom was quite visible flanked by his two best friends/brothers/cousins. They greeted the wedding party on the stage, but the bride never came out from behind the curtain.

After some time with everyone watching this big group of Kuwaitis talk with each other, the men's group left the same way they came in, drums pounding and music blaring. By this time it was about 11:30 p.m. Jo told us that the next thing that would happen is that there would be a huge buffet of food and then the party would be over. Since this was a school night, not to mention way past our bedtime, Suzanne and I left, making our excuses and thank yous to Majda.

What I inferred about this part of the world is that if you're a woman, the most important people in your life are the female members of your husband's family. If you're a man, it's the other men in your family. Women hung out together going shopping or to each others' houses, and the men hung out together generally at their family's diwaniya (DEE wah NEE ah) — a meeting room with low "couches" all around the perimeter of the room. Large screen TVs hung in various places on the wall. It seemed to me that a married couple rarely appeared together in public. The bride would be spending most of her time with the female relatives of the groom's family.

In each family group, consisting of possibly five or six what we would call nuclear families, one older male took the role of leader. He would be responsible for allowing or not allowing activities or behavior and making life decisions for everyone in the group. He would approve or disapprove a job that a family member sought. I'm guessing he would approve where the family would live, go to school and where they could travel, but no one ever told me that and I didn't ask. Much like the royal family in Saudi Arabia, when that man died, there might be a struggle between the survivors to decide who would take over. If there were several sons, handing over the leadership could be difficult, but eventually one man either took or was given the job.

So many things in Kuwait were culturally different from what Americans are used to. I was keenly aware of how I might appear to Kuwaitis whenever I left the house. I dressed modestly and when Stan was driving, I didn't put my foot on the car seat hugging my knee the way I did when I was in America. I was always focused on the task at hand: drive the car, buy the groceries, bring the groceries into the house. If I was meeting people at school, I always extended my hand for a handshake and I only remember once that a man waved me off, as a man isn't supposed to touch a female who is not a relative. Once at the Sultan Center I saw a young Western woman in short shorts and spaghetti strap tank top. While she wasn't forbidden to dress like that in Kuwait, her appearance must have riled the locals in their long robes and head covers.

The Persian Gulf has beautiful beaches, but it was painful to see whole stretches of sand where no one was sunbathing, swimming, or enjoying the sand and sea. Custom dictates that neither men nor women display themselves in public in swimwear, though once I saw a woman in a black robe walking in the gulf, robe and all. Fenced in swimming clubs had pools where there were hours for men to swim and later, hours for women, and I went to one once during the women's session. It was nice to get wet, but there were so many girls and women that it wasn't really much fun. That was the only way to swim.

*Women walking on the beach.*

## WORKING WITH LAILA

My favorite word in Arabic is "khalas." (khuh-LAHSS) When uttered, it means "finished" or "stop it" or "it's over." My colleague, Laila, who was the lead psychologist at the center and probably 20 years my junior, held a lot of sway with Mrs. Amani despite not moving cases forward in a timely fashion. She and her family were from Lebanon but had been living in Kuwait for several years. She was a beautiful young woman who dressed in completely Western style: pants, shirts, sandals, or occasionally dresses that were always professional. No head cover. Her English was flawless and she could listen and translate simultaneously which amazed me every time I saw her do it. I was often the person to whom she was translating. How can you hear what has been said, understand it, translate it immediately into another language and be ready for the next sentence? She was amazing and most of the time I really enjoyed working with her.

I heard Mrs. Amani say, "khalas" to Laila more than once, so I'm pretty sure Laila drove her about as crazy as she sometimes drove me. Laila was often on the phone with her 13-year-old son who apparently had his own ideas of how things should go and Laila didn't seem to agree with those ideas. They would argue in Arabic on the phone until one of them hung up on the other. Then Laila would pace around her office in a noisy fury until she calmed down.

After Laila did a psychological evaluation on a student, if the student's IQ was within the normal range, she would pass the case on to me and I would schedule another time to administer academic tests to determine the child's achievement level compared with others his/her age in vocabulary, reading comprehension, and written language. I could usually complete my evaluation in one session, compile my results and write up my report within a day or two. I'm a good report writer and editor, but Laila always found fault with what I had written or the way I had scored a particular assessment tool. We would work out a compromise on how the report should be and it would then be in Laila's hands to write the entire report. For her this process took at least a month. The reports would be approximately 10–20 pages long. She was a perfectionist and her excellent reports reflected that. Eventually the report would be finished and we would meet with the family, explain the results, and make recommendations.

After the first year I learned that Laila was really mad that I got to drive a brand new, red rental car provided to me by Mrs. Amani while she had to drive around in the Center's old, beat-up, two-door, dark green Fiat. When I arrived at the beginning of the second year, *I* was assigned the old, beat-up two-door Fiat, and Laila had the new red car. I have always said that my favorite kind of car is the kind that when you put the key in, it starts. In fact, that old beater might have saved Stan's life. When he drove through the intersection just before two contractors were killed, were the killers looking for any American to kill? Americans always had nice cars. Stan who was practically bald at the time could pass for an American or an Arab and must have looked like an Arab in that old beater.

The American professor with whom the school had a strong connection told me later that she hired me largely because she perceived that I would be able to get along with Laila. She was right. I did get along with Laila even though I wasn't able to help her move the caseload forward more quickly. When I left Kuwait, Laila said this to me, "I can honestly say that you are the nicest person I've ever met." I hope her son is doing well.

## KUWAIT HEAT

How hot is it in Kuwait? The high on June 26, 2003 in the shade was 46°C, which is about 115°F. But, it's a dry heat! I learned quickly to time my shopping and other trips for times when the traffic was light and I could be assured of a parking place in the shade or in underground parking.

Before opening the door to the outside, I'd arrange my keys, bag, water, and other paraphernalia, take a deep breath, open the outside door, and step into the open maw of the outdoor oven. Then, I'd move to the car as fast as possible, open the burning hot car door with something other than my bare hand and quickly start the car. The AC, always on MAX, blasted dry fire onto my face and made me feel like I was on the top rack just under the broiler. A steering wheel cover meant for Wisconsin winters worked just fine to protect my hands from the burning steering wheel.

I became an expert at dressing for the hot dry climate. All synthetic fiber clothes were packed away. Nothing but cotton on this body. Loose fitting, light cotton shirts with sleeves at least to the elbow were easy enough to manage. Back in Wisconsin I had purchased five cotton-knit, elastic-waistband skirts which hit me about mid-calf that were perfect: not too risqué for the conservative Muslim culture and absorbent for all of the sweat that seeped out.

And feet. Oh my gosh. My feet got crusty, dirty, and calloused. I remembered my Bible stories about someone being treated to washing of the feet. That story finally made sense. Someone washing my feet would be the kindest thing that could happen. At my house, I found the best place to wash my feet was in the bidet! I sat on the closed toilet, put my feet into the bidet, and washed away. Toes and heels became so cracked around the edges that they sometimes bled. This isn't good in an unsanitary environment like a desert. Every night after the ritual foot bath, I had to slather on the best lotion I could find.

## No Political Correctness

I adored my Grandpa Johnson, my mother's father. He was short, formerly red-haired, freckled, and a cigar-smoking man of few words. He was the first in his Norwegian family to be born in the U.S. I will never forget the time when as pre-teens, my cousin and I had been swimming in the lake in front of their house in Newaygo, Michigan. Both of us were staying with Grandma and Grandpa for our annual visit without our parents. One day I jumped off the neighbors' raft onto the soft sand in five feet of water and got a deep cut on the ball of my foot. I was crying and bleeding by the time I got to my grandparents' house and found out that my Grandma had gone to town for groceries. Grandpa treated my cut with loving care, if almost no words. He put on mercurochrome and a gauze bandage with adhesive tape. When he was finished, he gently held my foot in his hands, looked into my eyes and said, "Now, we're not going to tell your Grandmother about this."

It was a little conspiracy my cousin and I had with Grandpa. Our little secret. I'm sure Grandpa never told her and Grandma never found out. Their relationship had deteriorated to one word communications, generally at mealtime, "Butter" or "Salt." Occasionally we'd hear a whole sentence, "We'll go to town tomorrow morning." Sometimes this might be followed by a harsh, "I can't leave until after lunch because I'm painting the bottom of the boat." The response was, "Why can't you paint the boat on Thursday?" in a tone that felt like this was an ongoing fight and it was a disgusting thought that he had to paint the boat. She would storm away and they went after lunch.

As teenagers, my cousin and I would often be seeing boys while we stayed with Grandma and Grandpa. My grandma wanted to know where we were going and what time we would be back. My grandpa wanted to know the boys' last names.

When we told him, he'd say, "Oh, he's a Wop, or he's a Polack." The last name of one of the boys I dated was Thomas. Apparently that boy was OK because there wasn't an extremely disparaging and offensive term associated with his name. As a Norwegian immigrant, it's hard to understand how my normally fair-thinking Grandfather could use monikers like Wop and Polack, but he did. He didn't discourage me from seeing any of these boys, but something made him identify their nationalities by these negative terms.

Aside from those comments from my grandfather, I lived a relatively politically correct life. I didn't hear that kind of pejorative name-calling from anyone in my family, my work, or my social groups. I guess that's why I was bowled over by the way the people in my school in Kuwait talked about Jews. The hatred was plain, overt, and ugly.

Well into my first year at the Center, during a week when I didn't have reports to write or teachers to supervise, I worked on cleaning out my office which had held quite a few people in this position over the years. I dug down to a pile of catalogs of educational materials and samples of textbooks. I found several maps that I thought might be helpful to the teachers. I brought them to the staff room and put them in the center of the communal work table. I told the staff what they were and that they could take them. I would recycle what was left. One Jordanian teacher was looking at a world map published by an educational supplier. As soon as he unfolded the map, he looked in the center, shouted some Arabic words and threw the map violently back into the middle of the table. I asked Talal what was wrong. He told me that the Jordanian teacher was angry that the map showed Israel. World maps published in Arabic countries show only Palestine.

## CARS

One of the formal assessments I administered when trying to determine a student's achievement level was a vocabulary measure. I had a standardized assessment tool that contained pictures, one to a page. The first few pages were easy. Ball, dog, cup. About the fifth picture was a car. One six year old I was working with was doing fine saying, "Ball, dog, cup." When I turned to the page with the car, she opened her eyes wide, jumped out of her chair, pointed at the picture and shouted, "B — M — W!"

Only in Kuwait! I gave her that one.

## DIFFERENCES

One small office separated my office from the office of school director, Mrs. Amani. She was rarely in the building, but when she was, everyone knew it. Her aqua Jaguar was in the first parking place in the parking lot. The space wasn't exactly reserved for her, but no other staff member EVER parked in that place. And when she was there, everyone spoke in hushed voices walking with quickened steps.

I loved it that when she wanted to talk to me, she telephoned the office manager, Mr. Saleh (sah LAH); Mr. Saleh would telephone me (I could hear him say this without the phone) and say "Ms. Hoffman, Mrs. Amani will see you now." I would walk the five steps to her door and go in. She would ask me how things were going and if I needed anything. Actually our offices were so close, she could have said my name, "Carol," and I would have heard her. Or she could have called me on the interoffice phone. Instead, she called Mr. Saleh who then called me. I wasn't used to the formality.

## DUSTY

I'd been warned by my colleagues that the dust storms in Kuwait were truly treacherous. The first one I experienced made itself known far before the time it actually arrived. It looked like a brown cloud slowly marching its way along the ground to my neighborhood. I wondered if I should run over to the grocery store and lay in some supplies. In the end, I simply watched it get closer and closer until it finally swallowed my building. Once I was swallowed up in it, I was a bit disappointed. Based on descriptions from other expats, I wouldn't be able to see my hand in front of my face. Actually, I could see across the street to the other building, and I could see down to the street from three stories up. Yes, visibility was far less than usual, but in a country where the blue sky enabled us to see for miles, this simply looked like it was a cloudy day. I'd heard my car would be inundated with sand. Okay, some talc-like tan powder lay in the well of the windshield, but I could blow it out with a quick puff. I also heard that the sand would sting my skin. I had to walk to my car in one sandstorm, and while I can say a sandstorm is annoying, my skin didn't feel stung. Either sandstorms are not as bad as people made out, or no serious ones occurred while I was in Kuwait.

## RAIN IN THE DESERT

I was surprised that it *does* occasionally rain in places like Kuwait. The naturally growing vegetation, scruffy and low to the ground as it is, must get water from somewhere. About once every month a little rain fell from the sky. The rain came down just like it does in other places, but the kids in our school had a funny reaction. Everywhere else I have ever been, when it starts raining, people put up their umbrellas, cover their heads, or dash for an overhang. The kids in our school rushed outside, spread their arms to the sky, and threw their heads back so that they could feel the rain on their faces. The first time I saw this happen, I was delighted! After I lived in the desert, I now understand that rain is a gift. Even though I don't rush out and turn my face to the sky, I cherish every rain storm because I know what happens when it doesn't rain.

One day in February we got a rain storm just at the time when the kids were getting out of school. It was a real gully washer and everyone in it got completely soaked. The rain accumulated quickly, and soon the streets were flooded with cafe latte colored water. Cars were having difficulty navigating. It was impossible to even see where the road was. It was lunch time for me and I waited a bit before leaving school to go home. At about 1:30 the water where our Center was located had receded and I started out for the 15-minute ride home.

Not two blocks away I could see the traffic in front of me. It looked like every car in Kuwait was headed for the same freeway (there were only two) and the cars were creeping, inching along. The water had receded on the main roads; however, the side roads stayed full of water for hours after the rain. Cars were jammed on the freeway because no one could get off. The exits were flooded with water and cars that couldn't move.

The Kuwait Times published a long article about that storm. It was so unusual to have that much rain in so little time. I wouldn't have believed it if I hadn't seen it myself. By the next day an odd puddle or two were still evidence of the day before, but the rest of the water had disappeared.

## BACK TO SCHOOL

My younger daughter, Melissa who had dropped out of college and was waitressing back in Wisconsin, was never far from my thoughts. I remembered enough about my teenage years that if my mother told me to do something, I would find a way to do the exact opposite. So when I talked to Melissa, I never mentioned that I hoped she would go back to school and complete a degree. Apparently that was the right approach because in January 2002, Melissa told me that she had signed up for two classes at the UW in Wausau where she was living at the time. Could she hear the applause inside my heart? I tried to be nonchalant, "Oh, good for you," but inside I was screaming, *Thank God* so loud I thought she would get wet from the waterfall of relief. In fall 2003 she went back full time to the University of South Carolina where she would live and waitress part-time to pay the bills.

## DYSLEXIA AND ARABIC

As if students with dyslexia didn't have it hard enough, the students in our little school were with us because they had been having difficulty in their regular-education Arabic schools. A typical situation for a student with dyslexia learning to read English is to confuse a b with a d. While there are many teachable tricks to avoid this becoming a problem, think of these children who spoke Arabic and had to learn to read and write in that language which is written from right to left. Then they had to do mathematics operations generally from two directions: addition, subtraction and multiplication were right to left, but division was left to right. Plus they had to learn English which is read and written from left to right. The main language for our students was Arabic, but they had approximately 5 classes a week in English. Mastering the direction of operations in reading, writing and mathematics was really challenging for students with dyslexia.

## STRATEGIES FOR STRUGGLING STUDENTS

During the year that I didn't have a job and was restlessly living in Wisconsin and Florida, I created a teacher training workshop called "Strategies for Struggling Students." I tried to market this workshop by sending a brochure to international schools in places I wanted to visit. I got no responses, but I saved all of the materials and the syllabus.

When I got to Kuwait, I applied to the European Council of International Schools (ECIS) to present my workshop at their annual conference which would be held in Berlin in November 2002. To my surprise and great joy, I was accepted as a speaker. When I asked Mrs. Amani for permission to attend this conference at my expense she said yes.

The conference was held in November and when Stan and I arrived in Berlin, the first thing we did was seek out a place for some German beer and German food. We found Joe's Bar, apparently owned by an American, on the Ku'damm and drank the best beer either of us had ever tasted. Of course, there is no alcohol of any kind allowed in Kuwait though expats shared recipes for home-made alcohol, but I was never interested enough to try that. In fact, I heard that in one apartment building where the expat teachers from another school lived, an unmarried couple who each had to have their own apartment (for the sake of appearances) but lived together in one apartment, devoted their unused apartment as a distillery!

We'd been to Berlin before, so it was fun to revisit a few highlights in the few hours available for sightseeing, but the paramount moment for both of us was that delicious beer at Joe's. It still stands in my mind as the world's best beer.

The conference was energizing and my presentation went very well. The space they gave me for it was about the size of a large classroom in a typical American high school and not only was every seat occupied, there were about 12 people standing at the back. Good for teachers! They are concerned about students who struggle, and at that time many international schools had no provisions for special needs students. My point was that the non-existent special education teacher wasn't coming to take these students out of your hands, *so get busy and help them, here's how.*

After I returned to Kuwait, I got the idea to offer my workshop to the teachers at the many international schools in Kuwait. I framed it to Mrs. Amani that it would be an opportunity for teachers to come to our center and yet another vehicle for the message to go out that we offered services. She endorsed it. I enjoyed meeting the other teachers and offering them the benefit of my many years of experience in working with special needs students.

## AMIRA

Do teachers really have "pets?" In my experience most teachers do actually enjoy some students more than others, but they work really hard so that no one knows which ones are which. I certainly tried to do that, but some come to mind that were absolutely irresistible to me. In Kuwait one of the most remarkable students was Amira.

She was a skinny 4th grader my first year in Kuwait who came to school in the morning all put together: thick black braid tied down her back, dress sash knotted in a bow tie at her back, white knee socks tight up to her knees. Bean pole thin, she could run faster than any of the boys and frequently did. Because break time was a snack and then chasing each other around our small play area, Amira was the first one finished with her snack and already chasing the boys, whom she picked because they were at her running speed. None of the other girls could match her speed nor wanted to. After the morning break, Amira's lush hair, as if it were alive, started to escape the confines of the braid and loosened up, no longer tamable, her sash was loose and her knee socks were more like mid-calf socks. By dismissal time at 1:00, Amira's hair was a loose rubber band hanging down her back, her untied sash hung at her sides, and her socks were anklets. She was the most hands-on learner I've ever seen and had an absolute gusto for life. She was the first one to run out in the rain, and she had the heartiest laugh at the smallest funny thing such as when somebody dropped their snack or had an untied shoe.

When she wrote anything on paper, she had to stand at her desk, bend intently over her paper and, breathing hard, write each word as if plowing a cornfield with her pencil, often ripping her paper. Her eyes were gorgeous, brown pools of shimmer. She didn't know the effect she had on people because she couldn't help being so out of the norm.

The second year she came to school on the first day wearing a white headscarf. I was disappointed because I loved her beautiful hair. She said she didn't want to wear the scarf, but her aunties made her do it. It turns out those white "trainer" scarves are not so easy to keep in place. Now because she was taller, she could run even faster and she went home with her hair falling out, the scarf more of a shawl and socks still dangling around her ankles. Honestly, I could have taken her home, I liked her so much. Did I feel a kinship with her? She was anything but a teacher-pleaser and could be downright naughty in class. I had to substitute in her class one day and found out the hard way she was the same way in class as she was on the little playground, but I still loved observing her. Did I want to be her? Had I been like her as a child? I sure hated restraints and so did she. ***THIS IS WHY I CAME HERE,*** to try to make it easier for students like Amira to learn, feel successful, and move seamlessly into adulthood.

I can't imagine what life is like for Amira now. Was she able to conform to the strict role of women in Kuwait? Whatever family she ended up in, I'm guessing they have their challenges with her irrepressible personality. I wonder how she has met with the emotional bumps and bruises of adult life. Is she still full of joy?

## FUN WITH VISAS

My daughter Laura extended a business trip to London by coming to visit me in Kuwait on June 12. In order for Laura to visit, I had to secure a visa for her. No one could board a plane for Kuwait without one. We knew this for a fact. Mr. Saleh decided that I should go after the visa by myself. He said it would be better for me to go to the Ministry in person or maybe he didn't want to send his facilitator, Ashraf, so he filled out an application for me to take to the Ministry. I had to get Laura to scan the picture page of her passport and send it to me via email. Mr. Saleh explained that after I found the correct building — not an easy task for the directionally challenged Carol — first, I would have to go to a little house just outside the building where a bunch of guys are sitting at typewriters and I would pay them to take the information and type it on the official form. After I had secured this paper, I had to enter the Ministry building and try to find the right office to deliver this application. This is not an easy process as there are no signs written in English and it is a hopping busy place with people, mostly men, coming and going. Desks and offices were everywhere and cell phones were ringing and ringing with people loudly talking into them. I asked one person and then another, and pretty soon I ended up in the right place. The man at the desk said I had to come back another day because, in addition to my passport, the application and Laura's passport page, I had to have my salary document, an official paper from my work that stated my salary. OK, well at least I knew where the building was.

The next day, armed with my salary paper, I found the same man from the day before. He checked my papers again and sent me to yet another room. It was a big waiting room with one of those number caller machines. My number was 55. They were on 27. Twenty minutes later my number was called in Arabic and I knew I had to go somewhere, but that wasn't very clear either. Pretty soon, I could hear a woman calling something khumseh (five in Arabic) and I finally saw her sitting behind the big counter. She was my lady. It seemed that of the 25 or so people behind the counter, she was the only one taking numbers. I explained what I wanted; I would like to have my daughter come to visit me for four days. She studied my papers and told me, "You must have proof that she is your daughter because you have different last names."

Proof. What kind of proof? Documentation that she is your daughter. Her picture? No, something that says she is your daughter. I tried to think. Do I have anything in Kuwait that has my former married name on it? Is there anything Stan could send me? Is there anything anywhere that would document that Laura is my daughter? This woman was patient, but many people were waiting. I told her I didn't think I could produce a document that this darling young woman to whom I had read nightly for over eleven years, nursed through chicken pox and various other childhood illnesses and survived her teenage angst was my flesh and blood. So much and yet so little proof. She hesitated. I said, "She looks like me." I would have to go home, try to find or manufacture some kind of document (a letter from my mother? DNA?) and return here yet another day. Good thing I started this process early! I stood there. Finally, the woman said, "Or... you can see the manager." Ah, now we're getting somewhere. Where is the manager? She made a loose gesture with her hand in the vague direction of the hallway and I was off. I had another 20-minute wait there while at least twenty people (men) went in and out of the manager's office without sitting and waiting their turn with me, and finally I was ushered by another man into the manager's plush office, palatial by comparison. The usher man stood there while the manager scanned my papers. He looked up at me. I said, "I would like to have my daughter visit me for four days." He said nothing but took his red pen and signed the top paper. Had he seen those years of nurturing and keeping clean socks in the drawer in my eyes? I'll never know. He signed it. The other man ushered me out and back into the big waiting room. The manager hadn't spoken a single word.

This time I had number 133 and they were on 96. Finally, I got up to the counter and another woman took my papers and gave me a receipt. Come back in three days and it will be ready. Khalas. Three days later I went back and traded my receipt for Laura's visa. My American colleagues told me later I got off easy to get the visa in only three trips!

I faxed the visa to Laura. She had to present it in order to board her flight from London. On the day she arrived, I had to arrive at the airport early and give the original visa to the airport/passport control police. I kept a copy. When Laura went through passport control, they would match her faxed copy with the original and let her into Kuwait. And they want to start promoting tourism?

I waited for Laura at the airport Starbucks, one of the 18 in Kuwait, and knew her plane had landed when I saw a man walk by carrying a London shopping bag. Pretty soon, there she was! Glorious reunion.

## LAURA'S VISIT

Laura stayed just four days, but the things we did during that time show how interesting Kuwait really is. A friend arranged a small tour to the Grand Mosque. At the entry they supplied all the women with a black abaya (head and body cover), which we had to put on in order to go in (OK, just this once. I felt like a different person hidden under that black cloak and I didn't like it.) The Grand Mosque is an enormous room with beautiful tiled walls, the floor covered in carpets. This is the room where the men prayed. We asked to see the place where women are allowed to worship, but it was "not open." After gratefully giving back the abayas, we visited the National Museum, which had just opened for the first time since the first Gulf War.

*Laura, me and Liane in the mosque.*

We ate lunch at Andalousy's, a buffet of Arabic foods: tabouleh, three kinds of hummus, which our friend Jim called "buttered dirt," three kinds of cold eggplant, and two or three kinds of lettuce, cucumber and tomato salads. They brought a little hibachi grill to our table with raw chicken, lamb and kofta (a kind of spicy meatball) and mixed grill kebab for us to grill our own meat. For dessert there was cake, crème caramel, rice pudding and lots of other delicious stuff.

At about 2 p.m. everyone in Kuwait goes home for the afternoon rest. It is the only thing that makes sense in the climate. They come out again after the 3:30 afternoon prayer. Since Laura had spent the night on a plane, we went home for a rest too. I've asked several people if there is a word in Arabic for this "siesta" time, but other than raha (RAH-ha) which means rest, there doesn't seem to be a name for it. Anyway, we had one.

After our raha we picked up Liane and went to Souk Mubarakia, which is the old market in the old part of Kuwait. I never grew tired of going there. It's a huge, labyrinthine collection of shops through little alleyways where you can find so many interesting things and people. Produce, fish, meat (hanging from big spikes — I never went in that part), dates (Loosely covered by plastic in an attempt to keep off the flies. I ate them anyway, they were so delicious.), clothes, hardware, guns, dishes, pots and pans, rope, carpets, souvenirs, juice places, restaurants, perfume, and gold are just some of the things you can find there. Our destination was a pearl shop. Long ago, pearl diving was the main source of outside income for Kuwait. I had visited before but had never been able to find it again. I had directions from an American friend and former Kuwait resident, Bette, who did the best she could in an email from Wichita. Anyway, it was an interesting quest and we eventually found it. The man was so busy that we decided to come back later. The next time, he was closed! Oh well, it was fun just to walk around that place.

We met with three other people, Americans, for dinner at Mais Alghanim (MAZE al GAH num), which is the quintessential Kuwaiti restaurant. There is traditional furniture in a big dining hall with ferns hanging from the windows) and the food is traditional Arabic: humus, tabouleh, and grilled lamb, chicken and kofta. And they had a mint/lemonade drink that was quite good. Laura got a good taste of Arabic food and expat life.

On Friday (like Sunday) we went to church at the American Embassy where security was very tight. If I wanted to attend church there, I had to know somebody who could put my name on the list. I did, and that person added Laura's name for that day. We drove into the street where the embassy is located, parked in the outer lot, then walked the 100 yards to the entry. We had to wait in the heat while the people in the security office took our ID and checked to see if our names were on the list. We couldn't see into the office so it was like talking to a live machine. After we got our security badges, we would come one at a time into the little room where they would go through our bag. The duty soldiers would take our mobile phone, which they gave back on leaving, X-ray our bag and direct us through a metal detector. After a few trips to the embassy, we learned to bring a bag that contained a wallet and a candy mint, period.

A walk through the beautiful embassy grounds took us to the large group room where church convened. They were celebrating their one-year anniversary as a church body that day. This meant there was a meal afterward and the ambassador attended. It was an indoor picnic for about 50 people with barbecue sandwiches, sweet corn (such as it was — we Wisconsinites are pretty particular about sweet corn. Legend says, get the cooking pot for the corn boiling, go pick the corn from the field in the back and peel it while running back to drop the fresh corn into the boiling water,) baked beans, and cake. These things didn't taste the same as they would at home, but they looked right and it was comfort food. Afterward we visited one of the many indoor shopping malls in Kuwait. I think Laura was surprised by how many stores there were with the same type of merchandise one would find in the States. They even had a Liz Claiborne store just like at home except with higher prices. Evidently the women wear some stylish things under their abayas!

At 5:00 we went to the Friday market: a weekend outdoor market that might be compared to a flea market, except all the stuff was new. There were rows and rows of furniture, rugs, underwear, dishes — you name it. We missed the entry and had to walk way around the end to get in. We were each carrying a water bottle that I had frozen. These helped somewhat, but the wind was blowing up a dust storm and it was so hot. After we finally got in, we stayed only about an hour and that was enough! I bought a long dress that looks a little like a robe. Women in Kuwait wear these or apparently anything else they feel like under their abayas. One day I saw a lady who wore a pair of flannel pajamas under her abaya. Hmm, there could be some advantages to those things!

We drove south about 20 minutes to a city called Fahaheel to have dinner with Dan and Rose, then more shopping. Laura bought candy, nuts, Turkish coffee and Kuwaiti coffee (a small portion of coffee mixed with cardamom.)

On Saturday, the first day of the workweek, I had to give a presentation to the teachers at my school. To celebrate Laura's visit I sponsored a breakfast for the teachers after my presentation. In the late afternoon, I had to show up at work again for a little while, and then we tried to go to a place called the fabric souk (market). It is two entire malls full of fabric shops. Some are upholstery type shops, others are shops with buttons, ribbons, thread and various other sewing accessories. There were lots of tailors in Kuwait who created clothes from these fabrics.

Unfortunately, the traffic was so heavy that there was a big back up just to get into the parking lot of the mall so we ditched it. Later, we joined another friend for dinner, and after that we walked around the enormous Marina Mall. It was right across the street from an old souk which has gold shops, fabric shops, and an everything's 100 fils store, which is like a dollar store in the States only this one is only about 30 cents.

Kuwait is a small country, bigger than Connecticut but smaller than New Jersey, and I wanted to take Laura on a drive to the little farming area called Wafra, a collection of farms at the southernmost point in Kuwait. I wanted to show Laura that wild camels roam the desert, and I knew that on a drive to Wafra, we might be able to see some. However, it was June and the weather was beastly hot. If my little car had a breakdown on the way, we would be in serious trouble. No AAA in Kuwait!

So, I recruited an Arabic speaking teacher from our school who agreed to go with us to Wafra and help in case anything happened. He would be able to flag down another car which would be the only solution as the desert is, well, a desert. Mr. Mohammad, an unmarried Syrian, happily joined us and had a lively conversation with Laura. He taught us some Arabic and explained some interesting things about Kuwait. I'm pretty sure this was an extremely memorable day for him!

Luckily we did see two camels cross the road just in front of us and saw more when we got to Wafra. Mr. Mohammed took Laura's picture with one of them and I think Mr. Mohammed was able to tell his friends that he now had an American girlfriend.

After we deposited Mr. Mohammed back at school, we were off to the beauty shop to get henna'd. A woman paints flowers wherever you want them on your body. I've only seen henna on hands and arms, but I suppose there are lots of other possibilities. Anyway, ours looked good and we really enjoyed the woman who put it on. Mine lasted about ten days.

The market at Wafra.

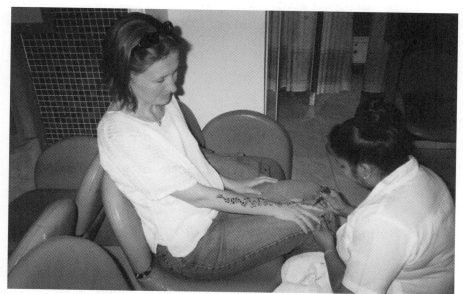

Laura gets henna'd.

Afterward, we finally got to the fabric souk and then just the two of us had dinner in a French restaurant called Paul's!

After Laura went back to the U.S., Mr. Mohammad wanted to send her an instant message. I gave him the number of her cell phone and told him that I didn't think she had instant messaging. He ended up calling and waking her up at 6 a.m. to tell her how much he enjoyed the trip to Wafra!

## WEEKEND TRIPS FROM KUWAIT

During the first year of my two year stay in Kuwait, I was on a special visa that required me to leave the country every 30 days. I learned this the hard way. At the airport on December 12, Stan and I were going home for Christmas. Ramadan that year fell during the Christmas holiday so we had booked a flight home.

When we arrived at the Kuwait airport for our departure, the customs official at passport control pulled me aside and told me to wait. Soon a uniformed man came to tell me that I needed to pay 45 dinars (about $150) because I had overstayed my visa. I patiently explained to the kind gentleman that this was impossible, I worked at The Center and that I was sure if they called my supervisor Mrs. Amani that this could be all cleared up. Stan stood a few yards away discreetly counting out 45 dinars. Well, what was Mrs. Amani's number? Long story short, we paid the 45 dinars and were on our way.

When we returned to Kuwait, I shared my story with Mr. Saleh who said, "Oh, Mrs. Carol, I'm so sorry. I thought you knew." OK. Never mind. Just how often do I have to leave the country? Every 30 days. Well, I thought, Middle East, here we come. We quickly planned a trip to Dubai in January because it was the only month when their temperatures wouldn't send my hot flashes to the boiling point. We also made plans to visit Oman, oh my God, so exotic, and Jordan which we especially looked forward to visiting for my 55th birthday.

Our travel agent in Kuwait, Mr. Yassar, set us up for these great trips with tours, lovely accommodations and a driver/guide in each location. Because it was 2002 and the possibility of terrorism loomed, tourism in these fascinating places was all but non-existent. Hence, we stayed in 5 star hotels for next to nothing and got great tour guides for extremely reasonable prices.

## NOT GETTING LAID IN PETRA

Our trip to Jordan was especially memorable. We went in late May just after my 55th birthday. We flew into Amman where we stayed at the stately, five star, Grand Hyatt Amman. What luxury! I was excited to be there and wanted to take a walk around the neighborhood before dinner. Stan didn't want to go with me so I set off by myself. Knowing my non-instinctive sense of direction, I started walking and made a loop around the neighborhood where I could always see the hotel. About 200 yards from the hotel was a beautiful residence with a policeman outside. I hesitated while looking at this palatial building wondering who lived there or what it was. The policeman who looked about 18 seemed to take an interest in me so I casually asked him who lived in this beautiful property.

"Are you American?"

"Yes, do you know who lives here?"

"Yes, it is the home of Queen Noor."

She was the famous and beautiful American, Lisa Hallaby who married King Hussein in 1978 and became his widow when he died in 1999. The king acted as a peace broker between various Middle Eastern rivals and was renowned for huge improvements in Jordan. In 2002 his death was quite recent and his widow's house was proof of her value to the country of Jordan. I was impressed that I could stand in front of the home of his widow, guarded by this very young policeman.

I told him, "I understand that she was a great queen and her husband was a wonderful king."

"Yes, she is very good. You are American. Would you like to lay with me tonight?"

I had heard that young men from the Middle East watch a lot of American movies and think that all American women are ready to drop into bed like they see in the movies. I think this man had learned this expression from his friends and was trying it out for the first time on the first American he had ever spoken with. Sort of like American boys learning "Voulez-vous couchez avec moi?"

"No, but thank you for the information about Queen Noor." I quickly walked away. Stan didn't know what he was missing. I told him all about it when I got back to the hotel. He didn't seem at all impressed that as a brand new 55-year-old woman I still had something! Ha!

The next day our guide picked us up at the hotel at 8 a.m. for our drive to Petra to visit the Nabatean ruins featured at the end of *Indiana Jones and the Last Crusade*. It was a two hour drive to Petra on a perfectly straight 4-lane highway with a grassless median separating the two roads. The highway took us through a flat gravelly desert with nothing to see for miles. After an hour or so, we noticed a police car ahead parked sideways across the road, lights flashing. Three other cars were stopped in each lane behind the police car.

We were the fourth car on the right side. Our driver/guide got out and spoke to the policeman who told him that there had been an accident up ahead and we had to wait here until it was cleaned up. More and more cars lined up behind us. Soon some of the cars that had been in line edged around so that they were now to our right and left instead of behind us. More and more cars and trucks began to do this so that soon the road looked like it was 16 lanes wide.

Eventually I realized that all of the drivers and passengers in these cars and trucks were men. I was the only woman. Should I be nervous about this? The guide was taking it all in stride and an official looking policeman stood very close to us so I decided that we were safe. I tried to keep myself busy while we waited. I rearranged my purse, wrote some work related notes and looked at the cars behind us.

About an hour later the policeman got into his car, drove it out of the way and all of the cars jockeyed forward to get the best position on the highway. Our driver wasn't the competitive type because he just cautiously made his way forward until we were safely on our way again.

On arrival in Petra, it was clear that this town was used to hordes of tourists. Now, however, the squares and pedestrian walkways were gapingly empty. Tables full of tourist trinkets displayed their wares to the blue sky.

Our hotel was a Movenpick and as soon as we had settled in, we ventured out to walk around. We came across five or six other groups of people who sounded like they were speaking German and we went to dinner in a restaurant the guide had suggested. On our brief walk that evening I noted a place with a sign that said Turkish bath with a price list for a bath and a massage. Hmm. *Maybe tomorrow.*

Our guide had arranged our walk through the Siq for the next day and had shown us where to catch our donkey ride to the entrance.

Visiting the Siq should be on everyone's bucket list. A six foot crack in 50 foot sandstone mountains wends for a kilometer down a sand path. At each turn it appears that the crack will join together and make a dead end. Finally at the very end, it appears that the path has ended but through a slit that looks too small for a human being to enter emerge the two empire state building sized sandstone peaks and an enormous open space which opens up to Al Khazneh, The Treasury, an ornate facade of a building carved into a rock face. It is actually only a facade that doesn't have an inside. This World Heritage site is breathtaking, but while the Treasury is the most beautiful facade, it is only 1/100 of the whole city of the Nabateans. The city which was built into the sandstone cliffs unfolds at ground level and continues up on the rocks. A whole day isn't enough to see it all. Schedule the donkey ride for the way out, not the way in because by then tourists will be exhausted. Get a guide for the entire visit to help explain the various features of this one of a kind place.

After spending the whole day in Petra, we returned to the hotel, tired and sweaty, and I wanted to go to the Turkish bath. Stan didn't want to go but said I should go ahead. It wasn't far from the hotel. I found it easily, entered and tried to understand what to do. I asked for a bath and a massage. After the male receptionist understood I hadn't brought a bathing suit, he gave me a clean, serviceable pair of shorts to put on with a skimpy towel for my top. Turkish baths may seem a little risqué, but they are all about modesty. Then I entered the large warm room that was the "bath." I was the only person there. I knew from my experience in Turkey that it is customary to enter the steamy room, sit down on a low marble slab, and pour warm water on your fully clothed body. Pretty soon the room was full of steam and I got a bowl from the water container and started pouring warm water on myself. The walk around Petra had been very tiring. Soon I laid down on the bench, sleepily breathing in the steamy air. I think I was beginning to fall asleep when a young man wearing only a loose pair of shorts came and took my hand and motioned for me to come with him. I was so used to people not speaking English, I followed him.

He led me to a massage room with two other massage tables and he used hand motions to show me how to lie face up on the uncomfortable marble slab. He never spoke. He massaged my lower legs, lower arms, shoulders and neck. All very chaste.

He motioned for me to turn over, face down on the hard table. I discreetly arranged the little towel on top so that it would open in the back for my massage. As I was turning over, my hand went off the table and I accidentally touched him in what should I say? His private place. I was so embarrassed and said, "Oh, excuse me." He started working on my back, I closed my eyes and as I relaxed, it felt good. I kind of went, "Mmmmm."

He spoke. He said, "You want dick?" I stopped breathing, I opened my eyes. Wait. What did I just hear? No, it can't be. Did I want Dick... the masseuse? Naive, Wisconsin girl, me. Why would they have a guy named Dick working here? I said, "Whaaat?" He said again, "You want dick?" Okay, now I got it. I said, "No." I was thinking *Oh, my God. What a hoot! I could get laid if I wanted to!* Then I started to smile and couldn't get back to the hotel fast enough to tell Stan that at 55 I had been propositioned not once but twice this weekend. I almost ran.

## OMAN

Stan and I visited exotic Oman for a long weekend. Mr. Yassar arranged a city tour and we loved it: lots of expat Brits, black sand, fairy castle buildings with arched windows and crenellated parapets. And unlike Kuwait, the Omanis worked jobs like mechanic, waiter, hotel bellman. In Kuwait the least acceptable job a Kuwaiti can have is policeman or firefighter; a teacher is OK, college professor is better, but most of the people work for the government. They leave jobs like electrician, plumber or shopkeeper to Bangladeshis or Indians. In Oman we were shocked when the taxi driver was an Omani.

After Stan returned to Wisconsin in the spring, I went for another Oman weekend the same time my friend Dixie and her husband were going there. I suspected they were trying to make their weekend a romantic getaway so I stayed in a different hotel and only made one arrangement to meet up with them on a guided tour of a wadi (dried river bed) that included a picnic.

When I arrived in Oman at the hotel, I was very tired. I had a small bag and wanted to head to my room to go to sleep. However, some Australian sailors were in town and staying at the same hotel. I rode up in the elevator with two of these young sailors. The larger man looked like he was holding his liquor well, but by the way he stood, tight lipped, staring straight ahead, it was clear there had been a lot of it. He made a little small talk with me and I answered nonchalantly. When I got off the elevator, he got off too. The other man could hardly stand up and slurred something like, "Come on, man. Let's go." The man who got off said, "I'll be there in a minute." I found my room, right across from the elevator and the elevator doors closed. The man stayed in the area just outside the elevator. I hurried myself into the room and closed the door, locking it.

Even though I was really tired, I felt uncomfortable with that man in the hallway. I peeked out of the little peephole. He was still standing there. What should I do? I kept my jacket on and sat on the bed. The man didn't knock on the door, but I heard him say something like, "There's a lot of beer out here." Was he thinking I was going to come out and join him? How could I get rid of him? I looked out the little peephole again. He was standing next to the elevator in what looked like a pose a soldier on guard duty might hold: eyes focused straight ahead and hands clasped behind his back. *Do I call security? That might make him mad.*

I just waited. Five minutes. I went to look and he was still there. Ten minutes; I looked again and he was still there staring straight ahead. Fifteen minutes, still there. Finally at 20 minutes, I heard the elevator doors open and watched him get on the elevator. I waited awhile and then rolled my suitcase out the door and got back into the empty (thank goodness) elevator. I went down to the check in desk and told the clerk what happened and asked for a different room. He was very accommodating. He said the Australians were "celebrating" and gave me another room on another floor. There was no sign of my bodyguard. I never told Stan that story.

The next day I enjoyed the trip to the wadi with Dixie and her husband. The weather was hot, but the drive through the desert to the wadi was comfortable in the guide's air-conditioned car. The Oman mountains/rocks get compared to a moonscape in travel books and based on photos of the moon I've seen, it's accurate. The jagged volcanic rock is interrupted every so often by salt flats. At the few oases, lush date palms cluster around the water. The black rock hills with the spring green of the oasis date palms were very different from Kuwait's flat stony desert with its scrubby olive green vegetation. The trip seemed other-worldly and the wadi water shone blue while the stony surrounding rocks discouraged hiking. No shoes I owned could walk safely on those rock outcrops and if one of us fell onto those rocks, we'd risk the chance of being impaled on a small scale or at least severely cut up.

For our picnic, our guide spread his little card table in the most shade he could find under some short palm trees next to the water, and we breathed in the beauty of the water, the rocks and the blue sky. The parts of the picnic that were supposed to be cold, were cold and the rest was bread, olives, dates and fruit. If we had brought our swimsuits and if we had been able to change into and out of them, we could have gone swimming. But of course we didn't and couldn't. Instead, we waded as deeply into the water as we could without getting our clothes wet. Sitting in the shade afterward next to the rippling water made us all homesick for the midwest where a picnic by a lake is as normal as a hamburger on the grill.

## THE NEIGHBORHOOD MUEZZIN (MOO AY ZIN)

I loved listening to the prayer calls we heard every day. The muezzin (person who calls the prayer) at the mosque that was really close to our apartment had a beautiful voice. Gradually I learned what time the evening prayer would occur and I would try to open a window or go downstairs and walk around the block so that I could hear him. I wondered if the notes of a musical staff were printed on the sidewalk. Did he look like a priest dressed in a long cossack who wore ballet shoes and tiptoed on the notes as he sang?

## WASDA (WAHZ-DA)

Because of oil wealth, if you're Kuwaiti, you have money. All Kuwaitis have money, it's just a question of how much you have. The Kuwaiti government has been subsidizing its people ever since oil was discovered there in the early 1920s. if you're a Kuwaiti, that you have money is understood. For a Kuwaiti, money isn't the issue; for a Kuwaiti the key is *wasda* or influence, and that's how your status is measured. Is one of your daughters married to the Emir? (He has many wives.) Are you friends with anyone who is in the royal family? Is your family in the upper echelons of Kuwaiti society? Do people listen when you have something to say?

If you're Kuwaiti, you might be white skinned or black skinned. It doesn't matter. I've never seen such beautiful openness between skin tones. However, if you're any other nationality, you're not qualified. In other words, a black skinned Kuwaiti is 100% accepted in Kuwait society, but an Indian, a Bangladeshi, a Sri Lankan or American unless through marriage to a Kuwaiti, is someone who can't become a Kuwait citizen.

## GOODBY KUWAIT

It was hard to believe that my two years were finished. I was of two minds. I was happy to be going home to Stanley and to trade desert for greenery, veiled women in black robes for women in shorts and tank tops, traffic noise for birds chirping, blow dryer heat for jackets in the evening weather, bottled water for a cold drink straight from the tap, club soda for WINE (!), mangoes for raspberries (OK, that one is an even trade) and one TV channel for what, 50? But, I also was trading the men in their white flowing robes for guys in baseball caps, the rich mixture of languages including Arabic in all its varieties, Farsi, Bangladeshi, the various Indian and

Pakistani dialects, French, British [!] and even a little German, for English-ALL THE TIME BY EVERYONE. I was trading the haunting prayer calls for silence, our wonderful travel agent Mr. Yassar for on-line ticketing, and our miracle worker Sabastina for our self-cleaning house that I would now be cleaning myself. Living and working in Kuwait was such an interesting experience. I had wanted to live in Europe and ended up in Kuwait instead, and I'm not one bit sorry.

BELARUS

# BELARUS

—◦›› ‹‹◦—

When my job ended in Kuwait, I decided maybe it was time for me to try retirement again. Stan was pushing me, too. He kept saying, "We have two beautiful places to live and I would like to live in them." I had to agree. I told him I'd try it for two years and I did. By this time in addition to our Florida condo, we had our condo in Door County. It was big enough for us each to go our own way and we did pretty well. It was great not to be working during that first year. My daughter and Christopher were engaged. They planned their June, New York City wedding by themselves.

My financial picture was a little different because I had started to draw my pension from my 22 years in Appleton so I didn't feel dependent on Stan for income, but I kept busy volunteering in schools daily just to keep current and, though I wouldn't say it out loud back then, I still wanted to be able to tell an interviewer that I was in schools every day.

*OK, I had tried it.* After two years, I was ready to go back to teaching overseas. While Stan didn't want to work again, he would gladly accompany me on another international experience. I decided against going to another job fair to spare me from the costs, both financial and emotional. From my experiences in Turkey and Kuwait I knew that there were always schools that needed someone at the last minute and with my three years of international experience, I liked my chances. I started looking in mid-July. On July 20, I saw that an organization called QSI (Quality Schools International) had two openings for English teachers in Ukraine. My teaching license says "English teacher-grades 6–12" so I contacted them. QSI has 37 international schools all over the world (qsi. org) and a 50-year history of success.

They responded within twelve hours. The short response time was impressive. Well, the jobs in Ukraine had been filled, but they had an opening in Minsk, Belarus. Would I consider that? *Yes, I would.* I knew that in the international school business, it is good to say *yes* first and get out the map later. Belarus is located between Poland and Russia and had been part of the former Soviet Union, hence the people spoke Russian. The school had an enrollment of about 20 kids from ages 3–16.

They asked me more questions about who would be coming with me and after they found out that Stan was a retired high school principal, they were *very* interested. It seemed the previous director of the school resigned, taking the other teacher with her. Would my husband consider working? Stan was in the room. I watched him wrestle his demons (for the very first time in 16 years of marriage) as he paced the room. He didn't want to go back to work, but he was intrigued. "Oh, all right." He joked later that he was trying to save his marriage (it wasn't at risk; I would have found another job), but I still believe he was happy to be begged to take a job.

He seemed to enjoy retirement, but he had very few interests aside from reading and making short trips to places like

WalMart or Publix. If he ever worried about his health, I wasn't aware of it. If I planned a trip, he was always a willing companion, but if left to him, he would have stayed home and sat in his chair. When I would go to the Outlet Mall, he would come with me and head straight for the Food Court with his book and would stay there the entire time I was there. He never complained about how much time I was taking. We also had spats and disagreements living together in retirement that were absent when one of us was working. He'd say, "I'm turning on the AC." I'd say, "I'm freezing." He'd say, "Get your sweatshirt on." Lots of these spats were about heat and AC. Remember that he was a high school principal for 27 years in a school where if he said the AC should be turned on, that's what happened. Also, he retired years before me and he wasn't used to my "input!" Eventually we worked out the hot and cold by having odd days and even days. On even days he controlled the thermostat and on odd days I did. It worked!

In addition to work being good for Stan, he was exceptionally good at what he did. He was a natural leader who had a "presence" that people noticed. When he stepped into a room, people sat up a little taller. He could diffuse a tense situation with a perfect question. He had a way of looking at problems as if someone were asking him if he wanted strawberry or vanilla. Cool and confident with parents, teachers and kids, he would ask a distraught male or female what the problem was. The next question was always asked in the calmest possible voice, "What have you considered doing about _____?" The person always had some ideas and just saying them out loud was usually a path to a solution. If the person needed further encouragement he would say, "What's the worst thing that could happen?" If he had angry parents in his office, he would let them vent and listen politely to what they had to say while taking notes which he would later throw away. If the parent kept on and insisted that they would sue the school, he would calmly write the name of the attorney the school district worked with and gave the paper to the parents saying, "Well, have your attorney contact our attorney." I know that this was a different era, but I think it speaks well for Stan that not one suit was ever filed. Everyone was always treated with respect and humor. He was full of self-confidence and negative things rolled off his back like water off a duck. I've always wished I had those qualities.

His favorite expressions were, "Trust the universe." And he did. "Accept grace." And he did. "I'm not worried about anything because the things I worry about aren't going to happen. Other things will happen but I don't know what they are, so I am not worried about them." And he wasn't.

When he was principal at Appleton-East, the staff, parents and kids loved him. He was calm, level-headed and funny. There was a tradition at East graduations. Each student in the senior class would give Stan a gift as he handed them their diploma. For example, the year he had a motorcycle accident, kids came with band-aids, bumper stickers that said *Watch out for Motorcycles,* or those tall orange flags that go on the back of the motorcycle. One year when Laura was in high school, Stan came to breakfast wearing a name tag from the previous evening's meeting on his bathrobe. We asked him why he was wearing a name tag and he said, "I didn't want you to forget my name." Well, Laura was dating a boy from Appleton East then who told his classmates about this incident so that year at graduation, each student came with a name tag with his name on it and pasted it on his suit jacket as they received their diplomas. Another year the students removed things from the school and gave them to Stan. He received a few clocks, staplers, scissors and one of the kids handed him a set of screws, saying, "Don't lose these." Another student later in the alphabet handed Stan the personalized license plates from his car. He was well-respected in the school and the community.

So a week after I applied for a job at QSI, we drove to Eau Claire, WI where we met with the QSI Director of Operations at a Perkins restaurant! I knew from the first minute this was my kind of organization. We weren't even back home yet when he called us with our job offers. We told him we'd call him back the next day with our decision. I was thrilled! We were on our way in less than two weeks.

## LIVING IN BELARUS

Our apartment sat on an eight-lane wide avenue in the exact geographical center of downtown Minsk, a city of approximately two million people. The wide sidewalks on our street teemed with people day and night. Cars (generally late model ones) in all eight lanes moved up and down the avenue in dry weather or in six inches of snow. They moved quickly and when I waited for the walk light on the corner nearest our apartment, I would always stand on the safe side of the large metal lamp post. That way an out-of-control driver might be able to hit me, but he would also severely damage his car on the lamp post.

*In front of our apartment.*

When we were there, the QSI school in Minsk was located inside another large, two-story Belarusian school. We were the only foreign faculty and the 20 kids were almost all the children of diplomats. They came from Israel, Lithuania, the United States, Germany, Poland, India, and Sweden. One family was from Russia and worked for the Coca Cola company. Belarusian students were not allowed by the local government to attend our school.

In observing the Belarusians who walked up and down our street, it seemed odd to us that no one smiled or waved to others and even if they met a friend, the perfunctory greeting couldn't be called warm. But the crowds of people kept moving, eyes straight ahead. At first glance, an outside observer would believe this was the unfriendliest of cultures. Yet the Belarusians who worked in our school shared with us and each other the warmest greetings, the friendliest banter and an unmistakable sense of family. When the same co-workers left the safety of the school, it was all business again: stoic faces, purposeful forward motion.

## STOICISM

Years of oppressive circumstances and fear of being watched spilled over into the way people behaved in public. One day as I was leaving school early, walking ahead of me was a woman holding the hand of what must have been her daughter. I assumed the mother had come to get her daughter before dismissal time for an appointment or something. I made my way gingerly down the snow covered steps and sidewalk in front of the school. As the mother and daughter walked full steam ahead, the mother was loudly clucking a blue streak of Russian to the eight year old girl. Mother was not happy having to pick up her daughter. The little girl's pale face puffed up and her cheeks got rosy. Suddenly whatever she'd been holding in spewed out. She vomited but she didn't stop walking and the mother started yanking harder on her arm and yelling something like, "Now, stop that, right now. Stop that." Still walking, the girl vomited again and the mother still kept up her punitive diatribe while pulling up on the girl's hand. The mother moved out ahead of the girl as if to say, "I can't believe you did that, you horrible creature." The little girl kept walking. There were no tears and no stopping for what would have put me on a cot. Apparently in Belarus, stoicism comes early.

## THE SCHOOL INSIDE A SCHOOL

Our little "campus," had already existed at that same location for 14 years. It consisted of seven small classrooms: language arts, art, music room, mathematics/computer room, preschool room, science room, a library about as big as a walk-in closet, two tiny rooms for small groups, a two-stall girls' bathroom, a one-stall-one-urinal boys' bathroom, and a closet sized office for Lena (LEH nuh), the school secretary. We also used the Belarusian school's gym on the first floor with its accompanying PE teacher. The gym was nothing like any gym in a modern facility in North America, but it was an indoor space where the kids could run and run and run which was so important in those cold winter months.

In addition to the gym, we also had access to the school's woodworking room and accompanying woodworking teacher, gentle Mr. Sasha, who adored our kids and was adored in return. We also used the football-field sized playyard right outside the school. It had one basketball court and nothing else but grass and open space. We were the only ones who used that field. The Belarusian kids stayed indoors. Their school had almost the same hours as we did as well as the same calendar and we all got along splendidly. We entered and departed with the students and teachers in the larger school, but that was the extent of our interaction. We had friendly hellos and goodbyes (zdrastvitsya and das vydania), but that was it, unless there was a problem. I'm sure they appreciated the rent we paid.

The only way in and out of our little second floor school-within-a-school was a sturdy metal door which we kept locked at all times. A little monitor showed us who was ringing the bell to be let in. We also kept the door locked to keep us safe from curious outsiders and to discourage the students from the Belarusian school from thinking they could come in. In case of a serious emergency, there was a bench/storage compartment below the window at the end of the long hallway with a rope ladder that could be employed to evacuate the kids one by one down to the ground. Luckily it had never needed to be used.

When we accepted the job, Stan and I thought we could handle the twenty kids. We could trade off, he'd take ten, I'd take the other ten and later in the day we would switch. Little did we know, there were already four other full time local teachers and three part time teachers for these twenty kids. If you counted the school secretary, Lena, our student to teacher ratio was 1.8 kids to 1 teacher. This didn't count the part-time staff: an attorney who did a lot of work for the school, the local accountant who helped with our books, the cleaning lady, and the security guard who arrived before we left and didn't leave until we arrived in the morning. Our little school was the best staffed school I've ever heard of, let alone worked at! My largest class had three kids!

The QSI International School in Minsk was the embassy school and had the endorsement of the U.S. Embassy in Minsk. Because of that official designation, someone from some U.S. State Department office that monitors schools had to make a yearly visit. Everything had to comply with State Department

*Teachers at a picnic at the Ambassador's house. L to R: Lena, Olga with daughter Arisha, Stan, Katya, Olga's other daughter, and Tanya, another teacher..*

rules for overseas schools. One of those requirements was that students and staff would be prepared for any emergency. To that end many years ago, the school had installed bullet proof windows throughout and the rope escape ladder. The plum job of school inspector was usually held by a former principal of an overseas school. During our first year a man visited, and all he seemed interested in was where we were going for dinner that evening. He especially liked the potato pancakes that were a traditional Belarusian food. At first I liked them too, all spicy and crispy fried. Later, I didn't enjoy the heartburn that was a little post-potato pancake pain! We took him to the place we called Patio Pizza and he was happy!

The second year a woman came to inspect the school. She gave the place a very thorough going-over and asked us to hold a fire drill. We did so and luckily she missed the part where I took the kids down to our emergency exit door on the first floor and which the Belarusians, for some reason, had locked that day. By some gift from the ghosts of my grandparents (who I've always believed are watching over me), the caretaker of the building was nearby and one of our Russian speaking kids quickly told him what was going on. He swiftly unlocked that door and the kids poured out while the inspector waited and watched from upstairs. Stan told me later that while he was talking with her during that fire drill, she asked to see an evacuation drill using the rope ladder out the window. According to Stan, he paused, looked at her incredulously, motioned her toward the window and smilingly said, "After you." I'm not sure if she laughed or was insulted, but that was the end of that request. Oh, he was a special man!

## OUR APARTMENT

While our apartment faced the grand six lane wide street: Praspiekt Niezalieznasci (Independence Avenue, Minsk's main avenue) and looked stately from the wide sidewalk below, the entry to the building was in the back and a polar opposite from the grand front. We used a key to enter and if you didn't know better, you would think you were walking into the worst slum in America. Poorly lit with a low wattage light bulb hanging by a wire from the tall ceiling, the hallway seemed black as we headed the 15 feet to either the creaky elevator or the stairs. The elevator would hold three to four average sized individuals who knew each other really well, but could hold only one Stan plus maybe one other reasonably sized person. Every time I rode it up to the third floor, I prayed a silent missive to God that the elevator wouldn't quit on this trip. I learned early on, probably the first day, that it was preferable to climb the 3 dark flights of stairs than take the elevator to our apartment.

In contrast to the creepy hallway, our apartment was bright, nicely decorated, and just plain homey. Our door opened to a hallway and coat closet. Straight ahead lay the second bedroom, and off that hallway to the left was the living room, to the right, the third bedroom/office. If we turned left at the entry, we would walk down the hall with the bathroom on the left and go straight into the kitchen. Our bedroom could be accessed from the living room or the second bedroom so that if we wanted to, we could walk in a circle around our apartment. It was maybe 1,200 square feet and quite comfortable.

The second bedroom and third bedroom/office faced the main street. Our bedroom, the living room and the kitchen faced the back which was a park like area with a few beat-up looking playground items, an orderly set of garbage cans, and lots of parking. We never understood why so many car alarm horns went off at odd times: beep-beep-beep. Was theft such a problem or did the alarm systems malfunction that often? These were so annoying at 3:00 a.m.

After we'd been there awhile, I learned that very late in the night or early in the morning, I could hear the subway pass by underground because the line (one of two) ran exactly under our building. It quit running between 2 a.m. and 5 a.m. So I kind of knew what time it was by whether or not I could faintly hear the subway. I always hated to hear that sound in the morning because it meant I would soon have to get up.

Flowery embossed wallpaper covered every single wall in that apartment, a different pattern in each room. The posters I'd carried from home to make our house feel like home wouldn't stick to the wallpaper no matter what I tried, and I didn't want to try so hard that I damaged the wallpaper. So I left the posters rolled up in the tube and carried them back home the first Christmas.

Our apartment was owned by a woman whose father had been a renowned Belarusian writer. She was very kind, if talkative, the few times we met her. I'm pretty sure this apartment was her pride and joy and that her living accommodations weren't half as nice. Every time we left for more than a week, she moved back in and left before we got back. How did I know this? A person like me leaves things just so. When I came back, they were not just so. Lots not so. There were different sheets and sometimes blankets on the bed, and shampoo in the cabinet instead of the edge of the tub.

The furniture was functional, not bad looking, and took up most of the space. The little kitchen had a decent sized refrigerator, a four-gas-burner stove with an electric oven, a washing machine and dryer that was the kind with a water collector that had to be emptied after each use. Two people could eat comfortably at the table there. The living room had a pretty comfortable sofa, two nicely upholstered chairs and a dark walnut dining table with six chairs. A white bookshelf

*How did this cat get on our 3rd story window ledge?*

housed some knick knacks that the owner or long gone tenants must have left, and there was a great stereo with one CD: Rachmaninov. The brooding melodies seemed to fit with the winter darkness and Belarusian stoicism. I could picture stone-faced Rachmaninov pounding the low notes on the piano to the beat of his anguish, the hard life Russians faced every day. Then after he expressed his torment, he'd remember the color of the leaves of birch trees in the spring and the fluttering of newly hatched butterflies while the music would lighten up and take me to a spring meadow. *Rhapsody on a Theme of Paganini* could carry me to that meadow and warm me with sunlight. Then back to the passion of his misery, Rachmaninov's low notes tumbled out. The listen was an emotional roller coaster that seemed perfect for this enigma of a culture. I listened to that CD almost every night and never got tired of it, sitting at the big mahogany dining room table working on one of the puzzles previous occupants had left behind.

I've never seen better windows than the ones that faced Independence Avenue. Clearly they were added later as they were sound-proof, beautifully sturdy, and completely functional. With the window open, the street noise pounded in. Close the window, instant silence. The windows in the back, on the other hand, were probably the original ones as they were framed in wood, leaky, dysfunctional, and downright breezy.

Off of the master bedroom was a glass door that led to a 12-inch wide outdoor balcony — not even wide enough to stand on. The fixtures on that door were wrought iron and after we opened it once, we closed it and never opened it again. A huge advantage to this apartment, besides its optimal location in the center of Minsk, was that it had been used by expats of all kinds for many years. This meant that it had its own water heater for use in the spring even when hot water for the whole neighborhood was shut down for two weeks for "maintenance." Yes, it's true. All of the water came from the government and if they wanted to shut it down, they did. Luckily when they shut down the hot water, our personal hot water heater kicked in. The locals couldn't afford such a luxury and would either go without bathing for those two weeks or go to their brother in law's uncle's house to get clean.

Another advantage was that our apartment contained a radiant heater. Shaped like an old fashioned radiator, it was free-standing, moveable, very new, and wonderfully efficient. Why did we need this? Because, like the water, the government also controlled the heat, and they didn't turn it on in the fall until they were good and ready. They also turned it off in the spring whenever they felt like it. Winter, fall, and spring are cold in Belarus and even when the heat was on, those drafty back windows could make the apartment feel like the bleachers in a hockey rink. That little heater got lots of use by this prima donna with her down comforter and silk long underwear.

## A TEACHABLE MOMENT

In our small school, Leah and Ocsana (both girls) were the only 7th grade students. In their literature book was a short story about a Jewish grandmother in New York who told her grandson about the time in Russia when she was a child and her town was attacked by Russian Cossacks. She and her family hid in an underground cellar and survived, but many of the other villagers died. I'm not sure you could get a better teachable moment because Leah who was Jewish read the story with Ocsana whose mother is Russian. Even at their tender ages, they understood how lucky they were that these two best friends who adored each other could read such a story and appreciate how much progress had been made between these two cultures.

When Julia arrived the next year, a transformation occurred. The two best friends accommodated their new classmate with an openness beyond their years. Ocsana and Leah had so many shared memories and so much love for each other that it was difficult to open their little circle. But open it, they did. They included Julia in most of their activities even though the comfortable thing to do would have been to exclude her. It wasn't long before Julia's arrival broadened the pair to a threesome and as difficult as that can be, Ocsana and Leah made it work — without any adult intervention.

## THE SOUND OF MUSIC IN KIEV

When we learned that QSI International School of Kiev (with some 500 students) in neighboring Ukraine was producing *The Sound of Music* for their spring play, those same three (now 8th grade) girls swarmed me like hungry great whites. They circled, they nudged, they enlisted the smaller fish until I agreed to accompany them to the show. We would take the overnight train on Friday night, arrive in Kiev around 10 a.m. on Saturday, get picked up by a driver from the Kiev school, eat lunch in their school cafeteria (not sure why they offered lunch on a Saturday) and be on time for the 2 p.m. matinee. After the matinee, we would get some dinner at McDonald's on the way to the train station and board the overnight train back to Minsk. Each sleeper car on the train contained two bench seats, one on either side of the car which made up into four bunks. It would be perfect for three students and one teacher.

If you've never traveled with three 8th grade girls, you've missed the chance to stand in the middle of a tornado. Bubbly Leah, social butterfly Ocsana, and quiet bunny Julia were so excited to (a.) get out of town (b.) get away from their parents, (c.) interact with some other kids (translate: boys) their own age, that they stopped walking and jumped everywhere on imaginary springs in their feet. These were the daughters of diplomats so they had to be good most of the time and try to be satisfied living in a country where their only age-mates who could speak English were the three of them. Going to another school with actual other kids their age was monumental.

In the days prior to the trip they talked endlessly about what clothes they would pack, the snacks they would bring, books they would read on the way (as if!) and most importantly, what music each one was responsible for bringing. On the day of our departure, they had to bring their things with them to school since we would take a taxi from school to the train station.

In the complex world of our school's finances, we often ran short of cash. We had plenty of money, but it wasn't cash. Our students were almost all from families of diplomats. All but our one scholarship student paid tuition by bank transfer, and the school used an American bank that was not in Belarus.

If we received cash, it was a small amount and the Belarusian cash economy, for complicated reasons, despite having its own currency, in reality ran on the dollar and in cash. Hence, we were almost always short of dollars. Whenever any school personnel went to Kiev or anyone from Kiev came to Minsk, they would bring back the legal amount of dollars. Our regional supervisor made two visits per year, and the staff went to Kiev each November for professional development. The legal limit of dollars that could be brought in was $2,000 per person so everytime we left, we came back with that much money in cash. The appropriate paperwork was handled by Lena and the QSI accountant who worked in a separate country with several QSI schools. So on this particular return trip from Kiev, I was carrying a lot of money!

On the train to Kiev the girls swirled around our little compartment like bubbles in a boiling pot. Who would reign at Eurovision? Another Greek? Did Daniel Radcliffe have a girlfriend? Was Justin Timberlake really in love with Christina Aguilera? Was Mariah Carey secretly married? If I ever have a daughter I'm going to name her Hermione. Then they all broke out in song with Queen's, "We Will Rock You" while clapping the beat with their hands on their laps.

Eventually the train attendant came to set up the beds. At around 10:30, I told the girls I was going to sleep. Due to my advanced age, I got the bottom bunk. Would they talk quietly from now on? They buzzed on for at least 2 more hours from the top bunk opposite me. I knew it would be silly to try to make them go to sleep, so I just let them burn themselves out which they finally did. I pretended to sleep and probably did.

The border of Belarus and Ukraine might as well have been Checkpoint Charlie back in the Cold War. On the overnight train, we crossed this border to enter Ukraine at about 3:00 a.m. We were awakened long before the border guards reached our cabin door. We heard a RAP-RAP-RAP on each door in our car. Because there is no lock on the door, the scary border guards opened the door, turned on the light, and asked their invasive questions, eyes boring into each passenger. Papers were checked, questions were asked, and each passport was poured over with a tiny magnifying glass that looked like a microscope. Then they exited to rap on the next door. Leaving Belarus to go to Kiev, this interruption by the border guards was a stressful annoyance.

But returning to Belarus could be worse, I feared. In fact, once on a train when Stan and I were returning to Belarus from Lithuania in the north, a man was removed from the train. He had a one entry visa into Belarus. He had exited Belarus and

gone to Lithuania on a one-entry visa and now he was trying to re-enter Belarus. He's probably still there on the border
with the guards asking him for his multiple entry visa.

The play was wonderful. The girls were excited about *The
Sound of Music*. They could appreciate how well done it was
with a cast of kids who came from all over the world. Our
three girls had met a few kids from the Kiev school and that's
all they could talk about. One of the girls they met also liked
Harry Potter and was an avid fan of Eurovision like our girls.
They had so much in common. I got to interact with some
staff and parents from the Kiev school and I picked up my
"package:" a brown manilla envelope which I quickly put
into my backpack.

We stopped for dinner at McDonalds which was absolute
heaven for the girls. (Of course there is no McDonalds in
Belarus). *Okay*, I told myself, *I could eat it just this once!* We got
driven back to the train station by one of the Kiev drivers.

When I went to the bathroom to change into my jammies, I
moved the money in the envelope to my money belt.

In the middle of the night, we were awakened long before
the border guards reached our cabin door.

We could hear the three or four guards knocking on the
doors of the train compartments down the hall from us. Slowly,
methodically, they moved down the car. Believe me, I was
awake. Door after door RAP-RAP-RAP. The money was safely
tucked under my pajamas. I waited. Finally RAP-RAP-RAP.
The guards opened the door and looked in at this unusual setting, three preteens and one adult. The girls were all sitting up.

Ocsana, a native Russian speaker, was serving as inter-
preter. I handed the guards the passports which I was also
carrying, (this wasn't my first trip with middle schoolers) and

one guard started examining them. Another started asking questions in Russian.

"Why you are in Ukraine?"

"We went to see a play, *The Sound of Music* at QSI International School of Kiev." I had letters of permission signed by the girls' parents in both English and Russian just in case we needed them.

"How long have you lived in Minsk?" This question seemed directed at me.

"Two years." Ocsana translating.

I was waiting for the question about whether I was carrying any cash, but they didn't ask it! The guard seemed to run out of questions. One by one the other guard gave the newly stamped diplomatic passports back. First the American one, then the Swedish one, next the Israeli one. They took an excruciating amount of time with mine. Luckily the girls had all traversed borders many times and knew the drill. Be serious. Answer the questions. Say nothing. Wait.

Finally mine came back.

"Hev a good evahneeng."

"Thank you, spasiba."

They shut the door. We held our breath until we heard them knock at the next door and let out a collective, if silent, sigh of relief. The girls went back to sleep, still exhausted from the night before, and I smiled a little smile lying there in the bottom bunk with my bundle of now sweaty money hidden in my money belt.

We got into Minsk in the dark of a northern Europe early morning and I headed right to bed. Two nights of little sleep and more stress about the money than I wanted peeled off quickly. The next day Stan and I divided the money into two piles and each carried one to school. I couldn't get there fast enough. Stan put the money in the school safe, but at the end of the day, he carried most of it over to the embassy where we kept a pouch in the embassy safe. Over the next weeks and months, that cash would be dispersed to the many vendors and service providers we dealt with. It's an odd economy where all of the serious transactions are carried out in dollars while the local stores and markets run on rubles.

The whole school knew these three girls had gone on a dreamy adventure. Ocsana, Leah, and Julia talked about nothing else for weeks. They oohed and aahed about Kiev, about the play, about the friends they made.

Ocsana in Minsk was a little like trying to keep a butterfly in a birdcage. Leah excelled at sports, and without competition and teams to play on, she was making do with her tennis lessons, but she was ready for more. Sweet Julia seemed happy to get back to where things were familiar and predictable. And how many teachers can tell a story like this about three students on a train together in Belarus?

*OKAY,* I thought, ***THIS IS WHY I CAME HERE.***

## NOT TOO SMALL FOR LICE
During one of the two winters we worked at QSI Minsk, the math teacher came to Stan and me one day and asked if either of us had ever seen lice? No, neither of us had, why? Well, he had seen a bug jump from one hair to another on one of the students, a girl with rather longish hair, a bug that looked quite at home living in and on her hair. We looked up a picture of a louse on line and figured, *yup, we got lice.* And apparently, you never have just one. We called the mother

who came to get her daughter, and Stan and I tried to decide what to do. I remembered from my grad school Educational Administration classes that no matter what the issue, if it involves others from the school, you have to send a note (yes, Millennials, a paper note) home with all of the kids so the parents know what they're dealing with. I contacted my friend Sue from Appleton and bless her heart, she sent me the text from the letter that her school sends home when there's an outbreak of lice, describing what to do: buy and use special shampoo, (yes, they had that in Minsk,) and wash sheets and towels. I copied the letter and each child went home with one. It was a Friday and on Monday I noticed that another little boy's hair which was usually pretty straight and flat looked like he'd gotten a perm that weekend. Eventually I found out that his family was taking no chances. Everyone in the family, including mom and dad had been treated with the anti-lice shampoo!

To our knowledge, the lice didn't spread to any of the other kids.

## BLESSED FRIENDS

We've been blessed with friends wherever we've lived, but the ones we made in Belarus were truly special. School directors shouldn't be friends with the staff or with parents, but in a small insular environment, these rules were easy to break. We counted the staff as true friends. We also got to know some parents, including an American elementary teacher, Amy who helped teach reading to our 5 and 6 years olds and her German husband, Thorsten. What a gift for their children to grow up in a family with two heritages to learn about. The kids spoke only English with Mom and only German with Dad. They will be so employable no matter what professions they choose.

We loved getting together with them and with other expat couples we met through the embassy. We saw them quite a bit at the embassy buffets sponsored by other countries that had consulates in Minsk. The most interesting event was Robert Burns night at the American ambassador's house. There were speeches, poems, a haggis as close as possible to the real thing that could be obtained in Belarus, and dancing, lots of dancing. Somebody knew how to do a special dance just for Robert Burns and we all tried to learn it. We had so much fun that we didn't want to go home.

*Robert Burns Night*

Though I didn't see it at the time, now I look back on the experience in Belarus in comparison to stories and movies about the English colonial period in India. An unspoken agreement was understood that, *here we are, all of us together. We've chosen this life. Let's make the most of it.* Luckily in Belarus we didn't have the social class issues the British had in India. The dinners and social events were just plain fun, and all of us expats were on an equal playing field — all of us there just for the experience. Stan and I were so happy to be included in all of it.

## EXCURSIONS FROM MINSK

It's a good thing we had wonderful friends in Minsk because there weren't many opportunities for tourism, travel, or excursions. The few local people who had money traveled abroad for their travel experiences and the local people without money went to the forests for picnics. The process for getting a visa to get into Belarus was complicated, and the intimidation from border guards didn't make it a coveted travel destination. We took one trip to the Nesvizh Castle, which was a residence of the Radziwill family. We could see the outside and a room or two inside. While it's a UNESCO World Heritage Site, it looked a little beat up. Ours was the only car in the parking lot. On the same excursion, we visited the Neman Glassworks factory store where we bought crystal wine glasses.

Vilnius was about a four hour train ride from Minsk and we loved to go there to escape the undercurrent of oppression which seemed palpable in Minsk. After I went to the annual craft fair in March of our first year, I knew I would want to go again the second year. A city of about a half million people, Vilnius is the capital of Lithuania (on the northern border of Belarus) and as delightful a European city as we would ever find. We always stayed in a converted convent that was extremely comfortable, if sparse. Vilnius' old city was charming and contained French and Italian restaurants — a welcome change from all of those potato pancakes. Their gift shops were full of amber, amber and more amber.

March 1 seems to be the beginning of spring for people of this area, hence the expansive craft fair plus other rituals such as burning the winter witch and jumping over a fire all dressed up in Halloween type costumes. In our experience in Minsk, true spring (warmer temperatures, green buds appearing, longer days) much like Wisconsin, didn't occur until later.

*Stan and his friends Sven and Alex.*

## BUGGED

The Belarusians we knew universally believed that they were being bugged every minute of every day in every location. Is that why their public interactions are so stiff?

Our Belarusian staff told us we should be careful what we said at home because they were convinced there were bugs in our apartment too. I told them I pitied whoever had to listen to us because they would find out just how boring we were. There I was in the evenings listening to my Rachmaninov doing jigsaw puzzles and Stan was on the computer or reading. We had a TV but we rarely watched it because what little came in English was so homogenized that it wasn't worth watching. During mealtimes we usually talked about one student or another or maybe the parents — pretty dull stuff for agents looking for us to be spies.

## THE CREAKY ELEVATOR AND THE DARK STAIRWELL

Sandra, from the embassy, and I took fitness classes from a svelte woman named Lyuda every Monday, Wednesday and Friday in the little fitness room at the embassy. Class started at 5:00 and ended at 6:00. When I walked home after class it was pitch dark as during the winter months it started to get dark at around 4 p.m. One day in January of our second year, I came home after Stan (who always took the creaky elevator). It was especially cold that day and I was all relaxed walking up the dark stairwell already feeling the relief of our warm apartment.

I was five steps from the second floor landing when I saw a large dark shape in the corner. In all of my walks up this dark stairwell, I had never seen anyone or anything on the stairs. In that split second I perked up with more curiosity than fear of this dark shadow. It looked like a blanket and I wondered why someone had put a blanket on the floor in the stairwell. Then the blanket moved. My curiosity flipped to fear. Why would a blanket move? As I climbed those few stairs to the landing, I made out the form of a human being — a hairy faced man — lying on the corner landing wrapped in the dark blanket. In one electric moment our eyes met. But I saw fear, not aggression. I didn't hesitate and give him a chance to change his mind and grab my leg; he was close enough to be able to do that. I just needed to put one foot on the landing and the other foot on the next step to get out of his way and up to our apartment. He pulled his wrapping away so that I could put my foot on the landing, turn the corner and head up to the third floor. I didn't run because I didn't want to seem afraid, but by then oh, yes, I was SCARED. I've never scaled a flight of stairs the way I flew up that one, listening for the sound of footfalls on the steps coming after me. Did I acquire a set of springs on my feet? Grow wings on my back? I didn't hear any noise as I bounded up the last flight and flew into the warm light of our apartment, quickly locking the door behind me.

I'm pretty sure I scared that man as much as he scared me. I doubt that he expected anyone to come up the stairwell as I was probably the only person in the building who didn't use the creaky elevator. I'm guessing that he was afraid that I would report him and he would end up outdoors in the subzero cold. Nope, not me. In the morning, he was gone. I checked.

I didn't tell Stan about the hairy man in the stairwell. He probably wouldn't have gone out there, as what could he have done anyway? But I didn't want to put him in that position. After I wasn't chased up the stairs, I simply figured that the man was cold, had found a way in and was planning to spend the night. I hope he did.

I kept using the stairs, much more watchfully now, but no other overnight visitors ever showed up.

## DRAFTS
At school, the idea of fresh air seemed offensive to the Belarusian staff. Drafts were treated like spoiled meat. Noses

turned up, shawls came out of closets and people gathered in the center rooms where no windows were open. If they had to, they opened the last window in the last classroom on the west side of the hallway and the first window in the first classroom on the east side. Little air could possibly exchange itself over the distance of that 80 feet.

At home, the drafts were a burden to me and Stan because there were so many of them. Our back windows that looked out over the parking lot and the little grassy play area let in enough air to make the gauzy curtains flutter. We examined those windows during that first cold fall and being a Wisconsin girl, I knew just what I had to do.

Number one: don't rely on a man to fix drafts. They don't care one breeze as much as I do. Number two: when we went home over the Christmas break for a glorious three weeks, I bought two 3M window sealing kits — remember those? It was a large sheet of plastic (I had pre-measured) and a roll of double sided tape. I stuck the tape to the wooden window frame and stuck the plastic sheet to the tape, much like covering a 9x13 cake pan with Saran Wrap. Then I took a hair dryer and blew it on the plastic sheet to make it shrink over the window. That worked great in the living room. The bedroom was more of a problem because of the narrow and drafty door that led to the one foot wide balcony. There was a piece of glass framed in metal and two smaller windows on either side. I did the best I could to cut and shape the plastic to fit around that drafty door and the two accompanying windows. It wasn't perfect, but in about 2 hours we were snug as a bug. Well, for a week or so.

One night as I was listening to broody Mr. Rachmaninoff, I suddenly felt a draft. What happened? I noticed that the upper left hand corner of the plastic was unstuck. Well, I could fix that. I got up on a chair, re-stuck the plastic sheet and wondered how it had come unstuck.

The next week the same thing happened. The same corner was unstuck. I stuck it back on and hoped the tape wouldn't lose its stickiness. Eventually I understood that the corner became unstuck on the days that our cleaning lady, Olya came. Apparently, uncharacteristically for a Belarusian, Olya wanted fresh air in the apartment. Should I tell her not to do this, or just let it go? You can guess my decision. Every Tuesday I put the chair up to the window so I could re-stick the plastic.

Olya was a friend of Lena's and when the previous school cleaner quit, Lena wanted to put Olya in the job. We agreed that Olya would be good and she started working a day or so later. I tried to communicate with Olya about the trash receptacle next to my desk at school. Please empty the things inside the bin, not the things on the floor. The next day the bin was still full but the things on the floor were gone. We tried again. She got it. Once at home, I had left the recipe for a delicious Thai peanut noodle salad that I had scribbled on some recycled paper on our kitchen table. When I got home it was gone. Olya was good, but she was the kind of cleaning lady you had to clean up for. Lena said she liked her because she was a good Christian.

## LENA

It's hard to write about Lena. She had a silly giggle that would have fit if she had looked up with puppy eyes while gently twisting her body and twirling a clump of hair. Sometimes she would giggle like that at Stan and say, "Oh, Mr. Ore," giggle, giggle. She dyed her hair a different shade of red every month or so and was the most dedicated school secretary I've ever worked with. The school was her life, the children, her children and the staff, her family. She loved to talk about the children. "I'm worried about Nicole. She is so skinny." "Julia is always reading." "Ocsana loves dogs so much." But she was also a businesswoman. She regretted that one family still in Belarus had decided to home school their children. "If those children came, we would pay off school debt."

Lena was the go-to person for bus stops. If we needed to go to Komarovski (kah mer AHV ski — translation: mosquito) market, it was the 4th stop on the number 23 bus. She regularly went to the market to pick up school supplies like toilet paper, bathroom soap, and water filters. She ferried all of these products in her shopping cart, one of those cloth bags strung on a frame with wheels. And she blew off the effort of acquiring these supplies. "Oh, I don't mind." With the sardine-can size, (and smell) of the buses, I can't imagine how she managed that shopping cart transferring twice to get to

*Komarovski Market.*

and from school. One day she came in with her cart and Stan greeted her with, "Well, I see you've brought your lunch."

"Hee, hee, oh, Mr. Ore."

In our little insular school, we tried to bring in as much variety and interest as we could. One of the things we did was to start a Pizza Day once a month. The little restaurant about two blocks away sold individual pizzas on their menu for a very reasonable price which came in a small pizza box. Lena talked to them about whether they could handle an order of about 25 pizzas once a month. They said they could, so we initiated Lena's least favorite day: Pizza Day. Kids had two choices: with cheese or with cheese and meat, literally little sliced hot dogs, but there were two different prices. Kids had to sign up for the quantity and kind of pizza they wanted and bring in the appropriate money to pay for what they ordered. The money amounts were odd and no one ever had the right change, so poor Lena had to keep track of each child's order, the amount of money, and provide change, which she did with no errors. Too bad it was such a hassle, but it was a huge hit with the kids and even the teachers, despite the pizzas being merely flattened bread dough with tomato sauce and some cheese or meat on top.

Lena also had all kinds of information about the health care system in Belarus. Doctors and nurses were not paid well and to receive good care, patients had to bring presents and money to their health care providers. She hated them for that because no other profession in Belarus collected payment in that way. She wanted nothing to do with them.

Lena attended the International Church in Belarus, the same one we were attending. She was a devout Christian and had been since she was little. Her unshakable faith told her that God was in charge and was going to see that life would be the best it could possibly be. When she was a teenager, she had had the opportunity to go to America and work in a church camp during the summer. She gladly took the chance and ended up in a camp somewhere in North Dakota. When she got there, she was told she would be the cook. She said she was so lucky because she had no idea how to cook. Another employee taught her what to do and then Lena took over.

After the first meal at the camp, Lena was observing while helping and noticed that some of the food that had been served family style to the campers had not been eaten. The woman teaching Lena the job told Lena that she was to throw away that food. Lena was horrified. Throw away perfectly good food? For a teenager who had suffered through food shortages and known real hunger as a child, this was an unbelievable shock. Eventually she got around to asking her pertinent question. Could she eat the food? Yes, of course, if she wanted it.

She did.

She gained 14 pounds that summer. When she stepped off the plane in Belarus at the end of the summer, her mother walked right past her. She didn't recognize her own daughter!

Lena also knew all of the cultural events in town. And we were lucky to live right in the center of everything. The circus building was about a block away to our north. The ballet theater was across the street and down one block. I saw at least seven fabulous ballets (including three times to Carmina Burana, O'Fortuna which became a ballet because of Belarusian choreographers) in that baroque space for only about $5.00 each. We also saw Swan Lake which was the time Stan said, "If they had shot the swans in the second act, we could have gone home." I either went by myself or with someone else from then on.

Lena also had many ideas for field trips for our students. Our most adventurous was a ski trip. Lena arranged a bus and all of the kids either skied or sledded down a local ski hill that had a T-bar. We had to plan in advance and of course, that day was a bitter cold -10°F. Thankfully there was an indoor shelter where we could get warm. Also lucky was that a few of the younger teachers actually wanted to ski with the kids so Stan and I didn't have to be outside the whole time. What a happy day for the kids! All thanks to Lena.

Lena had the complete history of the school in her mind. She remembered each of the different directors, the teachers and the kids. She said of one director, "He did a good job but after he got here, he sat on his suitcases."

Lena also knew the complete history of the 1986 Chernobyl nuclear power plant accident that had happened 20 years before. She and her then-husband came home from work that day not knowing about the toxic cloud that had passed over Minsk. The Soviets didn't tell the people there had been an accident. A few days later after some Swedish scientists noticed the cloud, the Soviets couldn't hide the accident anymore. They advised people to take off all of their clothes every day when they came home and take a shower. Their clothing should be laundered. I wonder how many people had washing machines? They also were told not to eat fruits and vegetables and foods like blueberries that grow close to the ground. I wondered if they really stopped eating the potatoes and beets that make up a large part of the diet in that area of the world?

When we returned for our second year, I noticed that Lena looked a bit thinner than she had the previous year. She was always interested in dieting and eating healthy so that's what I attributed her new svelte appearance to.

The next fall I was working in Brindisi. I learned In October that Lena had colon cancer. She was still working and the doctors were doing everything they could, but the cancer was pretty advanced and the doctors weren't sure they could do anything for her. Why hadn't she contacted them earlier? I *knew why.* She hated all doctors and wouldn't go to see one. *But why hadn't I said something about her weight loss?* Maybe I could have convinced her to go to the doctor early enough for a cure.

By November Lena could no longer work. She didn't have the energy. I refused to believe she wouldn't get better. I wrote her lots of emails. She wrote one back to me and Stan in October telling us, "I miss you so much and think of you very often. It was a blessing for me to work with you two years at the school. You are so wonderful, precious people. Of course, everybody misses you." She never said that she was ill, only that she had trained a new person as office manager during September.

I was heartbroken.

Dan and Rose, who had taken over at the school after us and were also part time pastor and pastor's wife, were the perfect couple to help Lena through that time. As Lena knew, God provides. Lena's faith was never stronger and Dan helped her make peace with what was happening. On December 30 Dan was reading to Lena from 2 Timothy 4:6–8

*For I am already being poured out like a drink offering, and the time for my departure is near. I have fought the good fight, I have finished the race, I have kept the faith. Now there is in store for me the crown of righteousness, which the Lord, the righteous Judge, will award to me on that day — and not only to me, but also to all who have longed for his appearing.*

Lena took her last breath, and the world lost one of the kindest souls we ever knew.

Lena

Was Lena's cancer a result of the Chernobyl accident 20 years before? How can we ever know? Something tells me that Belarus isn't keeping those kinds of statistics. Imagine the Soviets not telling their people about the accident? Is anyone surprised that keeping it quiet was more valuable to them than the lives of the people?

## GOVERNMENT DESPITE THE PEOPLE

Belarus is called the last dictatorship in Europe because of its president, Alexander Lukashenko. The director of a collective farm during the Soviet era, Lukashenko has been president since 1994. After abandoning term limits in 2004, Lukashenko was reelected with 84.2% of the vote in March 2006 while we were living there.

After the results were announced, people protested in October Square right across the street and down a block from our apartment. If we twisted ourselves just right at the closed window, we could look down the street and see the billowing light blue of the old and now banned Belarusian flags waving in the frigid air. The protesters set up pup tents and little fires in the big cobblestoned square. I still wonder how they didn't freeze to death. I guess you could attribute it to the Belarusian stoicism. Or maybe they were passing the vodka around.

On the fifth morning we looked out the window at the square, and it was as if no one had ever been there. It had been scraped clean. The protesters had stayed out there for four bitterly cold nights and got lots of international coverage in the media. According to the reports we heard, in the dark morning of the fifth night, when no foreign journalists were there to observe or record what happened, Belarusian soldiers arrived in buses and arrested all of the 460 protesters. Europe's last dictator survived that election and has won every election since with similar percentages. He's still the president.

Because the country of Belarus is controlled by a select few oligarchs, the rest of the people live in poverty and scramble to make a living. One of the families in our school had firsthand experience with this control and corruption.

Raj and Priyanka were the parents of two of our students. The family was from India and Raj was a businessman in Belarus. He'd been there about ten years when we got there and was quite well established as *the* man who could provide imports from India. Every year he held an exposition of Indian goods where anyone could go and purchase all manner of silks, pashminas, clothing, and those handbags with little mirrors embedded. Priyanka worked in our school as a preschool teacher assistant. A previous director had set up an arrangement that if Priyanka worked in our school and didn't accept a salary, there would be a reduction in the tuition of their children because they weren't sponsored by a government, NGO or private company.

We got to be friends with Raj and Priyanka and often accompanied them out to dinner to one of the many unusual restaurants they knew about like the Thai/Nepalese Palace.

Raj told us the story of the canned Italian tomatoes he sold in Minsk. One year he had the opportunity to buy a large quantity of canned tomatoes. He placed the appropriate bribes in the appropriate hands and made a killing selling the 2 tons of canned tomatoes. The next year he went to the same officials with similar bribes, but this time he was only permitted to sell 200 pounds of canned tomatoes. He didn't understand until he saw the same canned tomatoes in supermarkets all over Belarus. According to Raj, what happened is that the government let Raj make the initial investment and sale of the canned tomatoes. After that investment proved to be profitable, he was removed as a player and the oligarchs in the inner circle got contracts for the rest. No wonder the people live in poverty earning less than $5,000 per year.

## Arranged Marriage

After we told Priyanka and Raj the story of how Stan and I got together, they told us the story of how they met. Their parents knew each other and had many private discussions about whether Priyanka and Raj would make good marriage partners. After much deliberation, the parents decided it was time for the marriage to take place. On that special day when the two young people were to meet, Priyanka described getting dressed in her most beautiful sari and sitting in the room where the meeting would happen with all four parents. She said she was so nervous that she never actually looked at Raj or spoke with him. Apparently he looked at her and found her to be acceptable and the wedding proceeded.

Raj said that an Indian wedding takes about two weeks. Parties, galas, teas and outings have to happen. Finally after all of the festivities were over, Priyanka was able to look at Raj. When we knew them, they must have been married for at least ten years because they had a nine-year-old son.

Apparently their parents chose wisely because they said they were very happy together. In fact, they talked about how there was actually a lot of pressure on couples in arranged marriages to be happy. It was considered a bad mark on the parents if you couldn't be happy together so you did everything possible to make your marriage successful. They felt that arranged marriages are a good way to go.

## BEETS FOR DINNER

Despite the fact that we didn't have a car, we used to walk to the sprawling indoor/outdoor Komarovsky market each week. The indoor part was only indoor in as much as there was a roof overhead and walls surrounding the field house sized, unheated building. The outdoor space had a roof but no walls. Half of the indoor space was dominated by meat. I could only hold my nose and look away. It was even worse in the warm weather. One smaller section was devoted to cheese and some manufactured products such as the hummus we bought each week, the most yummy hummus I've ever spread on a cracker. Outdoors were vendors of fresh produce like tomatoes and scrumptious, not-at-all-like-American red, sweet peppers. Apples, potatoes, beets and other root vegetables were the only fresh vegetables available in the winter. In the fall, vendor after vendor sold persimmons, a tomato looking fruit with a large stone in the middle. The ripest ones tasted the best, so sweet, but didn't really look so good.

Going to this market on Saturdays was a pleasant outing for us and we always enjoyed our time there as well as the walk there and back. One winter day we were looking for beets. I was replenishing my hummus stash so Stan was on the beet job. He found some that looked slightly different than what we were used to. I got the hummus and we were on our way. Later in the week, one night we agreed that we would cook those beets with the beef roast Stan had bought at the meat section where they hacked off the piece he wanted from a carcass. (No wonder I couldn't watch.) Stan would do the cooking that night because I would be doing aerobics at the embassy until six.

The minute I turned the corner to the back of our apartment building that night, I could smell something horrible. Did something die around here? Were our neighbors boiling old tennis shoes? Rotten cabbage? Burned broccoli? Grilled rat? Yuck. Before I even had the door to the building open all the way, the full force of the terrible smell hit me. *Oh, this is horrible.* Slowly I started walking up the steps thinking hard, *"please don't let that putrid smell be coming from our apartment."* The smell got worse with each step. I unlocked our apartment door to a stinky steam bath that would have made a dog's encounter with a skunk seem like a picnic at Lake Michigan. I went immediately to the stove where the "beets" were gently simmering in a saucepan.

"Why do these beets smell so terrible?"

"I don't know. Yeah, they don't smell so good." Understatement.

I turned off the pot and took it to the sink where I ran cold water into the pan. I took one of the "beets" out and cut through it to find it was light colored inside.

"Okay, these are not beets and I don't care what they are, but I'm not eating them."

Stan took a small bite.

"Yup, me neither."

I put the beets into a double plastic bag and carried them out to the trash can in the back trying to figure out what else we had to eat. I admit, I opened that little corner in the plastic on the window to try to make that horrible smell go away. If any of our former neighbors are reading this, I am so sorry.

The next day I dramatized the story to our Belarusian colleagues. "Oh, you got some black radishes. Yeah, they would smell bad if you tried to cook them." Double understatement.

## SUNSHINE THROUGH THE GATE

Winters are brutal in Belarus. In January the sun rises at about 9:30 and sets at about 4:30. It snows practically every day and it's so cold that I kept getting frostbite on my forehead just above my right eye. Everything else was Gore-texed and goose-downed, but that area above my right eye got to me every time the Siberian winds blew.

On the coldest days, I would crack open one of my packages of Hot Hands — those little packs of what looks like charcoal that you can stick into your mitten or shoe. They stay hot for about 12 hours. On the coldest days I would keep one in my shoe all day. I don't understand this phenomenon, but for some reason if I put one in my left shoe, or boot, that foot would get warm and so would the right one. Without the little packet. Go figure. I also had two little reusable heart-shaped, pocket-sized plastic pouches of pink liquid that I could twist in a certain way and they would turn to gel and get hot/warm.

Every sidewalk in Minsk had a woman whose job it was to sweep the snow, leaves, or garbage off of a certain area. They used those old fashioned brooms that are about 3 feet tall and made of twigs-thin and bendable twigs, yes, twigs. They seemed right out of the Middle Ages. The women worked hard, bent over their brooms and seemed to pride themselves on how clean their bit of sidewalk was. Lena would tell us that her dream job was to be one of those women who cleaned the sidewalk because she was sure that it was a job with no stress!

So the sidewalks were relatively safe for walking, but while I was pretty sure on my feet, falling on a slippery patch was a constant worry for Stan. We learned about a new (at that time) product called Yaktrax that we could snap on our shoes to prevent slipping and ordered a pair for Stan that we had shipped to our house over Christmas break that first year. Until they wore out, those things kept Stan upright!

We were out in the elements every day during our 30 minute walks to and from school. And during a long part of the winter, we were walking, along with everyone else to and from work in the dark. If we saw sunshine, it was usually during the middle of the day and never lasted long.

By March the sky was beginning to lighten up in the mornings and we could walk home in the light. You can imagine the gift of a sunny, warm, okay, relatively warm, March or April day. One Saturday felt like one of those — sunny and warm. Oh, what joy to see the sun and watch the snow melt. I couldn't wait to get outside. I had made arrangements to meet an artist so that I could buy a painting that had been at the March art exhibition Maptayckir Katbl (March Cats) that I had so enjoyed.

I walked down the dark stairs to outside, through the back door, and through the thick wrought iron gate — imagine a medieval gate across a 10 foot opening in a 10 foot long corridor that led to the sunny street. The previous night there had been some kind of government function on our street that we'd been able to see as it paraded past our window, so the inner gate was only partially open. I could see the sunny street and I barreled through that gate, not understanding until it was too late that the inner gate had a bar across the bottom at ankle height that had been closed this one and only time. I went down like a tackled Green Bay quarterback and hit the sidewalk so hard I scraped the top part of my nose and skinned both knees through my jeans — right in front of a packed bus.

The street was still full of residual security personnel from the previous night's event, and a very kind, very young officer came to my aid. *Ow-ow-ow.* As soon as I got my bearings and spasiba'd (thank you'd) my wonderful soldier/policeman/savior, I turned around and defeatedly crept back upstairs to tell Stan, "I've been injured." My recovery took several weeks. I never got back the sunshine I'd missed, but I think I brightened the day of at least some of those passengers on the bus. I've always thought, If you're going to make a fool of yourself, you should have a large audience.

## COMING AND GOING IN BELARUS

Passport control when leaving or entering Minsk was always interesting. The scary looking guard at passport control would take our passports and use a tiny magnifier and go over every inch of the picture page. Imagine a tiny spyglass about the size of a piece of rigatoni and the passport control guard's eye on the microscope end and the other end on the passport going over back and forth until they had seen the whole page.

We always flew out on Lufthansa (a great experience if you're not familiar) to Frankfurt because that's where the only flight with a dependable airline went. Both Stan and I would let out a silent sigh of relief once that plane raised itself off the ground. That meant there was no more worrying that we were being watched or listened to. Stan was convinced he'd been followed for the first three weeks we were there. We didn't realize how oppressed we felt until we were off the ground. When the plane lifted off, so did the oppression.

## SUBWAY ADVENTURES

During our second year in Belarus, we learned to use the subway — the one that was literally 50 feet from our apartment! This was a big deal for two people from Appleton with its little bus system! Two lines intersected just on the other side of our apartment so it was pretty straightforward, that is if you could read Russian. We were both terrified that we would get down there and onto the subway and not know where to get off. We experimented slowly. My Russian teacher, Alla, copied the names of each stop along the north/south line and showed how the east/west line intersected it. First we went two stops to the large supermarket, Big ZZ. Prior to this we had asked a guy named Yuri to drive us to another large supermarket farther away from downtown. It seemed an imposition, to me, anyway, to get Yuri to take us to the store where he had to wait in the parking lot until we were finished. I've never been comfortable doing that and never will, I'm afraid, even though we paid him. But once we learned to take the subway to a supermarket near downtown, we had wheels!

Getting down into the subway was a twisty job. I learned to mark my direction outside and point my finger toward the direction I wanted to go. I would walk straight discreetly pointing my finger out — like a gun. As soon as I got to the escalator, I had to face another direction, so I would point my finger toward myself. Then, once I was at the subway station level there was another twist, so I'd point my finger out again and I would be able to tell which side of the tracks I needed to be on. Arrows on the wall pointed in the direction the train would be going. I found this method extremely helpful and used it for every subway trip. Then I used Alla's trusty translation of the Russian named stops such as Hrusauka, which was the stop for the supermarket. Molodyozhnaya was the hair salon where I got my hair cut. The station near us was called Kastrychnitskaya Octiabrskaya. These signs were are all written in Cyrillic script. Without my little cheat sheet, we couldn't have traveled this simple subway.

The largest thoroughfares in Minsk such as our street were treacherous for pedestrians to cross because of all of the traffic generated by the people in Minsk who were lucky enough to have cars. Underpasses at major intersections helped keep pedestrians safe. We heard that the Soviets used German prisoners of war after WWII to dig these underpasses, but no one could verify that. The first time we used the subway stop 50 feet from our apartment, we were shocked to see that a whole underworld existed down there. It was a huge space: dark, long, narrow, and low-ceilinged with all manner of vendors selling scarves, shoes, belts, jewelry, underwear, music, and make up. Not only that, it was warm down there. What a boon to be able to walk some distance down our street in a toasty marketplace until we had to poke our heads back up into the cold.

Shortly after we discovered the underground market, we received an invitation to a Valentine's Day party at the apartment of one of the American embassy families. We knew them because they had toured our school with their only child, a 9 year old daughter. Up to that point she had been home schooled, but the parents wanted to see our school to see if it was a good fit for their daughter. It was another disappointment for Lena when we learned that the girl would not be joining us. Lena said we could have paid off the school's debt and then some! Educators like us are usually not in favor of homeschool.

The invitation said "Cocktail Attire." We loved being included in these get togethers. It was fun to have something to do besides sit around in our apartment. So we dressed in the closest thing we had to "Cocktail Attire" and set off to walk to their apartment which was about a half mile from our apartment on the same street. I had their phone number on my phone and we had a general idea of the block where their apartment was. We were to call when we got to their block so that they could direct us to the right building and talk us through how to get to the back side and to the correct door. If all else failed they would come down from the 10th floor to guide us in.

Because I was dressed up, I didn't want to wear my boots, need I say — *nor* my silk long underwear, so I was wearing a skimpy pair of black flats and pantyhose (yuck, remember those?) with my party dress. OK it wasn't a party dress, but it was a dress. Snow was falling, but I figured I could make the short distance to their apartment and wouldn't have to deal with carrying shoes, changing my boots, blah, blah, blah. Stan was carrying the bag that contained the bottle of wine and hostess gift that we were bringing and I decided to throw my phone in there too so I didn't have to carry it in my hand.

After walking for a few feet, I was feeling the chill of not wearing pants, the accompanying long underwear, and my trusty Gore-Tex boots. Very soon my shoes were wet from the half inch of snow that hadn't yet been swept by the sidewalk ladies. When we got to the entrance of the subway, I had a brilliant idea. I would go down there and walk in the cozy underground market and meet Stan, who didn't want to go down there, on the other side of the street.

Down I went feeling very smart that I was warm and dry. Except this was a really new experience. I had only been down there one other time and I began to worry a bit if I would be able to find my way up to the other side of the street where I was supposed to meet Stan. For directionally challenged me, nothing was looking familiar, but I took a stab that the second stairway on the right was the correct one. And I did end up on the other side of the street, exactly where I thought I would. Back up into the cold I went, but Stan wasn't there waiting for me. I looked up and down the wide sidewalk, both sides, and didn't see him anywhere. His walk was unmistakable and I looked and looked but didn't see him.

By this time I was regretting several decisions I had made:

1. Throwing my phone into the bag Stan was carrying

2. No long pants, silk long underwear, or boots

3. Not double verifying with Stan our exact meeting point

4. Not carrying a key to our apartment.

I kept looking for Stan. Where was he? It was hard to see across the eight lanes of the street. Could he be over there? It was already dark out, but the street was pretty well lit. Lots of people were walking around but no one looked like Stan. Should I cross back? Walk to the block where the party would be? Go into the grocery store that was just a block down to warm up?

I didn't panic, but I couldn't see a way out of this dilemma. I decided to walk down the street to the approximate location of where the party was going to be. It was a wide sidewalk and if Stan was walking that way, I could spot him. I got almost all of the way down there and didn't see him. I walked back to the subway entrance. Still no Stan. Should I walk home and wait for him? Eventually he would show up and let me in. Right? By this time, I was cold, but so worried that I was almost sweaty. I walked back to our apartment and turned the corner to the park in back. No Stan. I waited. Okay, if he's not here in 15 minutes, I'll go to the grocery store to warm up.

We always had a rule, if we lose each other in a large place, go back to where you came in and wait. I stood on one foot and tucked the other one up the back of my leg. I scrunched my shoulders up even higher so that I could turtle into my coat. Why was I so vain not to wear a hat?

I looked up. There was Stan coming around the corner. He, too, had decided to go back to home base. Oh, thank heaven. Big hug. I think he was more worried than I was though that wasn't the kind of thing he would ever admit.

What had happened? He had waited and waited for me on the opposite side of the street from where I was waiting for him. We hadn't communicated that very well, had we? And here I was with no key and no phone, and even if I found someone with a phone with whom I could communicate, I didn't know Stan's number or the number of anyone else we knew. Stupid, stupid, and stupid!

Since that day have I ever left home without a phone? a key? undeniably clear directions about the meeting point? the phone number of at least one other person besides Stan? Not once. To this day my purse holds a piece of paper with the printed names, addresses and phone numbers of all of the people in my family and all of the friends I could fit in the three tiny columns of six-point font. If anything like this happens again, I'm more prepared. Especially if I bring my purse!

Did we go to the party? Of course we did! And we had a good time all dressed up in our "cocktail attire!"

## LOSING OUR RELIGION

I've been at best a reluctant churchgoer all of my life. When I was a child, I didn't understand the Bible stories, how they fit together, or how they applied to my life. Plus, my mother would always flit and dance around the house with a cheery voice after we got home from church on Sundays. By Monday, though, the black cloud that often followed her around was back. According to her, I was a bad girl for some perceived action I had taken or not taken. My sister had left her dirty socks in the living room. For these and other offenses, we could hear the pots and pans get jammed into the cupboards with a big slam of the door as she worked through the failings of her only two offspring. Church didn't have the power to change her life except for those few hours on Sunday. It didn't ring true for me.

As a teenager, I was convinced there was no God. I argued that if I prayed for something, I had a bigger role in whatever I prayed for becoming a reality than God. Say I prayed to do well on a test. Who actually got the good or bad grade? I was convinced that my good or bad achievement was a result of my efforts, not God's.

It was when I gave birth to my first child that everything changed. A miracle that was so much more than a miracle had happened. New air surrounded me. New tissue filled the space in my body. Wonder filled my brain. A love greater than any I had ever known encompassed me physically, emotionally and spiritually. These gifts floated down on me like gentle snowflakes, and encircled me like loving arms. I was merely an observer. Clearly this precious little being was from God. Oh, I cherished her. I still do. From that moment I acknowledged the existence of God. This gift of a daughter came through me but not from me. I had done nothing to deserve her. And yet, here she was all pink and wiggly, a precious presence in my life relentlessly insistent on being fed every two hours. For the first time in my life I had something I couldn't lose.

The coming of my second child was even more of a miracle because I knew what to expect: the joy of having her, the panic

over fear of losing her. It was as if God created this wonderful, precious bundle of human being and said I will give her
to you because you are also wonderful and precious and you
are the only person who will know how to nurture this child.
I loved that little girl, still do, with everything I had and more,
from the first moment. Her birth was all about God. It was
like He had given me another center, extra legs that could
walk straight upward, a second gift just as miraculous as the
first. With these births came also the knowledge that I would
love these two human beings unconditionally and if they
ever needed anything, anything at whatever cost — physically, emotionally, financially, I would provide it. (Except, of
course, the $70 jeans when Melissa was 14. Sorry, honey.)

After the birth of my second child, my relationship with
my now ex-husband was sadly not so miraculous. We were
already having difficulties and those were unhappy years as
a couple. Sometime during one of our separations, I started
to go to church. Voluntarily! Eventually through all of the
pain and trauma of my marriage ending, I became a regular churchgoer again. I attended Bible studies and tried to
be a good "witness" for Christianity. Except for the part
about Christ dying for my sins. I never really got that part. It
seemed to me that I had never done anything bad enough for
someone to die for and aside from my crazy teenage years, I
mostly tried to do the right thing. I kept attending, however.
I wanted to give my daughters a basis of religion so that they
could make their own decisions when they were old enough.
And as a single parent, frankly, I was glad to have the support of the church community. I had my work community,
my neighborhood community and my divorced/single parent community. One more couldn't hurt.

Stan, on the other hand, was always an eager churchgoer.
From an early age, he participated in all of the trappings a

United Methodist Church membership/education could provide like youth groups and church camps. He told me later that he found out that boy scout camp had only boys, but that church camp also had girls. That's why he went there! In fact his ex-wife was studying to become a minister when I started dating him. He attended the same church I did mostly because his ex-wife was doing an internship at the other United Methodist Church in Appleton, but I never saw him at church because he always went to the early 8 a.m. (good grief!) service.

## THE BEGINNING OF STAN AND I

One Sunday morning during that time, the minister mentioned that a new group was forming in the church. It was to be called "Single Again" for those of us who, well, you get it. I was immediately interested. After all, don't mothers always tell us to look for a boyfriend at church? No, seriously, I was always interested in interacting with others in my situation, male or female. Soon I found out that Stan would also be attending the organizational meeting of this group. He had recently divorced. That piqued my curiosity even more.

When I got to the meeting, Stan was the only person in the room I knew, so I sat next to him. After all, I had worked at Appleton East for 3 years and had gotten to know him professionally. That first night, as Charlie, the minister, who not only married us but also later became the husband of Stan's ex-wife, talked about Single Again, he said the group would need some volunteers to get it going: membership, program, and a group leader. I was already thinking there was no way I would be volunteering for any of those positions. I already had a heavy teaching workload, two pre-teens at home, laundry, meals and groceries to keep up with and a whole house to care for. No way would I take on another task. As Charlie spoke, Stan leaned over and said into my ear, "So do you want to be on the program committee?" In a nanosecond some inexplicable force turned my head to him and said, "Sure."

So Stan and I were all about church during those early years, and in fact, probably the closest thing we ever had to a fight occurred a few years later and it was about whether or not we were going to church one Sunday.

Back to Belarus. Many of the people we interacted with were humanitarian aide workers (missionaries). I'd heard nothing but holy things about missionaries my entire church life and held missionaries in high esteem. One of these "holy" people had been affiliated with our school before we arrived. Jack's wife had already departed for the States, but he had started a church in Minsk for local people and apparently, he remained behind to make sure it would stay viable without him. He was really helpful during those first days when we didn't know anything and were full of questions. "How can we find groceries? How do we manage the rubles? Which restaurants were acceptable? How do we buy things from the crazy department stores Zum and Dum?"

At first we enjoyed the time we spent with Jack. Over a period of a few weeks, however, we noticed that Jack kept showing up at dinner time. *Did he want to eat with us?* Well, sure. If it was a restaurant, we paid. Pretty soon we were trying to find ways to be somewhere else. Our missionary approval meter was heading toward 0.

We learned about the international church that met every Sunday in a building not far from our house. It was the only English speaking church in Belarus. We liked the pastor, who was also a missionary. (He was the one who told us that the Russian word for great-wonderful-beautiful was harashow and the way he remembered it was to think of horror show!)

We attended this church for about six months, and found that many of the participants were really, really serious about religion — more than we were comfortable with. When the minister opened up the floor for prayers, many of these people gave long speeches about things they wanted us to pray for. Later Stan would make parodies of what they would say, "Oh, Lord, I looked and looked but I couldn't find the mustard in the refrigerator. Please help me, Lord." Cynicism was his specialty.

The congregation was made up of English speaking Belarusians and expats, many of whom were also missionaries. One family had five children and had plans to keep expanding their family. These children were all home schooled. The missionary families could not afford the tuition of our school, nor stomach that the science books taught evolution. We got curiouser and curiouser about that big family. Wouldn't that many children put a burden on the church that sponsored them? One Sunday after church, we came home, looked at each other and said, "Does going to that church make you feel uncomfortable?" "Yes." "Me, too. Let's quit going," and so we did. Overall, I learned that missionaries were not any different than other people. I was still a strong believer in God, but church seemed like a completely different matter.

Apparently the Belarus government wasn't fond of missionaries either. Later we learned that the father of that big family with a ticket to fly to Budapest for a conference was stopped at the airport. Belarusian border guards took his passport and sent him to a room with no windows and locked him in. They held him there until just before the flight was ready to leave. At that time, they told him his visa was revoked and gave him two options: One: Get on the plane and don't come back, or Two: Stay there in that room and find out what happens when a visa gets revoked. He wisely chose option One. His wife, however, had to pack up all of their belongings, their five children and drive out of the country, never to return. The next year they also revoked the visa for the man who was the minister of the church, but he had more lead time. The vacancy he left behind was filled by Dan, Stan's replacement as director. With all of his previous experience in Kuwait, Dan was a natural fit for the part-time job as minister of the congregation and all reports we got were that he was doing a great job both as director of the school and minister of the International Church.

## VADIM AND HIS STORY ABOUT SOVIET TIMES

Vadim was the oldest student in our school. He was 17, and the next youngest was 14. Vadim was an Israeli but his parents were Belarusians who had immigrated to Israel during the waning years of the Soviet Republic when Jews were allowed to leave Russia. Like many of our students, Vadim was trilingual: he could speak, read and write Hebrew and English. He spoke Russian at home with his family but could neither read nor write it. He was curious about the world and a perfect student in that he wanted to learn everything.

Since I had been a high school teacher, I often worked with Vadim. I helped him complete the English, social studies, and economics requirements for a QSI high school diploma. He was a gentle young man who loved to play the guitar and listen to music. In 2006 no less, he helped me download music from a Belarusian website that had contraband music. He loved music from all genres, all artists. He wore his curly, dishwater blond hair long, often tied in a ponytail and he'd lost the gangliness of adolescence. He said he felt a little like a stick in our school of mostly younger students, but if he was unhappy about this, it didn't show. The Belarusian girls who attended the school in which our school was housed

used to come and knock on our door and say "Vadim," with their adoring smiles. Shy acting Vadim (not shy at all!) would smile at these girls and speak very briefly, but kindly, with them as if they were his younger sisters.

Through the days of our working together, Vadim told me the stories his father told him about former Soviet days. His father had worked in a Soviet automobile factory in Belarus. At the time there were very few automobiles anywhere in the Soviet Union. Everyone wanted a car, but getting one was extremely difficult. First the potential buyer had to prove he had enough money to purchase a car. The cost was an average worker's salary for two years. Then he had to go to a government building, wait in line, put his name on a list and wait his turn. Some bureaucrat decided just how often and at what time the buyer had to show up at the office and wait in line to tell the list-keeper that he still wanted the car. If he missed his time to renew his name on the list, his name went to the bottom and he had to start over.

Lada (LAH duh) is a famous Russian car. Each employee at the Lada automobile factory had a specific job to do. For example, let's say the job was to install the brakes. The brake parts came from another factory somewhere in the USSR and the Lada assembly factory often did not receive the brake parts. But the employees were still expected to get out a certain number of cars per day to make their quota. The employees would suffer if they didn't make that quota. So two workers would secretly leave the factory to go and find anything they could get their hands on to install some sort of brakes in those cars. Apparently they often went into the forest and got wood to fashion the parts to put in the cars so that they could drive the cars out of the factory. I suppose they knew how to do these things well enough. Did they paint the wood gunmetal gray so that an inspector couldn't tell that some of the parts

*Vadim standing between Stan and I.*

weren't the real thing, or was the inspector part of the conspiracy? The only requirement was that the car had to be able to be driven out of the factory.

So imagine the family waiting for the car. They've spent years waiting for this car. They've stood in line every two weeks in the snow and rain so that they can keep their name active on the list. They've waited as their name got higher and higher on the list. They've spent two years of their salary to purchase this car. On their lucky (!) day, they got a car with wood for brakes. I can't imagine it, but based on the stoicism I observed in the Belarusian people, that family would not be surprised if something like this would happen, and I'm sure they could find a way to make the car work.

Vadim enjoyed telling these stories as related by his father, and I enjoyed the easy rapport I had with him. I was seeing and hearing about life in another country that I would never have seen and heard in another way. It was moments like this that I remembered: ***THIS IS WHY I CAME HERE.***

## SHOPPING AND THE FIELD OF DREAMS

During Soviet times the Belarusians had to stand in line for everything. Our local staff told us that if a person was walking down the street and saw a long line, they would automatically get into the line because with all of the people there, it was clear that something good was at the end of the line. People told us they would stand in line and when they got to the head of the line, someone would hand them whatever it was. If it was a pair of shoes, people just took them. It didn't matter if the shoes were the right size or the kind the person wanted or needed. They just took them and went on their way. Later they would go to a large area out-side of town called "The Field of Dreams" where they could exchange the shoes for something they actually wanted or needed.

## WOMEN ON THE STREET

When we were there, beautifully dressed, statuesque, per-fectly coiffed young women would stride confidently down the main street of Belarus. After seeing the women of Kuwait covered in abayas, the pleasure of seeing the Belarusian women, especially the younger ones, wearing four inch spike heels with perfectly coiffed hair never got old. How those girls kept their footing on the sometimes cobblestoned sidewalks and streets is still a wonder. They walked like runway mod-els purposefully and determinedly shooting one foot in front of the other as if on a tightrope, eyes focused straight ahead with rod-up-the-back posture. Oh, they were gorgeous. The most beautiful woman I saw in Belarus was on Independence Avenue where we lived. This young woman was tall, thin, and stunningly beautiful. It was warm outside so she was wearing a tight, cropped top with no sleeves with a 6 inch gap between her low slung skin tight jeans and her top. From the back I could see the pencil thin thong of her underwear peek above her jeans and surround her skinny middle. The strap was covered with a row of tiny jewels that looked like diamonds. Those diamonds dropped seductively down into her jeans that complemented her inviting, sexy walk.

## DRINKING

Many of the walkers on the city streets, young and old, carried liquor: a beer bottle, bottle of vodka in a paper bag, or a paper cup of something. Their drunkenness was unmistakable. Once on the way to school at 7:15 a.m., I passed a man walking unsteadily carrying a beer bottle. I wasn't sure if his little party was left over from the night before or he was getting an early start on that day. We didn't see anything that looked like a bar anywhere in Minsk, and no one had money to spend in a bar anyway. The young people didn't have anywhere to go to drink indoors so they went to the many parks in Minsk. Even in brutal cold, they hung out in the parks because the apartments were so small, parents were rarely gone from home, and neighbors would have reported the kids anyway. Because of this, kids went to parks and stood around imbibing. Many times in the early morning on our route through three parks to school, I would see evidence left behind from someone who had had too much to drink. Once in the middle of the day I saw a girl in a party dress and high heels walking and laughing with her friends. She nonchalantly started to vomit but then kept walking as if she were spitting out a grape seed.

Our local staff members openly discussed how much alcoholism there was in Belarus especially for males. Since the end of the USSR, men felt emasculated. They couldn't work at the jobs they used to have and couldn't make enough money in the new economy to support their families. Maybe, under Communism, they used to install engines in the automobile factory. Now the factory was shut down or owned by an oligarch who didn't pay a decent salary or only hired his own people. In Soviet times the people were used to having their basic needs given to them: an apartment and food prices that they could afford. Everyone was in the same boat. Now, all prices were high. Unless your family was part of the president's inner circle, you had no chance of ever getting ahead. Older women stood at the entrances of Komarovsky market selling jars of pickles or crocheted doilies to put on upholstered chair arms. One of the teachers in our school said that the president would get his comeuppance after he died. She, and others must have felt so powerless.

## WORKING WITH STAN

Some couples might find it hard to work together. While Stan and I had our difficulties being retired together, working together was a dream come true. He took each job as if this was his "meant to be" job and was 100% engaged and committed to the job, the kids, the parents, and the other staff. From the first moment on, it was clear to all that he was there to ensure that everyone would do well, and that Stan was the one to stand behind them. Everyone loved him and I loved working with him. He was the real deal, and our opposite strengths and weaknesses complemented each other. He was budget and I was curriculum; he was International Women's Day and I was Parents Go to School Night; he was *I'll go home and start dinner* and I was *I'll stay at school and work on next year's schedule.* I also loved that I could make suggestions about what I thought we should be doing in terms of curriculum and activities, and he was right there saying, *Yes, that sounds like a good idea.* For example, in late spring I had the idea that if we were going to have sunlight until 10 p.m. in June, we should have a White Nights carnival at the end of our second year. *Yes, absolutely,* he agreed. *We should do it.* The other staff and I planned stations like: cake walk, jump rope contest, 50-yard dash. It was an outdoor celebration for the kids and parents. We got people to bring food, and we made a big party out of the extra daylight. Stan was game for it all, and it was really fun. It was so good to see him in his work mode again.

## NOSE BLEED PARANOIA PNEUMONIA

I had suffered from seemingly unstoppable, gushing nose-bleeds since 8th grade. They incapacitated me and scared me that I wouldn't be able to stop them. For years I was blown off by every doctor I ever asked about it who would say, "It's a nosebleed," as if, "It's a pimple, get over yourself." Dry indoor winter air and/or head colds made this condition worse. Over time, I learned that with ice and pressure at specific points I could stop the nosebleeds, but it always took about 20 minutes. Thirty-five years later, I learned that the cause of my nose bleeds was a curved cartilage in my nose that stretched the vessels on the left side of my nose. An ear, eye, nose and throat specialist cauterized that area of my nose a few years back, and that seemed to solve the problem, but I was always paranoid that the nosebleeds would come back. So in Belarus we bought a room sized humidifier that seemed to do the trick at home.

Late in November of our second year we took an overnight train to Kiev with the other staff from our school for a professional development session. QSI International School of Kiev's student population was about 500 kids compared to our scant 20, so we went there to participate in their professional development held over the Thanksgiving weekend. Yes, it's true, we were working on Thanksgiving.

Stan and I had our own room on the train for the overnight trip to Kiev, and it was hot in there. I'd had the start of a cold a few days before and I was worried that in that dry air, I could get a nosebleed. One remedy I had often used was to wet a washcloth, paper towel or kleenex and kind of make a mini-humidifier into which I would breathe while I slept. We had a little sink in our tiny compartment so I got the towel wet and spent a half-wakeful, half-sleeping night trying to keep that moisture near my nose while bouncing around with the motion of the train. We knew we shouldn't drink the water from that little sink, but I didn't think it would hurt to breathe it.

It was fun to meet some of the teachers from Kiev and Moldova, a school of about 75 kids just south of Ukraine. The sessions were interesting and it was good to share stories, information, and strategies with others in our situation. The Kiev kitchen staff even prepared a Thanksgiving lunch for everybody. Okay, potato pancakes weren't usually a familiar sight on our Thanksgiving table, but when in Kiev...

While there, Stan and I, not the school, treated our whole staff to dinner out at a pretty fancy restaurant. It was good to see them so happy and laughing at every joke Stan told. They knew they would each be carrying $2,000 on their person on the way home to resupply our stash of cash, and most of them teased that once we arrived in Minsk, we would never see them again. After everyone tried a different dessert, we returned to our hotel which the school paid for, and at the end of the next day we boarded the overnight train back to Minsk. Lena, Nina, Olga and Ludmilla shared a compartment and reported that when the border police came in to process everyone back into Belarus, the guard asked, "Are you carrying any money?" All four of these wonderful but-truly-poverty-stricken women burst out laughing, never actually answering the question.

They felt so burdened by that much cash (they were paid about $6,000 per year) that they had to get it out of their hands immediately. Upon arrival in Minsk, the first thing each one of the six people did was hand over all of their cash to Stan. So from the train station to our apartment, Stan was carrying $16,000 in his briefcase. Stan carried it all to school the next morning. I wonder if the Belarusians we passed on the sidewalk ever looked at him and imagined that he was carrying $16,000? At the end of the day he took it to the embassy.

By Wednesday of that week, I was really not feeling well at all and I took advantage of the embassy doctor, a Belarusian everyone called Dr. G. I'd heard Dr. G's name many times. He was the doctor for American embassy personnel and it was OK with the embassy for him to help us too if we needed it. A few of the kids, especially the girls, had lots of ailments that needed to be fixed by Dr. G. Once I met him, I could understand why. He was George Clooney — handsome with a Dr. Sheperd bedside manner, and he had a laser focus on me and my health. Well, yes, he said my throat was red, my nose was dripping fluid down the back of my throat, and I should drink twice the amount of liquid I usually drank and call him if I got worse. He would be in his office at the Belarusian hospital the rest of the week. He gave me the address along with some over the counter medications I should purchase. I did all of this and continued to work.

By Friday I wasn't getting any better and it was my turn to accompany the kids to the pool for their weekly swimming lessons. What a great thing! Every Friday after lunch Lena ordered four taxis and all of the kids piled into them. One teacher accompanied each taxi. We went to a local indoor pool and two of the teachers, one male and one female, stayed there to accompany the kids during their swimming lessons and in the locker room. Picture getting six three and four year olds into and then out of their swimsuits, monitoring all of the other girls while the Belarusian women pranced around the locker room in the altogether — our girls gawking. Usually at least one parent (bless them) also came which made things easier. The other two teachers who had accompanied the kids in the taxis were done for the day and could go home, back to school or whatever they wanted. Usually if I wasn't staying at swimming, I returned to school and had an entire afternoon to plan the next week's lessons. The parents picked up their kids from the swimming pool and our day was over. That was truly the best perk I ever had as a teacher!

Well, on that particular Friday, I sat in the very warm pool area still wearing my coat, shivering, then sweating with my head spinning. Something was quite wrong. I told Mr. Sasha who was helping with the boys, that I wasn't feeling well. He suggested that I needed to eat more salloh (a big slab of fat). I said *thank you* but thought to myself that I would eat cooked black radishes before I would eat salloh!

When the last child had been picked up, I rode in the taxi with Mr. Sasha who knew where Dr. G's office was at the Belarusian hospital. He dropped me there and I found the office. As I entered the anteroom, a group of four to five male and female staff (nurses?) stood crowded around a computer while one of them was operating the computer in the little glassed-in inner room that all medical offices have. I stood at the counter and said in English that I needed to see Dr. G. They gave me a nod and motioned that I should sit in the otherwise empty waiting room. Now I was feeling very woozy, shivery and weak. I thought I was going to throw up. I re-approached the counter where the little group dressed in white were still very interested in what was on the computer and motioned that I was going to throw up. They pointed in the direction of the door at the other side of the room. I noticed that the computer screen was a game of solitaire.

I made it to the bathroom without throwing up and kind of gagged in there, but didn't vomit. When I came out, Dr. G had arrived. He took me to his office. He looked in my ears, my throat, and my eyes. He took my temperature. I almost had to lie down because I was so dizzy. According to Dr. G, I had pneumonia. He wanted to put me in the hospital right then. I said, "Oh, no. I don't think so." I remembered the horror stories from Lena, and based on the blatant lack of concern the medical personnel had shown in the outer office, I wasn't ready to voluntarily enter that or any Belarusian hospital.

Dr. G shot me full of antibiotics, took me to his car and drove me home, stopping on the way to pick up some medicine. I gave him the money and he went in and purchased what he thought I needed. He helped me into the house and said he would be back in the morning for another shot, and I went to bed. There would be no more working for me for at least two weeks. Then it would be winter break.

For those two weeks, this was the routine. I could hardly stand up and Dr. G came every morning to give me a shot. He would return around 6:00 to give me another one. Stan was a big help, especially with groceries and cooking, but I got the impression his attitude was more like, "OK you dragged me over here to have your adventure. Now you are out of commission and I have all of the responsibility at school and at home." Who could blame him?

If I hadn't been so sick, I would have enjoyed Dr. G's visits. With Stan in the next room Dr. G would tenderly hold my hands, gaze into my eyes and ask me how I was. *How much water did I drink that day? How about my urining? Is that the right word? I should be going twice more than usual. What did I eat for lunch? Had I taken a nap? For how long? Tea would help me. I should drink a lot of it. Don't do any house work. You must rest.*

Had anyone ever cared for me so intensely? Not anyone I was currently living with. When I was ill as a little girl, my mother used to bring me a cup of hot lemonade made from fresh lemons. That might qualify, except her "cure" tasted like poison. Dr. G was so attentive! I began to understand why one of our students missed so much school!

When it was time for our 3-week winter break, we had reservations to fly to Florida to have Christmas with the whole family. I was going to meet my first born grand-niece who would be about a month old. I couldn't wait, but I sure wasn't healthy. By this time I was coughing like a chain smoker and barely had the energy to walk to the bathroom and back. On the appointed day, our driver, Yuri, came to get us, carried the bags down (I rode in the creaky elevator-that's how bad I felt) and took us to the airport. Thank heaven he accompanied us inside. I had never been this sick in my life. I could barely walk and after about 5 minutes standing in line, I had to sit down. Yuri and Stan waited in line and when it was Stan's turn, I got up and approached the counter. We checked our bags, walked to the gate and waved goodbye to Yuri. I made it to the plane where I could sit for many hours. Thank heaven for Yuri. He waited until we were through the gate and on the plane before he left. We flew into Tampa so Stan drove the 50 miles to Holmes Beach where I collapsed into bed.

The next day I went to Urgent Care and that doctor gave me an immediate treatment with a powerful antibiotic which was absorbed through the skin, a prescription for an inhaler, and a seven-day-pack of steroids. In about three days I started to feel human again and got to meet my new grand niece three days later. I didn't tell anyone in my family that I'd had pneumonia.

Did I breathe in some bacteria from that water on the train? It's all I can think of because I have never, ever before or since been that sick. Thank heaven I came home and got that extra medication or I'd still be over there getting my two shots a day from Dr. G.

Well, maybe that wouldn't have been *all* bad!

## EATING OUT

Eating out in Belarus wasn't as exciting as it could have been. First, we didn't have a car and didn't care to hire a driver to take us, so if we went out, we tended to stay in the neighborhood. The place we called Patio Pizza was just a block away, and its food was not bad for pizza, salads, sandwiches. Almost at the end of our stay in Belarus, a TGIFriday's, the first one in Belarus, moved in just a few buildings down from Patio Pizza. We went there one time with some other friends, but it was just plain wrong. The food didn't taste the same and the waitstaff looked out of place with their suspenders and buttons. Nothing we had seen in "buttoned up" Belarus was even close to those costumes, and their cheery banter was from another world.

Our favorite restaurant was one that served Lithuanian food and was like a big cafeteria. We took a tray and approached the various stations: meat, salads, desserts, and my personal favorite — a large bowl of cold pink soup. Beets, hard boiled eggs, dill, cucumbers, green onions and plain yogurt were the main ingredients of this tasty and visual treat that was served cold. It was called Holodnik, and I loved it.

## HALLELUJAH!

During my conversations with Melissa through the years in Belarus I learned that she was doing well in school and totally focused on graduating. The whole family attended her

*My mother, me, Melissa and Laura at Melissa's graduation.*

graduation (with honors!) in 2006 with a degree in elementary education. She was hired by the school where she did her student teaching. They saw what she could do and wanted her working with them.

## LEAVING BELARUS

A few weeks before we left Belarus, I invited all of the female staff at our school for tea at our house. I told the women that I had a number of things that I wouldn't be taking with me and I wondered if they wouldn't mind looking through them to see if there was anything they could use.

On the day of the tea, I had all of the things I would leave behind (turtleneck shirts, two pairs of pants, at least one heavy winter coat, a pair of heavy Gore-tex mittens and a goose down jacket (I wouldn't be needing those things in Italy where I'd be going next) on the bed in our bedroom which was just off the living room. I asked the women to take whatever they wanted or could give to the church and I left the room to get the tea ready. By the time I came out with a tray of tea and some snacks, these wonderful women had divided up the items and were calmly chatting. Not one item was left and each woman had a bag to take home. I really hope they used those things in good health because it felt good to me to leave my precious things in their capable hands.

## KHATYN (HAH-TEEN)

During the last month of our stay in Belarus, we hired a driver and Lena took us to the Khatyn Memorial. She said she waited until our last days in Belarus so that our visit there would not have a negative impact on our stay. The local staff were always afraid that we would leave and cause the end of their school. I hope they're more relaxed now as the school has grown from the 20 kids we had in 2005–2007 to 240 kids in 2019.

Khatyn was a small village of about 150 people that was destroyed by the Nazis in March 1943. Over the years of the war, the Nazis destroyed some 600 other villages in Belarus in the same manner. According to eyewitnesses, when the Nazis approached villages that supposedly were working with the partisans, they would gather up all of the people, including children, and lock them in the largest building in town, usually a barn or church. Then they set the entire town on fire, starting with the building holding all the people. The Nazis stayed until the fire was out. If the people managed to break out of the building, the Nazis gunned them down.

In Khatyn eight inhabitants survived. Six (five of whom were children) of those eight witnessed the massacre and though given up for dead, lived to tell about it. Khatyn is now a memorial for all villages in Belarus that were destroyed in the same way. The names of the villages decorate a plaque and are represented by artistic tombs in a cemetery of villages. In each tomb is a handful of soil from the annihilated village. Wherever a house stood in the village of Khatyn, now stands a foundation and a chimney with a bell. One of those bells rings every 30 seconds to commemorate a life lost in WWII. The bell has been ringing for many years and will continue to ring to commemorate each lost Belarusian life. The 30 second timing represents how little time there was between Nazi bombs.

A statue of Yuzif Kaminsky, who lost consciousness in the burned barn and later recovered to cradle his dying son, sits in the town square.

Belarus lost 25% of its population in WWII. Khatyn represents all of the war dead and destroyed villages. Local lore says that the Belarusians were very tired of the Soviets and at first welcomed the Nazis. But once they learned about the Nazis, the Belarusians began to fight alongside the Partisans. The Soviets which included Belarusians, called both World War I and II the Great Patriotic War, meaning a defense for one's homeland. The name was meant to motivate the population to fight against the invaders.

In today's Belarus, when a couple marries, after the ceremony, they drive around Minsk to the various war memorials and lay flowers at each one. I want to think that they are saying, "Because of your sacrifice, I am here."

Khatyn's peaceful setting belies what it symbolizes. From the moment I stepped on its sacred ground, I could only see through my tears. Every step was a contradiction. How could such an unspeakable event have happened in this utterly peaceful place amid these spring green leaves and papery birches? Did the birds and butterflies see what happened? On that spring day they were singing and flitting. I couldn't speak through the aching lump in my throat. A tissue wasn't enough to blot my nose. Khatyn's ghosts surrounded me as I walked the grounds, helping me to understand the horror of what happened. I was in a holy place where the unthinkable had come to pass. It changed how I saw Belarus. I was part of it now and I'm glad Lena waited until the end to take us there.

Living and working in Belarus was a special gift. The people we knew there are still in my heart. Having one last chance to work with Stan is still precious to me. It was like coming back to our origins and falling in love all over again.

# ITALY

—⋅≫ ≪⋅—

Even before the end of the first year in Belarus, Stan was ready to retire again. He accepted the job for me and once I got established, he wanted to opt out again. I asked him to stay one more year in Belarus and then I truly would be established in QSI which had 36 schools around the world. After the second year, I could transfer to another QSI school in yet another interesting location (Turkmenistan, Kazakhstan, China, Venezuela, East Timor, you know, more ultimate vacation destinations) so I tried to keep Stan happy and willing to stay for the second year. It didn't take a whole lot of convincing. While he would never have said it, I think Stan liked the sense of being in charge that came with being director of the school in Minsk. Truly, it's what he did best. The other part of him wished he had no demands and could do whatever he wanted. I, of course, thought the healthier thing was for him to be active and engaged, so to my thinking, staying in Minsk for a second year was positive in multiple ways.

International schools have to be constantly on top of their staffing needs. Hence, as a teacher or director, we had to let the administration know by mid-December if we planned to stay or go next school year. As soon as they sort all of that out, they begin to move people around and hire new staff. So by December of our second year in Belarus, I had already told QSI that I wanted to stay with QSI but move to another location, and Stan had told them he would leave. I could list my top three wishes for where I wanted to be placed, but there were no guarantees that I'd even get any of those. I knew that I had to take what they offered or say goodbye. I had listed that my top choice was the two-year-old little school in Brindisi, Italy; my second choice was Malta, and my third choice was Bratislava, Slovakia. I didn't think my odds were very good in any of these locations, but what did I have to lose in asking?

I didn't have very long to wait. By the end of January QSI offered me a teaching position in Brindisi, and I shot them a yes while I was still talking to Stan about it. While he didn't want to work anymore, he was fine with me working. He would accompany me wherever I went. I wanted to get my response to QSI before they could change their minds. And, finally, I was going to get to live in Europe. Oh, happy day!

In Brindisi, a new director, his wife, and four children would be joining the school along with another teaching couple and me. The director's wife would work part time as she had a one-year-old at home. Enrollment in the school was about 35 students. Most were from the United Nations Logistics Base located in Brindisi because of its deep water harbor. Those students came from all over the world. The other students were American, as Boeing had a plant nearby where they were making parts for Boeing's new Dreamliner aircraft.

## VISAS

I love watching the people go overseas to live in a foreign country on HGTV's Househunters International. They look at three dwellings and have to decide which one they will take.

This always seems silly that in this usually enormous local-
ity, the realtor can only find 3 possible houses or apartments.
They make it look like choosing a place to live is the hardest part of moving overseas. To me, culture shock or homesickness is a far greater challenge, but the true challenge is
obtaining a visa. In Turkey, the school had been in existence
for 70 years. They knew how to get visas. We had little to do
with the process, but even for our entering group, it was a
challenge. Remember that all 22 of our passports traveled to
Chios, Greece to be stamped? I have no idea where else those
passports traveled and even with all of those many years of
practice, we still didn't get our passports back for 6 weeks
after school started.

In Kuwait for the first year, I had the kind of visa which,
I learned the hard way, allowed me to stay in the country
for 30 days and then I had to leave. I could come right back
in, but I had to fly to Dubai, Oman, Jordan, Egypt, Syria, or
Bahrain because the only countries that abut Kuwait are Iraq
and Saudi Arabia. I couldn't go to Iraq at that time, and I
didn't want to go to Saudi Arabia where I would be forced
to cover myself. Ashraf took me on several trips to various
offices to secure my 30-days-at-a-time visa.

One thing I had to do in Kuwait was get a blood test to prove
I didn't have AIDS. (I didn't.) Ashraf and I stood in many lines
to turn in paperwork which someone at the office had filled
out, get a stamp, write my signature, or have my fingerprints
taken. Luckily for me, I enjoyed these little breaks in my usual
routine. I would line up with all of the other Bangladeshis,
Filipinos, and Indians. Ashraf would go to the head of every
line, shove his head into the window interrupting the person
standing there and speak loudly to the clerk so that I could go
to the head of the line and the clerk would shoo him away. I
always told him not to. I didn't mind waiting, and it seemed

very wrong to me that I would be allowed to cut the line, but he never stopped trying.

I'm not sure what magic happened the second year I was in Kuwait, because I got a permanent visa. But I also didn't get to take any mini vacations to the visa office with Ashraf in the middle of the day! I also didn't have to take monthly trips out of the country even though we still made quite a few trips that year, too. In fact, I came out of Kuwait with lots of great experiences but not much cash.

In Belarus because of the previous 14 years of experience, school secretary Lena knew what to do. We had to start with a single entry visa while Lena worked with the school's law-yer to get our multiple entry, permanent visas. The first year, because we didn't have our visas by the end of October, we couldn't go to the QSI annual administrators' conference in Phuket, Thailand.

The process of getting a visa to work in Italy was the most fun. I came into Italy as a tourist while Daniela, who was in her third year on the job as school secretary (because that's how old the school was,) tried to figure out how to get work visas for foreign staff. Up to that year, no one had received a work visa. I suppose if the government had wanted to, they could have come to the school and deported the entire foreign staff because up until that time no one had a proper work visa. But, seriously, this was Italy.

As it turned out, at my last doctor appointment in Wisconsin before leaving for Italy, the doctor had looked at a little spot on my ear that looked a little suspicious for the kind of skin cancer that is not fatal (basal-cell carcinoma). He had taken a biopsy but I only learned the results after I arrived in Italy. A nurse I talked to told me that while this wasn't life-threaten-ing, if it were her, she wouldn't wait until Christmas break to get it taken care of. So, I booked a flight home. Stan was still in Wisconsin. He wasn't scheduled to get to Brindisi until the end of October so he picked me up in Chicago and drove me home to Door County. I got my spot removed and a clean bill of health. Daniela had been coaching me about the fact that she thought I could go to the consulate in Chicago and get my visa that way. There was something online that she had arranged that said I was all approved for a visa. I just had to show up at an Italian consulate outside of Italy to pick it up. So from the first day I got home, I began to email and phone the Italian consulate in Chicago to get an appointment. I left voice messages. I emailed. I left more voice messages. No one ever picked up the phone. After about the 15th call, finally someone answered.

Impatiently, "Hello, yes?"

Calmly, "Yes, hello. My name is Carol Hoffman and I need to make an appointment to pick up a visa to work at QSI International School of Brindisi in Brindisi, Italy."

Very impatiently, "Madame you have to stop calling here. We have no visa for you. We cannot help you."

More calmly, I said, "Our school secretary, Daniela _____, says that the visa is available on the _____ page of the _____ on line."

Frustrated now the man said, "Madam, there is no visa for you here, you must stop calling."

Totally calmly, "Please look at the _____ page of the _____ on line where the visa is available."

Almost yelling, "Madame, there is no visa." And then in a more normal voice, "Oh, there it is."

"Good. I will be in Chicago on Thursday. May I pick up the visa then? I have a return flight to Brindisi on Friday."

Cranky voice again, "Madam, I cannot guarantee that you can get your visa. That is only one day. It depends on if we have time, if the printer is working and if we are not too busy."

"Thank you. May I see you on Thursday morning to see if I can get the visa?"

"All right. Come here at 9 a.m."

"Great, thank you. I'll be there."

By the time we found the consulate, got through security at the entry of the building and found their tiny office, I felt like I'd already put in a whole day's work. The door was locked and we had to ring a bell and wait till they buzzed us in. The waiting room was about as big as the entryway of a small house and there was a door to the offices in back and a small sliding window like the kind in a doctor's office where it looked like a secretary should be sitting.

I stood at the little window and said, "Scusi."

After about 5 minutes the harried consul, a tall black-haired Italian walked quickly to the window.

"Hello, sir. I am Carol Hoffman. We spoke on the phone. I have my documents for my visa."

The consul said, "Hello, madam. Like I said, I cannot guarantee that we can have your visa by tomorrow."

"Thank you for trying. I fly out of here tomorrow at 5:30. What else do we need to do?"

He looked through the documents I had brought. "You need 4 copies of your paperwork, 4 passport photos and a check for $50.00."

"OK, I will go out and get those things and bring them back to you as soon as I'm finished."

"Yes, but I cannot guarantee that you will get your visa tomorrow. Put your paperwork in this basket when you get it. Come back on Friday and if it is finished, it will be in this basket."

"All right, thank you so much."

We scurried around the neighborhood to find a Kinkos to make the copies and photos, and I wrote the check knowing I would be reimbursed for it. We rushed the completed paperwork back to the consulate and left it in the basket. There was still no secretary and no sign of the consul.

On our way out, Stan said, "It'll be ready."

On Friday morning we got buzzed into the consulate, and this time the secretary was sitting behind the sliding glass window. I told her my name and asked if my visa was ready. She handed it to me without a word.

Out we went.

In the pack, I noticed that of the items I had to get from Kinkos, they had used only two photos and none of the copies! Whatever!

When I returned to Brindisi, after missing only a week of school, Daniela was thrilled because now she knew the visa process. From then on she hounded new hires to get their paperwork to her so that she could make the arrangements for them to pick up their visas from the consulates in Chicago, New York, Los Angeles or Dallas. She told them not to bother to come until they had their visas. Even Doug and Therese who came from New Zealand received their visas from New Zealand.

Over the 5 years I worked in Italy, I made at least 10 trips to the visa office in Brindisi. These too were like mini-vacations from school. Daniela would drive me there and take care of everything, and I would sign, put my finger in the little sensor machine or show my passport. While we waited, Daniela and I would have lovely conversations. Her family, my family, whichever teacher on staff was on the s___ list this week, or scuba diving, Daniela's passion.

In Armenia, one of the oldest schools in the QSI system, they had the visa process down. Sarkis took care of everything behind the scenes, but about twice a year we all piled into cars to make a pilgrimage to the visa office. We had to go; there was no other option. We'd stand outside the office and go in one at a time to get our visas. We would all talk smart outside the office but then follow blindly as some government functionary stamped our papers, asked us our names, and checked our passports.

## WORKING IN BRINDISI

The first days in Brindisi started out pretty well. I bonded immediately with the other teaching couple. We hung out, shared confidences (wine) and enjoyed working together. Working with the director and his wife was another story. The director spent most of his time with the three high school students. His wife who was supposed to be working half time, rolled in around 1:00 and taught what seemed to me like one class. They had brought a nanny and I supposed the nanny was home with her sleeping baby. The first week of school I taught kids all seven hours of each day and had no preparation time. The director kept saying he would even out the schedule, but he didn't get it done. While I'm a hard worker and dedicated teacher, I could see that what I was supposed to do wasn't sustainable. At the end of the first week, I told him that something needed to change or I wasn't going to make it. Luckily he heard me and I got at least one hour of prep every day.

Over the fall months, parents and the other couple and I grew more and more disenchanted with the director and his wife. When they planned a five day long field trip for the six middle school kids, they figured out the costs of the trip and split those costs between the six kids. The kids' parents were shocked at the high cost: gas, hotels, food and admissions. It seemed that the director and his wife would get a free ride at the cost of the kids' families. When the trip actually happened, the director, his wife, all four of their children, one of their own parents, the nanny and a friend of their parent's accompanied the group. There were more people accompanying the group than there were kids. After the middle school parents found out about this, they suspected that the high fees they had paid helped support the director's family's trip and they were really not happy.

Apparently calls were made because soon the regional supervisor made an appearance in Brindisi. The way things shook out, the director could stay until the end of the year, but then he would be out and they asked me to take over as director. I said yes.

I'm not sorry I said *yes*, but I am sorry for the price I paid for the opportunity. From that day in January, the director's wife didn't speak to me, and the art teacher who was her friend didn't either. The wife of the other teaching couple also stopped speaking to me and while I held out hope that she would come around, she didn't. So I worked in a tiny school with three women who wouldn't speak to me for the rest of that long year. Because of its prime location (compared with Kazakhstan, Kyrgyzstan, Turkmenistan) teachers could only stay two years in Brindisi so there were new teachers, Doug and Therese from New Zealand, after the second year, lovely people who became my good friends.

## THE BUILDING

The Brindisi school was in a rented location that we were told was meant to be a school for children with disabilities. For some reason it was never used for that and we were its first occupants. QSI did minimal renovations to adapt the space to QSI's needs. The building was built around a small courtyard in the middle and consisted of 5 classrooms that surrounded a large, vaulted-ceiling, communal room which served as lunch-room, winter and spring performance space, all school morning meeting room (where we hyped the QSI Success Orientations such as Trustworthiness and Concern for Others), spillover classroom space from the classrooms whose doors opened out into it and physical education when it was raining outside. We all dreaded rainy days because when PE was inside, the noise carried everywhere else in the building.

The boys' and girls' bathrooms were perfect with three stalls and two sinks. There were also three very small rooms; one had no windows so we used it as the bookroom. Another became a very small classroom, and the third one became the office of the director. There was also a very tiny kitchen. It was big enough for a sink, refrigerator and one small counter space. If anyone needed a truly private conversation, that's where they went as there was only one frosted window to the outside. If that window and the door were closed, no one could see or hear what went on in there.

The outside of the building was painted pastel blues, greens and pinks, and all of the rooms inside were painted a differ-ent pastel color: blue, pink, yellow or green. The doors were made of a bright blue formica with white plastic trim. They weren't very well made and often wouldn't close, closed too tightly or simply didn't fit inside their frames. All of the floors were either white or very light terra cotta. The overall effect was calming and cheerful despite the door malfunctions.

*QSI International School of Brindisi.*

The first year we didn't have any heat or air conditioning. The building was outfitted for heat with radiators in key spots, but the director couldn't get the city to hook up the heat. So during the winter months, we froze in there. Brindisi winter daytime highs are usually in the mid-fifties. It's true there is a lot of sunshine, but that wasn't enough. I was glad I hadn't left my silk long underwear in Belarus because I used it every single day that winter. By the end of the day my legs felt like sticks and when I drove home I turned the heat in the car on high and kept it there all the way home so that I could thaw out. On the top I wore at least three or four layers, with a wool blazer on top. My suggestion to the director to resolve the heat issue was to go to the government office that was holding up the heat with about five of our preschoolers, discipline them loosely and stay until there was a promise from somebody that the heat would get turned on tomorrow. He didn't take my suggestion though he kept trying. On an 85 degree day in May the heat finally got connected.

Air conditioning in that part of the world isn't as common as Americans might think. And there wasn't any in the building at all. Over the years I was there, we installed over-the-window AC units in one room at a time beginning with my second year. The first room to get a unit was the one that got the most afternoon sun.

## DANIELA AND CRISTIANO

Anyone who has ever worked in a school knows that the two most important people in the school are the school secretary and the school engineer. If those positions are filled with willing, capable, dedicated people, most other problems will be small. Daniela was the secretary in Brindisi, and she was invested in the school. It was in her interest for the school to succeed. She was smart and good to the parents and kids, but very capable of saying no if the situation required it. She was also drop-dead gorgeous.

Daniela's favorite thing was to plan historical field trips for the kids. Because Puglia (POOL ya), the region/state where Brindisi is located, is a buyers' market for historical sites, planning trips for the kids meant choosing the best among great options. The trip she planned to Matera took us to a site where people had been living in caves for 8,000 years. In 1952 the Italian government forced the inhabitants out of their caves due to inferior living conditions that caused illness. Since the 1990s the caves have been rehabilitated and repurposed into gentrified, sanitized hotels, restaurants and residences for the very wealthy. Stan and I made a memorable weekend trip there later.

Daniela was an incalculable asset to the school. In addition to her school duties, which at times were overwhelming, staff, parents, and students counted on her to make translations for doctors, police, landlords or other non-English speaking Italians. She helped people find things they needed.

*Where can we find bubble wrap?* At Carrefour.

*Our dog died last night. What can we do with him?* Daniela called a veterinarian who had several suggestions for expensive graves at pet cemeteries. *No, that wouldn't do. Too expensive.* Well, come to our office and we can discuss other options. Daniela went and the veterinarian opened a freezer full of grocery bags containing dead pets. Apparently some man would come every month or so, pick up the frozen carcasses in those bags and bury them in an undisclosed location for about ten Euros. The parents didn't like that option either and ended up burying the dog in their backyard under cover of darkness.

*Tyler has an earache. Where should I take him?* To Dr. Pierrola at the medical center in downtown Casale.

Gradually Daniela took over the school library, checking out books for the kids and processing new books that got donated or ordered from Scholastic. I was especially grateful for Daniela managing this task because up to that point it had been my job.

The school was surrounded on two sides by apartment buildings of eight stories. A six foot tall wall ran around the perimeter of three sides. The entry to the school from the road was a sliding gate that could be opened and closed with a remote control device like a garage door opener. Each parent who wanted a remote could pay 50 Euros and get one for their car. (They would get the 50 Euros back when they returned the remote to the school.) Otherwise they had to park on the almost non-existent shoulder of the road, get out of their car and buzz for Daniela to open the gate (there was a camera so she could see who was out there). One parent who had a remote in her car did a lot of volunteering at school, especially when we were transferring from one library checkout system to another. She figured out the system and hand catalogued each of our books one by one into the new system. We were so grateful for her help. She came and went on her own schedule. One day she went outside after she was finished for the day and came back inside to ask if any of us had borrowed her car? No one at the school would have done that. *Have you seen my car?* No, we've all been here the whole time. *Well, my car isn't there.*

She said she always left her keys in the car because she felt that it was completely safe in our parking lot. Apparently someone in the apartment building adjacent to us must have understood that her car was there everyday with the keys inside.

Poor Daniela. That incident cost her so much time. There were police reports, and trips with the mother to the police station numerous times. Updates on the status of the investigation. The mother was disappointed to lose the use of her car and the set of hundreds of music CDs that were also in there. The absence of this mother's volunteer hours was also a loss to the school as she was so central to cataloguing the materials in the library.

Months passed. The end of the year came. The car was not found. The mother was resigned that the car was lost forever and as it was the family's second vehicle, they hadn't insured it against theft so the only way she could have obtained a new car was to start all over and buy one. Since their time in Brindisi would be up the next school year, they didn't replace the car. We all pictured this car in a chop shop, all of its limbs and internal organs now transplanted to other vehicles.

In the middle of the next school year, miraculously, the car was found. It was still intact, parked only a few blocks from the school. The keys weren't there, but the CD collection was. (The thief didn't appreciate her musical taste?)

The theory was that a young person had jumped the fence, hopped in the car, used the remote to get out of the parking lot and gone joy-riding until the gas tank was empty. There was even a shirt belonging to the owner still in the back seat. The mileage on the odometer wasn't much different than when it was stolen.

After this incident, we had security cameras installed around the building. Daniela made the arrangements for them! And they called her if they suspected something happening, some-times in the middle of the night. Sometimes she would have to drive to the school and sort out the difficulty.

Daniela also helped new teachers purchase cars. Many of the foreign staff on their way to new loca-tions would sell their cars to new teachers coming in, but sometimes there weren't enough cars to go around. Voluptuous, raven haired Daniela would go to a car dealer and help new hires get a car. I'm pretty sure she got them a good deal!

As wonderful as Daniela was, the maintenance side of the school was sadly lack-ing. The school hired a con-tracting company who sent us cleaners. Not many of

*Carol & Daniella 2009. Guess which one is Daniela?*

them stayed long and we had no continuity or buy-in from their workers. Teachers complained, the building didn't look clean, and anytime we had even the smallest kind of electrical, plumbing or other mechanical task, we had to pay someone to come and fix what was wrong. And things went wrong all the time.

When I met Daniela's brother in law, Cristiano, I got an idea. He and his wife had just moved back to Brindisi with their 5 year old daughter. He needed work. He had worked in a cookie factory in Abruzzo for several years and was a mechanic, caretaker, and general go-to guy. He loved children and was passionate about doing his best. I met him at a party at my house and liked him immediately. He had the cool of an Italian Tom Cruise, complete with mirror sunglasses and leather jacket, the looks of Lin-Manuel Miranda but the personality of Mr. Rogers.

The next day I asked Daniela what she thought about asking him to come to the school to take the job of cleaner, fixer, gofer. Could she deal with that? While she didn't jump at the idea, she didn't immediately dismiss it either. I asked her to think about it and give me an answer the next day.

She thought about it and decided that it could work for her and for the school so I called him and we had a talk. We would try this arrangement for a month and see how it worked out.

Well, what can I say? He was fabulous. The kids loved him immediately and I had a safe feeling with him in charge of our building and grounds. Over time I learned about the difficulties he'd had growing up and I think he found a refuge in me. To this day I consider him my "adopted" son and he calls me mom.

Cristiano loved Broadway and kept up with past and current musicals. He had performed when he was a teenager in restaurants for tourists in Sardinia where he grew up. He would always joke with the kids saying, "Keep eating you vegetables and you grow up to be strong Sardinian man like Mr. Cristiano." One year he convinced all of the older kids (boys included) to do a dance for the end of year performance to the song, "One" from the musical *A Chorus Line*. He taught the kids the whole dance, which he choreographed. Little by little, they learned it, not so much because they wanted to do it (though some did) but because of the force of Cristiano's personality and their dedication to him. They wanted to make him happy. And oh, did they! Yes, some of the boys were never going to get all of the steps right, (think seven boys facing right and one facing left,) but the performance was more darling because of it.

*Cristiano and Jamie.*

## THE BRINDISI BREEZE

I had started writing a one page summary of the week's school events when we were in Minsk. When I became director in Brindisi, I continued the practice with a weekly newsletter that I named *The Brindisi Breeze*. (See appendix for an example.) Every week I wrote about events that happened in little bullet points on a one sided sheet of paper and sent a paper copy home with the kids on Fridays.

When I got a new regional supervisor, she said I needed to expand the one sheet, include photos, and display the Breeze in a layout. That was all fine and good, however, if I had known how to do that, I would have already been doing it. Well, luckily the supervisor had a suggestion. A young man from another school would come to Brindisi and show this technically challenged person how to do it.

So Robert came in 2011 and showed me how to take my photos, drop them into the simple format he had set up on my computer. He watched me do it a few times, and I was in business. He also brought his device that he called an iPad and showed me what it could do. To an old dinosaur like me, it looked like he was doing magic tricks on a blank ouija board. A year later I had my own.

Over time I got pretty proficient at using the *Brindisi Breeze* to show parents what their kids were doing at school every week. If a class was giving presentations, I'd take a photo of each child giving his or her presentation and that would go into the Breeze. Playground shots, PE class, lunch time: parents got a good view of what was happening.

One week the 5–6 year old class of about 10 kids were giving presentations on their home countries. With the help of their family, the kids made posters that included photos, maps, special features of their country, and what language(s) is spoken. Several of the kids in that class were from the Balkans: Bosnia/Herzegovina, Kosovo, Serbia, Croatia, Macedonia, Albania and Montenegro. That week two of the kids who made their home country reports were from two of those countries, but as I was including the photos of their home countries, I hadn't written down which one was which and while I hate to admit it, I have to say that I don't know the particulars of the history of that area. I know horrible things happened: savage fighting, ethnic cleansing, rape, other atrocities and even now they have no lasting plan for peace, but I didn't have the information about which countries liked each other and which ones did not. In fact, I made it a point to treat each child as an equal and to be truthful, didn't want to know, for example, if they were from the country that perpetrated harm or that received harm. Everybody was equal in my eyes.

As I was trying to remember which of those countries this child was from, I knew it was one of two and I didn't want to go to that classroom and interrupt them on a Friday afternoon. I took a chance and labeled the photo with the country I thought he was from. It was only about 3:00 on Friday and I was very proud of myself for finishing the *Breeze* a little earlier than the usual 5:00, 6:00, or 7:00. It kind of depended on how the day had gone. Not 5 minutes after I had sent the *Breeze* to all of the families of our 37 students, I got a call from that boy's father.

"Oh my God, something terrible has happened." He was truly in distress.

"What happened?" I was really worried. Had his house burned down? The children were still in school so I knew they were OK. Was his wife ill? Had his parents been in a car accident?

"The *Brindisi Breeze* says my son is from _____. We are from _____. This is terrible."

"Oh, I am so sorry, Mr. _____. It's my mistake. I will fix it. Thank you for bringing it to my attention."

I went back to my version of the *Brindisi Breeze*, fixed the terrible mistake and had to send the new version saying that people needed to ignore the first one. Ouch. I changed one word. If anyone noticed, I didn't hear about it, but my one little faux pas caused one proud father unnecessary anguish.

*(See sample Brindisi Breeze in the Appendix)*

## LIFE IN PUGLIA-WORK
Brindisi is located in the Italian state of Puglia in the region of Salento which includes all of the area in the heel of the boot of Italy and a strip of land above the heel that extends to the Gargano Peninsula.

Employed Pugliesi have it made. Once a Pugliese is in his/her job for more than 2 years, the law dictates that the employee would almost have to commit murder on the job for the boss/company/organization to be able to fire him or her. That job belongs to that person for life. If the person became ill, had a lot of absences, or proved ineffective in that job, it's still theirs. The work day begins early, but by 1:00, people go home for the afternoon where they share a large meal with their whole family. Then they rest during the hottest part of the day. Summer or winter, they still rest. Italian families must be together in the middle of the day; there is no other option. Some employees have to go back to work at 4:00. At least that's the stated time, but the time they show up is more like 5:30 or 6:00 and they have to stay until about 7:00. The woman who owned the graphic arts business which the school used for all of our printing needs posted the hours ``5:00 to 7:00" for her evening hours.

One day I volunteered to go there after work with something that we needed to get printed. I arrived there about 5:15. Our good friend Stefania showed up sometime after 6:00 to re-open the door of her shop. It's a different work culture.

People who didn't have to report back to work showed up downtown for the passeggiata (pah SAY gee AH tah) (nightly stroll) where Pugliesi greet friends, stop for a quick stand-up coffee or aperitif, and enjoy a leisurely stroll. By 7:00 the streets are virtually empty because everyone has gone home to prepare and eat dinner.

With one exception, the Italian staff in our little school were aware of the employment laws but worked with our 8:00 to 4:00 schedule, showed up on time and dedicated themselves to our students and our school, despite rarely having a class-room they could call their own. One teacher occasionally brought her son to school when he was off school, but she (mostly) stopped doing that after I let her know that it wasn't acceptable. Walk into any restaurant in Puglia and the entire family of the proprietor is there, sitting at one of the tables, the television is on and parents are trying to get the children not to chase each other.

The one exception to our hard-working staff was a music teacher who only came on Wednesday afternoons to teach three music classes. One of the additional jobs of the music teacher was to prepare the students to present a winter and spring music performance. I hadn't hired her and she never asked my advice about what to do with the kids, but at least once a month she called in at noon to tell us that she couldn't make it for her 1:00 class because she had a stiff neck.

Now what were we going to do with the kids who were sup-posed to have a music lesson? No one else had free time to take these students for the class period. For most teachers, this was their only preparation time in a whole school day. They needed time to plan lessons, meet with other staff, set up their classrooms and go to the bathroom! When I learned about the Italian law about the two year arrangement, I made sure the music teacher understood that her contract was up at the end of the second year. Despite the difficulty in finding a music teacher in a foreign country, we couldn't keep this teacher whose track record was missing at least one day out of four in a month. Teachers have an unspoken culture with each other and rule number one is that you don't take someone else's precious prep time. Though she was a very nice person, these absences didn't endear her to me or the other staff.

## MASSERIA

The other reason Pugliesi have it made is because they have farmhouses.

In Italian that's a masseria (MAH sir ria) and every country road has one. Ambitious entrepreneurs have bought up the old, (14th century or so) farmhouses, maximized each one's architectural features, and turned them into hotels and restaurants where a Pugliese with enough money can stay all night and eat like a king.

My favorite, well, the only one I really knew, is Masseria Coccioli near Lecce, a town which should be on your bucket list if it isn't already. The parents of two of our students had bought the Masseria several years before and were in the process of turning it into a B & B. They had owned businesses (advertising and real estate), had worked in hotel management, banking, and nonprofits in Sweden and got tired of the rat race. They sold the businesses, quit their jobs and moved to Italy.

Sweat equity didn't begin to describe how hard Jan (YAHN) and Wenche (VEN-kay) worked on their place. When Wenche would bring the kids to school in the morning, she would be dressed in her work clothes which were always adorned with some kind of jewelry, a brooch, a large silver bracelet, a green necklace shaped like a butterfly that coordinated with her sweater on which you couldn't miss the dog hair. She'd return in the afternoon to pick up the kids still wearing the brooch but with paint on her hands, cement on her jeans, or tiny flecks of mud or paint in her bushy blond hair. With her larger-than-life personality she regaled us with the stories of what was being done that day: a contractor pouring cement for the floor cooling system, pipes running under each guest room through which would be pumped cold water that would obviate the need for AC, converting the old guard tower into a guest room by exposing the old masonry wall, installing a door where there hadn't been one in at least a hundred years, or digging out the hard ground to install patio pavers for sidewalks from the pool to the dining room.

They were artists, those talented people, and all of this time they were hosting people every day, cleaning the rooms, getting breakfast for them and seeing to their every need. After my second year, they started raising chickens on their property to be able to serve their guests truly fresh eggs for breakfast every day.

That beautiful setting, just 20 minutes from Brindisi, became a tremendous asset to our school for end of year parties, welcome dinners, and getaway weekends for parents and teachers. (One time we had an activity there and 40-year-old Daniela had to call her father to let him know she had made it safely!) By the time I arrived in Brindisi, Jan and Wenche had completed 5 guest rooms, a large dining room, installed a gorgeous blue tiled swimming pool, and were working on 5 more guest rooms. Masseria Coccioli (translates to shells) was positively heavenly for an overnight stay. Wenche and Jan didn't regularly serve any other meals aside from breakfast, but guests could ask, and if it was convenient, Wenche would serve a dinner they wouldn't soon forget.

During the last two years I worked at QSI Brindisi, I used my own money to pay for a dinner at the Coccioli for the foreign staff at the beginning of the school year before the kids showed up. The teachers could stay all night at their cost if they wanted to, or return to Brindisi if they didn't. The pool was wonderful for swimming and happy hour in the hot August afternoon. We would bring our own beer and snacks. Later we would go to our rooms for a short rest and show up at the outside tables for dinner at 8:00 under the starlit Italian sky.

A beautiful meal served on a warm August night in southern Italy with the clear black sky overhead pin pricked with star dots was just intimate enough to get the staff to bond and almost any human being to recall this as a perfect evening. Dark brown figs stuffed with white mascarpone, topped with

*Masseria Coccioli.*

a walnut (from a nearby tree) served with a chilly Proseco was the antipasto. Roasted peppers wrapped with prosciutto served with orecchiette pasta accompanied by Primitivo, a full bodied red that made no apologies was the primo piatto. Local bass poached in white wine and smothered in herbs and lemon slices with a crisp fruity Fiano was the secondi. Pesche Con Crema (Peaches with Cream) was dessert followed by piquant limoncello (lemon liqueur the color of sunshine) in a tiny, icy glass. Could a person want anything else?

Lucky Pugliesi have this in their own backyard. Family, food and wine — in that order. I miss it so much.

## LUNCH TIME AT QSI

As in all elementary schools, lunchtime is a big deal. At the given signal, the kids tear out of their classrooms, grab their lunches out of their backpacks, or run to be the first in line for school lunch (served by Cristiano), inhale what they want, and wait agonizingly to rush outside to play. The teachers and other staff need to eat, too, because keeping those darling children engaged and learning throughout the afternoon takes a great deal of physical and emotional energy.

As director, I could have assigned rotating lunch duty to the small teaching staff or even hired an aide to come in every day, (which was too expensive for our small budget,) but having been a teacher for many years myself, I didn't want to require teachers to take lunch duty for several reasons. First, some teachers ran lunch hour like boot camp and fired off commands like drill sergeants so that the stressed out kids looked more like inmates than students. Other staff were so loosey-goosey that the kids didn't know what the expectations were and took advantage of every opportunity to pick on other kids or chase each other around the playground until one of them was hurt. Some teachers never showed up at all, "forgetting" it was their day or week. Plus, most of these colleagues were really hard working and didn't get to sit down to eat lunch. I took pity. Eventually, I began to eat my own lunch before the lunch hour, and I joined Cristiano and the preschool teacher assistant for lunch duty.

Adults had to help the little ones if their lunches brought from home needed warming up in the microwave. Since the students came from all over the world, what they brought for lunch was also international. Jason's mother was Japanese, and his lunch came from home every day in a little bento box. The colors and creative square bits of sandwich, red pepper sticks and coiled carrot peels could have made the cover of Bon Appetit. Almost every day, each teacher would find a need to enter the lunch room and saunter by Jason's table to see what his masterpiece lunch looked like that day. Nicole, who was from Germany, always had tasty looking brown bread, so thinly sliced and dark brown, looking a bit like a square Oreo. Meat and potatoes, usually with sauce always accompanied those little squares of brown bread and more than once I wished I'd been invited to have dinner at her house the night before. These leftovers smelled so good and Nicole paid so little attention! Little Eugene always brought a box of chocolate milk. He hated milk but had already suffered two broken bones in his short life, hence the calcium-laden chocolate milk.

It was Cristiano's job every day to pick up the school lunch from the caterer. He loved serving whatever lunch came from her. He didn't *have* to do it; he *wanted* to do it and truth be told, wouldn't *let* anyone else do it. He loved heaping up the plates of those students and telling them, "Now you eat all you lunch today. It make you big and strong like Mr. Cristiano," doling out encouragement as he ladled on the ragout. He also complained bitterly when the caterer didn't provide enough food for what Cristiano deemed was the right amount for growing children and the prices we paid. "Carol, loog at theess. Why she can't give enough for the cheeldren?" On those days, after lunch he would get on the phone and have a loud Italian conversation with, presumably, the caterer and then storm around the building three or four times talking to himself before he calmed down.

After the kids ate, we had a specific time when they could go outside and play. When that time came, I went outside and monitored the playground. I tried to keep the rules consistent, preempted a lot of fights and got to observe the kids in a more natural setting. I like to think I helped the little ones learn to share, play safely, and have good clean fun. The slow eaters stayed inside with Cristiano.

We all dreaded the days when it was raining too hard for outside lunch recess. Over the five years I worked there, I either ordered things in our yearly shipment that came from America or carried things in my suitcase for kids to do during inside recess time. I'm sure my bags looked strange to customs inspectors: Play doh? Nerf balls? Uno cards? Marble Works? Eventually we accumulated quite a large stash. Those toys were kept in my office and could only be played with at inside recess so the kids wouldn't get bored with them. Those marble chutes that could be put together to build large structures that could be built differently each time were really popular, especially with the boys. Once they built the structure, they would send a marble down the chute and watch it propel itself to the bottom where it usually fell to the floor. Another popular pastime was Play-doh. Oh, I was so careful, OK, obsessive, with that stuff. It was expensive, heavy to carry and could all be turned brown by the right mixture of colors. I would selfishly hand out a small can of pink to one student, yellow to another and so on. "Don't mix the colors, please. Give it back to me when you are finished and you will be able to use it again next time." As official floor washer, Play-doh was Cristiano's nemesis. I tried to help keep everything clean, but those weren't his favorite days.

When I first started in Brindisi, the outside playground was about as big as a good sized backyard in the States. It was fenced in on three sides and the two swings, slide, merry-go-round, and teeter-totter, none of which would ever have passed a safety inspection on an American playground, were all clumped together in one small space. The third side of the play area was the school building and there was always the fear that a child would sneak out either from the front or the back of the building and escape to the parking lot.

The area in back of the school was a weedy, uneven mess about the size of a soccer pitch and behind that was an Italian day care where the children were never let outside. Eventually we worked with the daycare and cleared the field to expand the play area. That field was perfect for soccer matches, PE classes, and outdoor projects of all kinds. With the typical good weather in Brindisi, the field, our outdoor gym, was in constant use.

*Soccer at lunch time.*

Once we were able to use the field for soccer matches at noon time, there was always a game on. About once a week there was a situation that ended up in my office. "Samar kicked the ball at my stomach and he did it on purpose." "Fahad said we had one point, but we had two." "Graham hit me. Right in the neck." "Jeffrey called me a dumbhead." I'd always try to give each student his or her say where the other one couldn't interrupt. Usually things ended with an apology or an agreement that it was an accident.

Name calling was always a problem. It was usually the kid who got called a name that swung the first punch of a fight. I tried very hard to help kids understand that the person who did the name calling was the guilty party. Two students, almost always boys, (sorry,) all sweaty, crying, wiping snot and dirt from their faces, making accusations at one another would be standing in my office. "If Noah calls you a dumbhead, does that mean you're a dumbhead? Who's in the wrong here? Noah, what do you need to say to Eddie for calling him a name? Eddie, do we ever hit anyone for any reason? That's right, no. OK, apologize to Noah. Can you play without any problems tomorrow? I don't want to hear about you calling anyone names. OK, good. Now go to class."

Sometimes there was an injury, a skinned knee, a sore ankle or a bruised elbow. This is where Cristiano became Dr. Cristiano and the child felt like the most important person in Italy. Dr. Cristiano would ever so gently hoist the child up on the counter by Daniela's desk and examine the wound. In the world's sweetest voice, "Oh, I sorry you fall down. Let me see what happen. OK, I see. Don't worry, Dr. Cristiano can fix that for you. This will only take one minute. First we wash this right here. Is that OK? Does that hurt? Now we put the band aid. OK, one and two." He would gently float the child down from the counter. "You are all better. Do you want to go back outside? OK, you can stay here. Dr. Cristiano will stay with you. When you ready, you go back outside."

When recess was over, we had a handbell that we rang and like Pavlov's dogs, the kids would come running in, go to class and settle down. For the next 30 or so minutes, the building was a machine, humming with productivity and I was humming right along with them. I thought, *OKAY, THIS IS WHY I CAME HERE.*

### A BIG ITALIAN FAMILY

I had an office in the school that was about 9 ft by 9 ft. The previous director had purchased a portable air conditioner, an R2D2 look alike, that could be used in that little space, but it was cumbersome, noisy, and ineffective. I learned early that it wasn't worth the trouble, and during August before school started, I would set up a table in the breeziest place I could find in the school, which was just in front of Daniela's desk. I had my back to the center courtyard and I faced the street and found that I could work there quite well. If new parents came, we sat in that space and discussed what the school could offer their students.

One day the parent of a new preschool student stopped by and he sat facing me and the indoor courtyard while I faced the front of the school where there was a terrace surrounded by a short wall. The preschool class often played on that terrace as it was right next to the outside door of the preschool class.

I had shown the father the preschool classroom and the play area for that group and now we were sitting discussing the paperwork. As I was speaking with him and looking at him, to my horror, I saw a large rat walking on the short wall of the outside terrace making its way toward the preschool classroom.

I don't know what I spoke to that father about after that, but my whole aim was to keep him focused on me. *Whatever you do, don't turn around.* The rat moved out of my vision. Where was it now? In the preschool room? *Please don't let this father want to take one more swing around the preschool room to see the puzzle collection or the play kitchen. Please let the rat and any friends he might have brought with him go somewhere other than the parking lot where this father would soon be getting into his car and leaving the school.*

Some miracle prevented any of the mishaps I was envisioning, and the father left happy that his daughter would be joining the school. The minute he left, I found Cristiano in the Kindergarten/First Grade classroom on the opposite side of the building and told him what had happened. We went out on the terrace to see if there was any sign of the rat. Over in the corner of our property the grass had grown quite tall and the ground was uneven. Cristiano suspected that's where the rat had come from. He had heard on the news that there had been a rat infestation in the Sant Elia neighborhood where our school was located. He would call the city and have them come out to "take care of the rats." How many rats do you think there are? He teased me saying, "Remember these are eetalian rats and eetalians have big fah mee lees!"

## GARLIC AT MIDNIGHT

While it's true that Italians eat dinner very late, I'm pretty set in my ways and I usually kept to my 6:00 dinner time. In fact, we found a pizza place that opened for pizza on Friday nights at 6:00. That became our favorite restaurant. All of the other restaurants opened at 8:00.

In August Italians eat even later because of the heat. I would be there in August still suffering from a little jet lag having just returned from summer break. I would have a little stress about the new school year and a little misery from the intense heat with no air conditioner in my bedroom. Night after night, just when I was hitting the hot sheets, I would wonder what I was smelling. It was earthy, pungent, and hungry-making. The first time I smelled it I couldn't identify it or where it came from. The next night I looked out the kitchen door and smelled the source of that delicious food intoxication. It was the house on the south side of my apartment building, where apparently an outdoor kitchen existed and the woman of the house was sautéing garlic. Gobs of garlic. Whatever she was making, every night, she started with garlic. Every night. *Oh heavenly aroma, give me more!* Why didn't I ever go down there and invite myself to a late dinner?

Well, first, I didn't speak their language and was pretty sure they didn't speak mine. Second, if I ate dinner at that hour, especially one with that much garlic, it would be a long night and I needed all of my wits about me for the upcoming day.

I couldn't afford to lose any sleep. Third, that house was also surrounded by a big fence and unless I wanted to climb over it, I wasn't sure how I could get in. When I go back to Italy, I'm going to get over that fence, knock on that woman's door and tell her how much I appreciated those heavenly aromas back then. Maybe she'll invite me to dinner at midnight.

## LOCAL HIRES

In international schools, the foreign staff come and go, but the local staff are the glue who hold the school together. To my thinking, the issue of local hires is multi-faceted and there isn't a clear right or wrong about it. If you're a certified teacher who has been hired from the U.S., Britain, or another English speaking country, you are considered a foreign hire in an international school. If you come from and live in the community where the school is located, you are a local hire. The foreign hires command much higher salaries than local hires. If an unmarried person starts working at a school as a foreign hire and later gets married to a local, that person's status is changed to a local hire. However, the person still makes more than a person who has lived in that country all of their life. If an American, British, Australian or New Zealand trained teacher happens to be in a foreign country because of their spouse, that person is considered the same as if s/he were married to a local. These practices were common in four of the schools I worked in.

The advantage of paying local hires less (yet still more than they would make if they worked in a local school) is that a school can keep its costs down and deliver an educational program at a high level because of the local hires. For example, in the QSI schools, the preschool teachers were always local hires. Yes, they spoke with accents, but they were all highly motivated and effective teachers. At that time in the U.S., a preschool teacher didn't usually make as much as a K-12 teacher. In addition to preschool teachers, local teachers can provide instruction in subjects like art, physical education, and music. Each school also had a foreign language program so that the Pakistani/Nepalese/Swedish/American/etc. kids living in Brindisi could learn Italian from a native speaker.

One of the disadvantages to this system is that the local staff may feel some resentment that they are working as hard and long as the foreign staff but aren't paid commensurately. It can lead to a sense of elitism among the foreign staff. Luckily I was able to take steps against this happening while I was director in Brindisi. I used to invite everyone over to my house on Fridays for pizza. We would all gather and somebody would make a pizza run (I usually paid, but it was quite inexpensive — under 20 Euros) and often people would bring things like beer, wine, special cheeses or fruits. I knew of other larger schools where the director would invite the foreign staff to his/her house on Fridays but not the local staff. I was glad to include all staff, and I loved the way our staff worked together.

## GOOD SPORTS AND BAD SPORTS

I was always trying to make connections with Italian schools. Our Italian teacher Anna Maria (yes, that's really her name and yes, I brought her a t-shirt that says Anna Maria Island) helped us make a connection with a group of six high school students from one of the high schools in Brindisi. Our kids got to visit their school and their kids came to visit ours. Communication was really a challenge. Our kids' Italian wasn't good enough for teenage chit chat and their kids' English wasn't either. However, we had two native Spanish speakers and they helped the group communicate because of the similarities between Spanish and Italian.

Our kids joined with that school for an intramural volley-ball tournament. What a successful event in which our kids tried their best and competed at about the level of the other teams. They won some matches and lost others. It was competitive but good clean fun.

One year the elementary schools in our neighborhood put together an international program in which each school represented a foreign country. For example, one school was to represent Japan. Their girls wore clothing meant to look like kimonos and painted their faces white. Another school represented the United States. Those of us who were American cringed at their depiction. Some of the children wore cowboy hats and holsters with quite realistic looking toy guns. The other children wore Indian headdresses, beads, moccasins and carried fake Jim Bowie type knives. Their whole performance was the cowboys chasing and shooting at the Indians and the Indians trying to stab and scalp the cowboys. That's what they think of us? Yikes!

Our kids had learned the song "We Are the World" and performed it for the group. The kids from the other schools definitely recognized the song if they didn't know what the words meant. The program seemed to go on forever and for some reason (I think because our hot lunch was being delivered), we had to leave the program early. While we tried to explain why we had to leave, I can imagine the visual of those arrogant foreigners leaving before the program was over. If they had successive programs, I don't know, but we didn't get invited again. I wasn't director then but I was humiliated by our early departure.

Another activity we tried was a basketball game between our school and the nearby middle school where we sometimes went to use the gym. Other than our precious soccer field, our little campus didn't have anything close to a gym. Our PE teacher worked with the PE teacher of that school and organized one afternoon when our boys would play their boys in basketball. I tried to make my vision clear to the other school's PE teacher: two teams that were mixed, some of theirs and some of ours on each team. He let the kids play one game like that, but our kids complained the Italian kids wouldn't pass the ball to our kids. Then their coach split everybody up into an Italian team and a team of our students. Sadly, that match up didn't work out well at all. We had so few older boys that we could barely make a team of six. Their team had 4 times as many kids as ours and they had a school of 1,500 kids from which to draw players. Their kids looked at our little team like one of their elbows would wipe out the lot of us. Our kids could see that the deck was stacked against us but played anyway because they loved to play. We lost every one of those games and our kids came back defeated and disgusted with the Italian kids. This was not at all what I was hoping for. However, that wasn't my last attempt at cross-cultural experiences. Afterall, an eternal optimist wasn't about to be defeated.

The next attempt was an elementary exchange where a fourth grade class from another Italian school matched up with our kids who were third, fourth or fifth grade and the kids sang some songs together. This was much more friendly! On another visit, their kids came to our school and the kids all made art projects from our construction paper. Although there was lots of trouble communicating, all of the kids went home happily carrying their animal puppets.

### ANTONELLA AND THE HEALTH CLUB

With help from the locals, I found a health club just two blocks from my apartment. They had step aerobics classes at

5:00 on Mondays, Wednesdays and Fridays. I joined the club after my first trial class. The instructor was Antonella, who was either a misplaced middle school PE teacher or a hopeful choreographer. She encouraged us some of the time, but most of the time she hollered at us and demanded that we try harder and stay with the beat. Antonella only spoke in Italian, so I learned numbers 1–8 the first day I attended. She created a new routine every day and taught it to us one little bit at a time so that by the end of the hour long class, we could do the whole thing. Not only did we get a work-out, we got a short opportunity for self-expression. I loved her class.

Because she couldn't speak English, Antonella didn't know that the CD version she had of Cee Lo Green's song, "Forget You" was the explicit one. While I don't go around with a stomach ache because of all of the swear words I've swallowed, I lived and worked in an environment where that language wasn't tolerated, so it became very funny to me to be doing my step workout to "F—-You." The other members of the class often sang along. I smiled and I did my L steps.

Another benefit of Antonella's class was that I made friends with my fellow class members, especially the ones who could speak English. Francesca and I became good friends. We started doing activities together and soon our husbands came along, too. She and her husband called the women in our fitness class "Desperate Housewives!" Their daughter was finishing high school while I was there and then entered college in Milan. She was so beautiful that she had already done some modeling work. I went to Taranto to watch her participate in the Miss Monde competition that seemed a little like a Miss America pageant. (She was a finalist.) Sadly, Francesca won't travel by plane so she probably won't ever come to the U.S. to visit, but I wish she would. She learned English from working at the American military base in Brindisi that was established in 1960 and decommissioned in 1994. When I knew her, she worked at the equivalent of a county courthouse as an assistant to several judges.

The other friend I made at the health club was Barbara. Barbara was also a fluent English speaker and a fitness fanatic. In addition to Antonella's aerobics class, Barbara taught yoga. She was so thin, I thought her bones were made of glass.

Barbara included me in her weekend hiking group. Someone in the group of about 30 adults would plan a hike that had historical significance, challenging paths, and no environmental impact. We'd usually drive to the start of the hike on a Saturday or Sunday morning, begin the walk, stop for our bag lunch where someone was always sharing a special treat: home-made wine, walnuts from a backyard tree, or home-made pastries. Despite their not being able to speak English, this group was welcoming to me, and I enjoyed the walks and the camaraderie. One time a man who could speak English joined us for the day. He and I had quite a talk. He was the owner of a Salumeria (deli) who lived in Lecce and was not married. To me he seemed kind and intelligent and when I got to school on Monday I couldn't wait to tell single Daniela about him. I had even taken a surreptitious photo of him. I talked him up to Daniela and showed her his picture. *Nope. He wasn't her type.* Too bad.

## TO STAY OR TO GO?

Living in Brindisi, I knew that at some point, though I wouldn't want to, I, too, would have to leave. The transitory nature of our school population gave me a chance to think about this potential departure every time one of our current families had to move on. I felt tangible sorrow for the departing family and tried to reconcile what it would be like when the departing family was me. I had settled into my comfortable apartment, knew where to get my groceries, and couldn't envision the day when the bakery wasn't within walking distance of my house. I loved the friends I'd made. Our sweet little school was just the right size for me.

Every fall when Stan would arrive in November, we would sit down to discuss whether this would be the last year. We would take four sheets of paper to help me visualize what I was trying to figure out. Advantages of Staying — Disadvantages of Staying — Advantages of Leaving — Disadvantages of Leaving. As we discussed and listed all of the reasons, one page would come out full of reasons and the decision to make was clear. Stan was always supportive whatever the outcome would be. Even if we weren't in the same physical location, we talked everyday on Facetime. And because of his many successful years as a school principal, he was a big help to me in dealing with difficult situations.

*Therese in class*

One disadvantage of being in Brindisi was that I didn't have much social life. I never had much contact with the UN employees, though I wish that I could have. Making friends with the QSI staff was difficult because I was the director. The two years when Doug and Therese from New Zealand taught there were my most comfortable. Doug and Therese used to come over for a beer on Friday nights and we'd talk about the kids and QSI, make jokes, and share our wonder that George Bush could speak the way he did and still be president. (Little did we know!) I had a huge affinity for those two wonderful people and wish they still lived down the street like they did in Brindisi.

The other adults I knew were parents of our students. Being friends with them definitely wouldn't work out. I began to long for the days when we lived in Belarus where we had at least two couples from the embassy with whom to hang out. Neither couple had children or other connections with the school, so we were free to be friends. Also in Belarus, we were invited to many events at the ambassador's house. They were really good to us. In Brindisi there wasn't an equivalent role at the UN, and the CEO there changed frequently. They barely knew we existed. Another organization with many Americans was Boeing, but those people really stuck with themselves. Not to mention, either Stan was with me in Brindisi or he was back home. I couldn't make friends with singles or couples very easily. I made a few lovely friends, but truly, only a few.

When a student left our school in Brindisi to move on with his/her family to a new location, at about 5 minutes before the end of their last school day, we gathered up all of the kids and staff and lined them up starting at the door in two lines facing each other and hands joined overhead going out to the parking lot. The student who was leaving was held back by his/

her teacher until the sign was given that everyone was ready. Then the child had to walk/run through the line hearing good wishes and goodbyes from everyone currently in the school. If the parents were there, they ran through the arches as well. Doug and Therese gave us that idea and it became a tradition.

*Goodbye, Manuel!*

## VISITORS

In Brindisi we were visited by any number of friends and family. We enthusiastically invited a woman from Wisconsin we only knew professionally to come and visit us in Italy. She loved to travel and took us up on the offer to spend time with us in Brindisi. We picked her up at the Brindisi airport the runways of which abutted the end of our little street (our apartment was the last one on the street.) Stan loved to sit on our balcony and watch the planes land and take off. She arrived jet lagged and a little woozy. She said she was worried about some food her cleaning lady had prepared for her to eat on the plane that had reached room temperature in a Tupperware container long before she ate it. Just two hours after she arrived, that food came to a bad end and the poor woman was up most of the night getting it out of her body in not nice ways. The next day she stayed in bed. When we asked her how she was doing, the response was, "I can't believe what I've been through." The day after that she felt ready to go out with us to a restaurant for dinner. She was able to eat a bit and it seemed like her visit would be okay.

Stan, being Stan, would make plans with her the night before and they would be going to see the white city of Ostuni or the trulli (domed houses) in the city of Alberobello. Ever the early riser, Stan would be up by 6:00, finished with breakfast by 6:30 and out of the shower and dressed by 7:00. He would take me to work so that he could have the car for the day and on the way home stop at the bakery to procure some fresh rolls for our guest's breakfast and his mid-morning snack. Our guest would roll out of bed around 10, luxuriously, who could blame her, partake in the rolls, drink coffee (which Stan had made-Lord help her!) and be ready for her shower at around 11:30. By the time she was ready to go, Stan was out of sorts because, again, Stan, being Stan, had been ready to go at 8:30 a.m. At 2:00 he was more inclined to nap than drive an hour to a tourist site he'd already seen 3 times. Apparently this pattern repeated itself for several days. On the weekend we would all drive to Sorrento, our favorite getaway and show her yet another quintessential Italian city. Perched on a cliff overhanging the Mediterranean, Sorrento meant staying in our favorite hotel (the Ullise Hostel [for Ulysses]), walking the narrow alleyway that paralleled the main street and was full of touristy shops and sit-outside restaurants (all so predictable) and eating in La Lanterna ristorante with its salmon colored walls, salmon ambient light and salmon colored upholstered chairs. It was like being in another world. Nothing bad could happen here.

The drive to Sorrento was a long haul, usually 5 hours and we left on Friday night. Saturday and Sunday were sunny and we all had a good time. It was enough to patch up the previous days, for me, anyway. Stan's patience had already run out. So when we got home late Sunday and our guest discovered that the prized bracelet which she had been wearing was missing, you would have thought the world was going to end tomorrow and the only way to stop it was to get the bracelet back. She wasn't sure where she lost it but it could have been at one of the rest stops where we had stopped to either get gas or use the bathroom, of which there are probably 25 between Brindisi and Sorrento. Which ones had we stopped in? Absolutely no idea. It was 9:00. I had to go to work the next day. Could Stan drive her back there tomorrow?

I had to explain the difference between Wisconsin and Italian culture. If you lose something in Wisconsin, the finder will usually try everything in his or her power to get the object back to its rightful owner. If you lose something in Italy, the finder will think he or she is having a great day. *Well, could we call all of the rest stop gas stations that we could have stopped in?* How would that even be possible? They don't have names and we didn't remember where we stopped, not to mention we didn't have the kind of Italian vocabulary required for such a task. *Well, could I ask the bilingual school secretary to call them?* I said, okay just to make it stop. When I came home that day, I told her I was sorry but the school secretary wasn't able to find a single number to call. A blatant lie. I hadn't even asked her.

On the day before our guest's departure, Stan once again tried to make plans to take her somewhere, but he later reported that she said she wanted to be sure she was all packed before she went anywhere and ended up spending the whole day in her room. Maybe she was at the end of her patience, too. As visitors came and went over the years, we tried to be good hosts and find the best in each guest.

## A VISIT TO ASSISSI

The first year we were in Italy, Stan and I made plans with my sister and her husband to spend my spring break somewhere in Italy. We consulted with Daniela about where to go. Tuscany was too touristy, we'd already been to Florence, Venice, and Rome, Daniela suggested Abruzzo where we could see Perugia, Assisi and Umbria. We found a rental house that would meet our needs and then some. Laura couldn't come, but Melissa could, so we had three bedrooms and everybody would be comfortable.

The house, owned by an English couple, was described as situated on a "white road" (gravel) and we used the owners' instructions to find it. When we got to the white road, we were so happy because we had finally found the road and looked anxiously to the left and right to see where the house was. The instructions were a little less perfect from there. Basically, the white road was one lane that led into a forest beside a large hill. Tall trees towered all around as the road was barely a ledge on the side of the hill. Our car, Pablo, the Citroen Picasso, was fairly wide by European standards and as we slowly, painstakingly made our way down into that gorge, we learned that looking straight ahead was the only way to keep our lunches safely tucked in their designated spots. We decided that the only "white" part of that road was our knuckles as we tried to drive on that narrow strip. Finally, finally we arrived at the house, a large two story with one tiny place to park the car, facing in with the front wheels at the edge of the gorge with a skinny rope extended from two poles to keep the car from driving into the gorge (as if!)

We had passed other houses on that road and the one with the caretaker was just 50 yards away. What would we do if we met one of those other drivers on the trip back to the main road? Would one of us have to, oh my God, BACK UP? Goodbye Pablo!

It was cold that April and we tried to figure out how to turn on the heat from the elaborate instructions left by the owners. Both Larry and Stan tried to make sense of the little pins that had to be moved from one hole to another, but nothing they tried worked. Finally they gave up and we called the owners who were back in the UK.

"Well, it's really quite simple." Really? Then why are there three single-spaced pages of instructions? After about ten minutes, they got the heat working and it was a good thing because that night it snowed! Now the road was "white" but no one wanted to drive on it.

I guess we were younger then because we did venture out, and we toured the whole area. My sister got the idea that it would be cool to go to church on Easter morning in St. Francis' Cathedral, so we tried it. We had to stand in line to enter and the whole scene reminded me again how differently people of other cultures react to the idea of personal space. We were jammed in line and eventually jammed into the entryway. I immediately lost Judy, Larry and Stan and tried to make my way forward. After what seemed like hours but was probably 10 minutes, I was only 15 feet inside the cathedral, I turned around and headed for the exit. Outside I found Stan sitting on a bench. Had he gone in? Yes for 2 feet and then immediately exited. Not long after, Judy (who put her hands on my shoulders after her first day in Europe and said, "I will never see things the same way again,") and Larry popped out. It was even too much for them.

The St. Francis Cathedral seemed to me a contradiction. On the walls of the cathedral were all of the pictographs of St. Francis in his simple robe tied with a rope, his poverty and his love of animals displayed so beautifully. Would he approve of this multi-million dollar cathedral or the 200 tourist shops that sell all manner of trinkets with his name on them? I think he would tell all of those people to go outside, smell the air, feel the sunshine on their backs, and listen to the birds.

Melissa would be arriving on Easter and we took advantage of the owners' advice and made reservations at a local agriturismo (working farm that offers meals) for Easter dinner.

## DINNER AT THE AGRITURISMO

We arrived a little late at 1:10 and the entire place was full. We were the last arrivals. Wine was poured, plates were brought out and we began what for me was the longest meal of my life. Three antipasti, three primo piatti, three secondis and three desserts. We had to leave before the third dessert was served because we had to go to pick up Melissa from the train station at 5:00. We left the agriturismo at 4:30 and they weren't finished yet!

While the food was so good, each plate could have been a whole meal for me. I don't have the kind of patience required for sitting for a 3-1/2 hour parade of plates of food that after the first 4, I had no interest in eating. We spent an entire afternoon sitting at a table eating and drinking. The image of this meal may sound deliciously decadent, however in reality, though I'm glad we did it, I was ready to go after an hour.

## RESTING MY EYES

On the last day in the rental house, I was closing up a garbage bag and while doing that, as I pushed the air out of the bag, something flew into my eye and started bothering me. I took a shower and while in the shower, something happened to that eye that caused it to be completely blurry — like I was looking through a piece of plastic. I could see light and shapes, but no detail. *None. Oh, dear, what to do?*

Judy and Larry were moving on to other tourist sites, Stan was going to drive back to Brindisi by himself and Melissa and I were going to take the train to Rome. Okay, I figured I would stop in a pharmacy in Rome and get some eye drops.

The pharmacist in Rome told me to go to the hospital. She didn't have any eye drops that would help. Well, that didn't sound like such a good idea so Melissa and I finished our day. She left for the airport to return to the States and I left for Brindisi by train. The next day Stan drove me to the hospital and Daniela met us there. She explained what the admitting doctor determined was wrong and they admitted me to the hospital. I needed to rest. My eye was full of blood and they couldn't tell what was wrong. I should rest in the hospital and they would give me blood thinners to help dissipate the blood in my eye.

I was put in a triple room. I had the bed next to the window and an older woman with a bandage over one eye who seemed very kind was in the bed nearest the door. The middle bed was empty.

In the wee hours of that night another woman with a large entourage came in and took the middle bed. It was noisy and crowded in that little room for a while until most of the people left. The woman in the bed must have been in quite a bit of pain because she did a lot of groaning and another female was speaking to her in calming tones. Any sleep I might have had pretty much ended right then and I spent the night feeling bad for this woman while listening to the groaning. I tried not to think about how much rest I was not getting.

Breakfast the next morning was a package of two zwieback and a cup of tea with milk and sugar. I know Italians eat light for breakfast, but I couldn't see how that little food would get me to lunch at 1:00. When Stan came, I left the room and bought a kind of cinnamon roll in the hospital coffee shop. *Yuck! No wonder the hospital stay was free.*

When it was time to see the eye doctor, I had to line up with all of the people who were in the hospital because of eye problems, including the other woman in my room with the eye patch and wait to be seen by the eye doctor. When it was my turn, I had to put my face into a face shaped frame and try to rest the edge of my eye into a little eye frame. There had been so little time between my time in the room and the previous patient, I wondered if that little frame that was touching the whole outer edge of my eye had been sterilized. The doctor looked in my eye for 5 seconds and I was finished. The next patient cycled in. According to Daniela who later translated, the doctor still couldn't see in my eye, it was too full of blood. I needed to rest and continue to take the blood thinners.

I'm not sure what time it was when I decided I'd had enough of the hospital, but I got my clothes on and told them I was going home with Stan.

Well, they didn't recommend that but they couldn't stop me. At home, I called an eye doctor in Florida and told him the story. He couldn't give me a diagnosis but would see me if I got myself to Florida.

Next I asked Daniela to see if she could get me an appointment with a private eye doctor in Brindisi. She found one and scheduled an appointment for two days later. Meanwhile I stayed home and the kids at school were muddling through with the mother of one of our students serving as a substitute.

When I went to the private doctor, Daniela went along. I had to pay 75 Euros cash (about $100) before I met with the doctor. I just about fainted when I saw the doctor walk into the examining room. It was the same doctor from the hospital! All of a sudden, I was the most important person in the world. He took at least 15 minutes with me, looking at everything but still couldn't see in my eye because there was too much blood. The diagnosis: I needed rest and blood thinners, which they couldn't administer outside of the hospital.

Stan was going back to Florida in four days. I bought a ticket to accompany him and scheduled an appointment with the eye doctor in Florida.

When I got to Bradenton, I went to the eye doctor's office. Dr. Pope took one look into my eye, with sterile equipment I was sure, and said I had a torn retina. He could numb my eye and fix the tear with a laser. I was out of there 45 minutes later good as new, vision restored. He told me to go home and be very quiet for 24 hours. Two days after that I could fly back to Italy. Be careful wishing for socialized medicine! And, if you have a major medical problem in Italy, go home to get it taken care of.

## THEADORABLE

On Mother's Day during my third year in Brindisi I got a call from my daughter, Laura, who was living in Philadelphia while her husband Christopher was working on his Master's in architecture. Both she and Christopher were on Skype which was unusual; Laura generally called when Christopher was at school. They wanted to tell me something.

Laura was pregnant and the baby was going to arrive in December, on the 17th if the calculations were correct. All I heard was "baby" and I was crying/laughing/exploding with joy. Oh, my God, I was going to be a grandmother. Aside from the two birthdays of my daughters, was there ever a day happier than this one? I'd never really talked to my girls about having children. It didn't seem appropriate. They would or they wouldn't and the less I said about it, the better.

After months of talking about the size of the baby: a lime, a peach, an eggplant, December came and I went to Philadelphia. I had 2-1/2 weeks to get this baby born. I house sat for one of Laura's friends. Stan didn't come, he felt he'd be in the way and he already had seven grandchildren, so for him, this wasn't a big deal. Soon Melissa came too, but she slept on the couch at Laura and Christopher's little row house near downtown. Every day Melissa, Laura and I went somewhere fun, including one doctor appointment during which the midwife said that if the baby didn't come by December 31 there would be a mandatory inducement. I had to leave on the 30th. *Come on,* I kept thinking, *let's go!*

On Christmas Eve we wanted to go to church and figured the Unitarian would be the most likely to have the shortest service which is what we were after. It all looked good. Real, lit candles hung from each pew in this 18th century church. What a beautiful touch for a candlelight service. We squeezed into one of the old straight-backed pews. Laura was on the aisle and told us later that about once a minute the candle from above her head dripped wax on her neck.

The music was lovely, if almost unrecognizable. The small low-ceilinged room got hotter. The unpadded, straight-backed pew got more and more uncomfortable. The minister started his sermon. Wait a minute, on Christmas eve, wasn't it supposed to be a lot of music and a short, short sermon? Not to these Unitarians. He went on and on. At an hour and 15 minutes he came to his third point. At an hour and a half he finished up. We burst out of there like trapped miners. Laura, Christopher and Melissa went back to their house and I headed over to Emily's. Tomorrow would be Christmas and we were all ready: stockings, presents and ingredients for a Yorkshire pudding dinner that Christopher would cook.

The next morning I was awake early and made my way to the shower. When I came back to the bedroom, I could see that there was a missed call from Laura. Standing in my towel I called back.

"My water broke and I'm having contractions."

"Woo-Hoo! Oh, my God. It's happening. Once your water breaks, there's no going back." I was overjoyed, not only that there was going to be a baby, but because I was going to be able to meet him or her.

"The midwife said to get dressed and get to the hospital."

"I'll meet you there."

Melissa had brought along our Christmas stockings so we had a little Christmas there in Laura's room. She was managing pretty well but didn't look like my Laura. Later she decided that it was time for her to concentrate on getting this job done without the extra people in the room so we went to the waiting room to WAIT.

It was a long day especially in the late afternoon when the contractions were much stronger and Laura was trying to do without all of the pain maskers. Christopher's parents arrived from New York City about mid-afternoon. This baby was their sixth grandchild but my first. We waited. I paced.

We didn't hear any news. No one came to update us. I paced up and down the hallway. At 7:20, I saw Christopher walking toward me. He looked a little worse for wear with a serious look on his face. I thought he was coming to tell us that there was progress. Instead he told us, "It's a boy. Mother and baby are fine." Joy, tears, relief all around.

In a few minutes the baby was going to be cleaned up and we could go to a viewing station behind glass to watch our new grandson get his first bath. All pink and wiggly, he was gorgeous. He responded to the touches of the nurse bathing him. His eyes weren't open but his little arms and legs were stabbing at the air. I couldn't stop looking at him. He was going to be called Theodore (my grandfather's name). I don't know if I've ever felt happier in my life than I did at that moment. From that first moment, my life which had been riding down the same highway for 51 years, jumped into a new trajectory of happiness and joy that continues to this day.

Two days later he came home and we finally had that Yorkshire pudding dinner and opened Christmas presents.

In March, little Theodore and his parents came to visit us in Italy, and I went to Philadelphia for spring break in April. Oh, he was adorable so I called him Theadorable. I told Stan there was a new man in my life but he had nothing to worry about. Laura Skyped about once a week so I could see this darling boy and all of his week-to-week changes.

## THE DOG'S NOSE

For some reason each of the buildings in Casale, the little neighborhood where I lived, sat in the middle of a walled-in yard. A locked gate in the middle of the wall allowed anyone holding a key to enter, but it was always puzzling to me because the wall wasn't that high and a determined climber could have easily scrambled over it. Some houses had parking inside the wall so there was a sideways retractable door with an electric motor that could be operated with a device similar to a garage door opener. My building looked like a large four-story house. It sat on the corner of a quiet street that dead-ended into the airport. The four stories held four apartments — one on each floor. The basement apartment had a large wall of windows that faced a tiled terrace. Several different renters lived down there during my five years in Brindisi. Romeo, a technology expert from the Philippines, lived below me on the first floor and above me was a two story apartment that belonged to the daughter of the owner of the building, Mr. Rohde who lived across the street. Isn't it funny that I lived in Italy with a downstairs neighbor named Romeo who was from the Philippines?

My apartment and Romeo's were exactly the same with 3 bedrooms, 2 bathrooms, a kitchen, large living room and 3 balconies. One small balcony (3'x6') was off the third bedroom just about the right size for a drying rack. Another small balcony off the kitchen held the washing machine and the largest one (6'x12') off the living room had a white plastic table and 6 plastic chairs. (at least it did until the table blew off in a winter storm) The street below the large balcony was the dead end where we angle-parked. Off in the northwest direction lay the Brindisi International Airport. Stan learned when a landing was imminent by watching the ground crew reposition the staircase from its usual spot out to the area in front of the airport out to where the airplane would be parked. They had no jetways. More than once I'd be sitting at my computer and could overhear the communication between the air traffic control tower and a pilot ("Al Italia flight 238 you are cleared to land...").

A raving red bougainvillea burst out of the garden of the apartment owner's house across our little cul de sac. Those colors were more vibrant in spring, but were visible all year. Mr. and Mrs. Rohde lived in one half of that large building and another of their four daughters lived in the other half. Traffic was almost unheard of in Casale, except during the one yearly festival in the fall, so the neighborhood was mostly quiet. Except for one thing: since a wall surrounded almost every building, owning a dog served at least two purposes: companionship and protection. Dogs of all sizes, colors and dispositions lived in the neighborhood and barked out their warnings from behind their respective fences. As a natural born pedestrian, never afraid to walk, day or night, I knew by heart which yards contained the meanest sounding dogs. I would plan my walking route based on staying on the opposite side of the street from the meanest sounding barkers.

The dog across the opposite street was the most fun. Though I never actually saw that dog, I saw part of him. If I walked anywhere near his building he would start barking, not in a mean way, more like, "Hey, I'm over here. Why are you out there? What are you doing? Let me out of here. Take me with you." After only three barks, somehow he would manage to lay his head sideways and slide his long nose out from under the retractable door. I only ever saw his nose and mouth barking like he was being held against his will and needed to get out right now to see his sick uncle in the next village. How did he configure his body to get his skinny snout to fit under that door? His head had to be sideways so that he could still open his mouth to bark. What did he look like from behind? A downward facing dog? Poor baby! Though I'm not a dog lover (there's a long story about a dog we had when we were kids that contracted rabies) I always wanted to open the door and let that dog out.

## VINO

Italy is nothing if it isn't about wine. Puglia farmers scratched out their livelihoods with grapes, olives, and artichokes, and most recently solar farms! I knew what produce was in season at Brindisi's open market by what was piled high on the market tables: artichokes, red peppers, grapes, and if I was lucky, delicious peaches. Olives, having been brined and processed, were available all year round and though I'm not that big on olives, I'm told that once you've had an olive in an Italian market, every other olive you'll eat will be inferior.

Our favorite winery was Due Palme (DOO ay PAHL may) located next to two tall palm trees, hence the name, in Mesagne, the next town over. Their wines had won awards and we loved to go there and buy a stash. Of course, the most fun thing was to bring our own jug and they would fill it for us from their table wine in big vats that resembled gas pumps: we called it the wine gas station. We could get a five-liter container — about the size of a gallon milk jug — for eight Euros. We learned the hard way that this table wine was really good, but after a week or so, even if you refrigerated it, it was not so good. By then, it was probably still drinkable but kind of sour.

One spring I learned about a wine festival that was being held in Taranto during the same time that Laura, Christopher and little Theodore would be visiting. For sure we would be going. Much like such events in America, tables with canopies were set up and each local winery had one. I was the driver for the hour and a half to and from Taranto with such precious cargo (Theadorable) so drinking any of that wine was prohibited to me. This was my own rule after I almost caused an accident way back in Appleton after drinking one, I swear, one glass of wine. So I went to each booth and picked up a brochure. Laura and Christopher got lots of tastes!

Those brochures became a true treasure during the next years. When I first started in Brindisi, Stan would come and stay most of the school year, however, over the five years we were there, he began to shorten the amount of time he spent in Italy. From October to May to November to April. When he was there, we would get up on Saturday morning, pile into our little Peugeot 206 (named Tootsie-I traded Pablo in after the first year) choose one of the wineries to visit, and put its address in the GPS. Those excursions took us to places we never would have seen and we bought bottles of wine from each one. Wine in Europe can be cheaper than bottled water. Then we might ask the winery staff where we should go for lunch and they would direct us to a local locanda where we would have an authentic meal: spaghetti alla cozze (pasta with mussels) for me, lasagne for Stan or whatever else they offered.

*An Italian winery*

Puglia isn't really that large, but these expeditions allowed us to see a lot of it. Over the five years we lived there, we saw more and more fields of solar panels. Could these be more profitable than artichokes? Easier than olive trees? Way to go, Italia. Wake up, America!

## JUST THE WAY YOU HERNIA

During the summer of 2010 Laura, Theodore, Christopher and Melissa came to visit us in Wisconsin while we were home in America, enjoying Door County. They all arrived the same day. Just before dinner Melissa was passing out the beer for happy hour. She handed one to me and had another in her hand for Laura. Laura, who has never said no to a beer in all of her adult life, put her hand up to refuse the beer. Melissa understood before I did. There were a lot of hugs, screaming and jumping when we realized another baby was on its way.

Theodore kept growing, "talking" to Grama on the phone (skype.) I would read him books, show him toys, sing songs. He was with me, eyes focused, constantly watching. I'm not sure if he was thinking, "Who is this crazy woman who keeps singing off key and showing me pictures of giraffes?" but he looked like he got it.

Laura kept getting bigger and I scheduled a trip to Philadelphia for Christmas and spring break. If all went as planned, even though I wouldn't make it for his/her birth, I would be there when this baby was about a month old. I could live with that.

On March 2 our precious Jamie was born all tiny and squiggly not looking anything like his brother Theodore did. Oh, happy day! I couldn't wait to hold him.

Two weeks later Laura called. There was a small problem. Jamie was in the hospital and they were going to operate on him tomorrow. *Oh, God.* The bottom fell out of my chair. What kind of surgery?

He had started to scream uncontrollably the previous day. They couldn't comfort him no matter what they did. They headed for the ER where he was diagnosed with a hernia and would have the minor surgery to correct it the next day. As mother/comforter I was all, "Well, that makes sense. Yes, they need to fix that now. That will be fine. Don't worry, honey, they know what they're doing." Christopher would call me when it was all finished.

When I hung up, though, a fear like I had never known encompassed my whole being. *He was two weeks old. Oh, God. The things that could go wrong. I had watched ER.* I believed he would be fine, but I didn't sleep all night.

I knew the surgery would be at 9 a.m. which was about 4 p.m. my time. I bumbled my way through the day not knowing if it was Monday or Friday, September or February. Finally after the kids left the building, I waited. At 5:00 I called Laura but there was no answer. I kept calling every 15 minutes. No answer. I was afraid to go home in case I would miss a call while I was driving.

Cristiano, my hero, stayed with me. He kept checking on me, telling me that everything was going to be fine. Somehow that day so many jobs at school had to be done and he had to stay late: change lightbulbs, fix that leaky toilet, clean the dirt out of the track of the sliding windows. Finally at 7:00, I called Christopher and he answered.

"Jamie is fine. The surgery went well. Jamie is a little groggy but he's nursing just fine and he'll go home this afternoon."

"Oh, great. I knew everything would be okay. Is Laura there? Yes, but her phone won't work in this building."

"Oh, can I talk to her on yours?"

"Hi, Mom." She was sobbing. So was I, silently.

Composure restored, "I'm so glad everything went well, honey. He'll be fine."

"Yeah, I'm sorry about my phone. It doesn't work in this building."

"Oh, don't worry about that. I'm so glad everything is okay. Now is when you need that beer."

"I'll get one when I get home."

"Good idea. Me too."

"I love you, Laura." Catch in my throat.

"I love you, too, Mom." Catch in her throat.

"See you in two weeks."

After I hung up, Cristiano was there hugging me and I cried until the crying was finished. So did he.

"It's OK, Jamie is OK. Don't worry, he grow up to be strong Sardinian man like Cristiano."

When I met Jamie two weeks later, you would never know that anything unusual had happened to him. If there had been scars, they were already gone and Jamie could belt out an unhappy cry like a tornado siren. He didn't like to be carried upright, only laterally on my hip. I walked back and forth that way with him looking at the lights as they passed over his eyes. He was gorgeous. Big eyes that looked like they would be blue. If two year old Theodore noticed that Jamie was even in the house, he didn't let on!

## Another Wedding

During the summer of 2011 Melissa married Rick, an elementary school counselor who was living in Columbia, SC. The two of them met through a mutual friend and pretty much knew in a few minutes that this was the relationship they were both looking for. So we all came together in SC to surround them in good wishes and love. Wow! Both of my daughters were married.

## My Favorite Places to Visit in Puglia

### Otranto (OH trahn toe)

The drive to Otranto is the first spectacular part about this visit. South of Brindisi we would float along a coastal road that soars at least 300 feet above the cobalt blue sea. I couldn't drive all the way to Otranto without stopping at least once to stand on that cliff and stare off into the water waiting to point out the best place I could build my million dollar house perched on the cliff overlooking the water. Once we were in Otranto, we parked in the city lot and did not have to walk far to get to the city center. Just on the main street with a view to the basilica, there is a restaurant that's only open during the summer. There are about eight tables inside, but most of the tables lay outside in the cool shade surrounded by a half glass, half wood barrier where I could get the most delicious plate of spaghetti a la cozze (COAT say) I will ever taste. The house wine was a perfect pairing.

### Lecce (LEH [like "let" only without the t] che [like Chet only without the t] )

Getting to Lecce was easy and took about 30 minutes in all. It's a fairly large city for Puglia so we had to pay attention to where we were going to get to the old city, but when we did, we would stroll around the white stone streets, looking

*Our favorite restaurant in Otranto. Note the pile of empty mussel shells!*

at each building for its own gift to the world. In the middle of the city lay half of an old Roman amphitheater. A bridge divided it and the other half was still underground, but the part they dug up is at its most remarkable during Christmas. The entire 500 ft by 400 ft. half-oval was transformed into a life sized Bethlehem with life-sized papier mache human and animal figures, a specialty of Lecce. This Christmas display looked like the closest thing I've ever seen to what I think would have been the real creche. The cats who roamed the site freely made the site come to life and put us at the birth of Christ.

To mark 12:00 noon every day, a loudspeaker blasts about two minutes of a male opera singer doing a fine rendition of Ave Maria in Piazza Sant'Oronzo.

### Matera (muh TERR uh)

People have been living in the Matera caves for 8,000 years. The people were poor and often ill because of the poor living conditions. In 1952 about 15,000 people still lived in the caves, but the conditions were so unhealthy that the government forced the remaining people out and into proper houses in the town. Since then the caves of Matera have been gentrified and transformed into luxury hotels and a unique tourist destination. Because it was carved out of rock, moving around in the curvy Matera streets presents a challenge for the most able bodied and it's easy to see why Mel Gibson chose the site for his 2004 *The Passion of the Christ* when Jesus carries his cross down the via della rosa to his death.

A museum shows a typical family home in Matera. Its one "room" shared by the whole family including the livestock is about the size of a living room in a modest American home. The bed was the dominant feature and apparently everyone slept in it because otherwise there was only a crib. Under the main room was a cistern for fresh water. There must have been outhouses somewhere, but that wasn't abundantly clear. With the large families and animals purportedly living there, it was easy to see how these dwellings were hospitable places for disease. Stan and I spent a weekend in Matera staying in a cave room in a refurbished luxury cave hotel. Our domed room had 3 little windows high on one wall that we could shutter for complete darkness, but I have to admit that despite the lush white linens on the bed and the spa-like atmosphere of the bathroom, I couldn't have stayed 5 minutes in that room without opening one of those windows. My

*The caves of Matera.*

ultra-sensitive nose detected that about three hundred mice had died in there over those 8,000 years and while workers cleaned it up, they missed one little mouse. The open window made the tiny odor undetectable and all was well. At that hotel, Stan and I had the most romantic lunch I've ever enjoyed. A quiet jazz CD of *The Girls from Ipanema* flowed all around the rough vaulted ceiling and wine kept getting poured into my glass. The stone floor felt so solid under my feet. We went back to our cave room for the afternoon rest. It was a great afternoon, if you get my drift.

### Santa Maria di Leuca (SAHN ta MUH ree ah dee LAY OO ka)
We took at least one day trip every weekend and Santa Maria de Leuca at the tip of the heel was one of our favorite destinations. The drive there, again through the Santa Cesaria cliffs, was a way to see life through a different window. Of course we had a favorite restaurant in Santa Maria de Leuca. We always sat outside because we could see the sea just across

the parking lot. On our day trips, I would usually drive to our destination where we would dine on typical Puglia fare, orecchiette, the shell-like pasta endemic to Puglia, with olive oil, garlic and tomato sauce (margarita) or plates full of antipasti. Most restaurants in Puglia and Italy in general seem to have much the same food, but it's all so wonderful. After lunch we would walk across the street to the beach and go exploring. Though Italy has some great beaches, I'm so spoiled by the pristine beaches of Lake Michigan and the Gulf of Mexico on Anna Maria Island, the beaches in Italy didn't hold my interest for long and we'd be on our way.

Lucky for me, Stan would drive on the way home and I would catch up on some of the sleep I'd lost that week! I would start out the trip making comments about the stunning cliffs and pretty soon my chin was trying to reach my chest and I'd give in, slam the seat back and get my nap, complete with open mouth!

### *Polignano a Mare (PAH lig NAHN oh ah MAHR ay)*
About an hour north of Brindisi on Strada Statale 379 sat Polignano a Mare, a little old city right on the Adriatic which had such an intimate feel that I thought it invasive to walk through its little streets. It was as if we were walking through someone's backyard. At the end of the street, there was a thick sea wall built right down into the water with a fence on top where we could look over and watch and hear the waves crashing 30 feet below. On a windy day we'd get wet.

### THE OVERLOOK
One of my greatest pleasures was the simplest. I would walk from my apartment four blocks to tiny downtown Casale where I passed the three salumerias, the tobacco shop, the indoor fresh market, four coffee shops, and the bank. I would

*Laura, Theodore and Jamie on the Casale side of Brindisi Harbor—*
*Note the Ferry on the Brindisi side—far right*

come out on the top of the overlook, where across the narrow harbor I could see the outer edges of downtown Brindisi. Six ships sat permanently on the Brindisi side of the harbor, and beyond them stood the apartment buildings that fringed the downtown area of Brindisi. Several restaurants and smallish hotels faced Casale on the lovely cobblestoned riverwalk. To the left I could see the narrow inlet where those six ships could make their way out to the deep blue water of the Adriatic and then to the wider waters of the Mediterranean.

From the overlook, my favorite place in all of Italy, I could go down the 60 steps to the ferry dock. Then I would use one of my ferry tickets (which I bought at the tobacco shop) and ride over to the little peninsula that was old Brindisi and walk to the main street (which oddly enough is quite reminiscent of downtown Sarasota). The ferry ride took almost exactly two minutes and once there I would walk up one of the cobblestone streets, jog right then left past the cathedral, turn right at the little grassy square where an old city gate lay half buried, take a left and in one block be walking on the smooth stones of the main street. Turning right on the main street leads to the train station. Turning left leads to the dock where cruise ships to Greece take on or let off passengers. Sometimes I went with Stan, sometimes met someone for coffee, sometimes went to a restaurant with someone or often just walked the main street for the sheer pleasure of it.

Going back to my apartment in Casale, I would swing down another street back to the ferry dock and stop at Bar Betty, the best gelato place in, well, all of Italy, to my thinking. Bar Betty had more flavors of gelato than anyplace else in Brindisi and in fact its only competition that I ever registered was a gelato place in Sorrento. I liked Nocciolo (hazelnut), Stracciatella (chocolate ripple), cioccolato (chocolate), and especially Limoncello (lemon) when combined with fior di latte (vanilla). Bar Betty had both an indoor and an outdoor restaurant where we could order lunch, ice cream or a big dinner. Most take out counters in Italy operate on a cash first basis. The customer would go to the cashier, tell him or her what they wanted, like two gelato cones and then they would pay for them. The cashier gave them a receipt which they took to the gelato bar and gave to the person making the cones. It was the same for coffee at a coffee bar. The customer would go to the cashier and say, "Cappuccino decaffeinato," pay, then go and get their coffee at the coffee bar.

Bar Betty was right on the water so I could get my gelato and monitor the little ferry. Once I saw the little blue and white boat plowing its way back across the water, I had to hurry because it only took two minutes to get across the quarter mile of water. I could never be exactly sure of the ferry schedule. If it was early, the boat would sit at the dock, but if it was late, it would disembark its passengers, embark anyone waiting right there, unfasten its moors and be gone before I could say "Scusi." Going back, once I was across the water, of course, I had to ascend those 60 steps, but I was always so happy that I had been downtown, I never minded the return, especially if I could still taste my gelato!

Other times I would simply walk to the overlook to absorb that this woman, me, from Appleton, Wisconsin was standing in this magnificent place, doing this fascinating work. I was seeing, hearing, learning something new every single day. How lucky I was to receive this gift. How can I imprint this moment in the flow of my memory so that it can never be forgotten? ***THIS IS WHY I CAME HERE.***

When I left Brindisi after five years, (that year the "Advantages of Leaving" page came out the clear winner) the parents and staff gave me a painting of the overlook. Even now I can stare at it and hear the sound of the ferry boat, smell the pine trees that grew next to the steps, feel the breeze on my face and hear the sound of Brindisians running down the steps to catch the ferry.

*The painting of the Overlook the parents gave me when I left Brindisi.*

# QSI

# QSI

—⋅≫ ≪⋅—

Belarus was our first experience with QSI schools, and it turned out to be an organization we would stay with in the coming years. This collection of schools is playing a valuable part in the education of children all around the world, and I was proud to be a part of it.

## THE ORIGIN OF QSI

The founder of QSI, Jim Gilson, graduated from Seattle Pacific University where he roomed with Dwayne Root. Apparently the two of them conjured up the idea of starting a non-profit school somewhere in the world. Somehow they came up with the idea of Yemen for the location of their school. Was it the Christian community service component of their university that compelled them? The lack of Christianity or a school in Yemen? Those two things seem logical, but I found absolutely no evidence of this concept during all of my nine years with QSI. Non-profit and non-religious: these were two of my favorite things about working for QSI.

After Jim graduated, he worked for an international school in Taiz, Yemen, but a civil war broke out, the families were evacuated, and the school closed. This experience led him to believe he could start a school in Yemen, and he began to work toward that goal. He met with people in Sanaa, Yemen; hired a teaching couple; found a rental property that would serve as a school campus; gathered up the materials that would be needed for a school; got those materials to the school, found a few families willing to send their children to the school, and got a job teaching for high paying Aramco in Saudi Arabia. None of these were easy tasks. Jim's relatively high salary from Aramco would take care of his own family's needs and pay the teaching couple. Over the course of that first year, 1971, word of the children's academic success spread around Yemen. More children joined the school during that first year and by the end of the year, with an enrollment of 25 children, Jim determined that he could quit his job with Aramco and he and his wife Marjorie could replace the man and wife team they had hired for the first year. The school continued to grow and prosper for 20 years. They built their own building starting in 1976.

When the Soviet Union fell apart in the early 1990s, many more diplomats were being stationed in the former Soviet Republics. One such country was Albania where one of the ex-pats approached Jim to form a school in Tirana, Albania similar to the one her children had attended in Yemen. That's when Jim partnered with Dwayne Root and they formed QSI. Now there are 37 schools around the world. The overall enrollment of these schools goes up every year. QSI designates class placement by age: 6-year-old class, 12-year-old class, etc. The curriculum is very similar to what students would experience in an American school.

Expat communities like it when an organization comes in to run a school. Otherwise, the parents are on their own to start a school, get a school board, acquire a site, order materials and get them shipped to the country, recruit the teachers and run the school. Over time, they found that key board members would leave, consistent quality was difficult to maintain, and the whole process was a huge time, effort, and emotional drain.

QSI has a process. They only create schools where they are invited. They work with local authorities and the expat community to find a rental site, send a school start-up package, and pay the bills until the school is up and running. Those bills and the cost of the start up package are then called the school's debt which the school, once it's making some money, must start paying down. Over time the school can pay down its debt and either lower tuition or decide to build its own school. Most schools want their own building. If the school pays down the debt of its building, then it can lower tuition. However, I don't think this would ever happen because then the school decides it wants a gym, a tennis court or a new wing.

These are some of the advantages of having QSI run the school:

- QSI hires all of the teachers, who must be certified with a demonstrated record of two years of successful teaching experience

- QSI has policies and regional supervisors to handle sticky situations, of which there are way more than one would think!

- QSI can finance the school's debt

- QSI can finance a new building if the debt is paid off or almost off

- QSI can be blamed if anything goes horribly wrong!

- QSI has a system of keeping the curriculum current by having a rotation of renewing each curriculum area every seven years.

The curriculum pretty closely matches what is happening in American schools. When it's the year, say, for mathematics curriculum revision, selected, current QSI math teachers get together over the summer to work out how the curriculum will change and how it will stay the same. They review sets of mathematics textbooks and select a set that will help teach the concepts that they've determined need to be taught and that everyone can agree with. Then they go off to their various locations and start working on the new curriculum while they are teaching in their classrooms during the next school year. Sometime in the spring, they meet up again. Over the course of a week, the curriculum writers finalize the new curriculum. I was lucky enough to meet up for the Reading and Language Arts Curriculum in Sanaa, Yemen in 2007, before Yemen was torn apart (again) by civil war. What a great opportunity for me.

QSI's motto is Success for All and its mode of operation is called Mastery Learning. The student doesn't fail, s/he simply isn't finished yet and must keep on working on a particular concept or concepts before the teacher can determine that the student has mastered the concept or skill. This is a controversial method for parents who want A-B-C-D-F grades and say that on a job you don't get to keep working on a concept until you master it, you simply get fired. It's also difficult for teachers because potentially each student in your class could be working on something different. It can be done, but it

*Breakfast in Yemen.*

*Fairy castle architecture in Yemen.*

takes lots of time and meticulous organization. My thinking on Mastery Learning is that it's one of several operating systems. Each system has its advantages and disadvantages, so I can work with any of them. I can say as a school director, however, it would make a director's job easier if the system were A-B-C-D-F! It takes a lot of time to patiently explain the QSI system to every parent.

As a not-so-stellar student in math however, I'm not sure how Mastery Learning would have worked with me. Kids who don't get it, usually know they don't get it. Does it help to watch your classmates soar ahead to multiplication while you are still working on subtraction? This is an age-old problem that can't really be solved with any educational system that still relies on the traditional classroom. Did I not do well in math because I couldn't do it or because I didn't care about it? It wasn't interesting to me — still isn't!

## YEARLY CONFERENCES IN PHUKET

Every fall QSI hosted a conference for all school directors in Phuket, Thailand. Apparently the owner of a hotel there, the Kata Beach, had children in the QSI International School of Phuket. The end of October and beginning of November is at the end of the monsoon season so business is slow. The owner offered QSI some very special rates to hold its annual conference there every year. Stan and I were hired at the last minute, so we weren't able to go to this conference our first year in Belarus. The second year, we were all set to go and Stan's mother died right before the conference. I told Stan I would do whatever he decided — go to Wisconsin for his mother's funeral or go to Phuket. He said that he could hear her saying to him, "Oh, go to Thailand for heaven's sake." So that's what we did. During the nine years I worked for QSI I think I went to Phuket five times. One year they held the conference in Ljubljana, Slovenia. I really enjoyed it: same time zone, short trip to get there and archetypal European city. I never asked, but I imagine that Ljubljana didn't prove to be a popular location for the annual conference because the year after that it was back in Phuket!

Here's what Stan said about Phuket: "They fly us halfway around the world to one of the most beautiful locations on earth and shut us in a room with no windows all day." When I became director of QSI International School of Brindisi, I can testify that this is true. I would wake up in Phuket where the temperature was a balmy 80F. A huge breakfast buffet of tropical fruits, omelets, breads and many other dishes was set in the main dining room/reception hall which was open on two sides, but I could take my breakfast out to the deck and enjoy the sunshine, the turquoise water, and sit in my some-what professional clothes while other guests were wearing their swimsuits. At 8:15 I would have to show up in the con-ference hall upstairs that truly does not have any windows, ready to take in the important information of the day.

I could get out at lunch time, but not for long — we used to go right across the street to eat yummy green curry with veg-etables, #1 spicy, every single day. After the general meetings were over at 4:00, we had to meet either with our regional supervisor, other directors regarding people who were going to be moving to our school next year or with the director of finance regarding our budget for the current school year and the projected budget for next year. Sometimes we had to meet with someone in QSI management about next year's school calendar or about an upcoming accreditation, a very big deal in international schools. Meanwhile, we had to stay in communication with our school to find out what was hap-pening and try to resolve any issues that came up. Staying for a whole week was a hardship for our schools because everybody either teaches or has an oversized workload. And this didn't allow much time for resolving those little day to day playground fights, ranting parents, prospective students whose parents are in town and want to visit the school in 15 minutes, or the music teacher who didn't show up again.

While it was a bit of a disadvantage with the long flights to get there and the jet lag, being in Phuket was still like going to heaven for a week. When we finally got to the hotel, a one hour — in good traffic — ride from the airport, the check in agent gave us a cold wet towel with an orchid so that we could wash our hands and smell the orchid. The large reception room was about the size of a Walgreens with walls on only two sides. The back part of the room was completely open to the pool and deck which spilled out onto the beach. Parrots, javan green magpies, and wood storks, all squawked from the trees above. Breakfast on the deck was to listen to a

*Kata Beach Resort, Phuket, Thailand.*

bird orchestra tuning up, cawing, cackling and tweedling just like flutes, oboes and piccolos before a symphony. Look anywhere and see palm trees, lush bushes, green grass. Gentle breezes kept people cool enough to walk around to the little shops, restaurants, nail salons and massage parlors. Every plate served in the Kata Beach Resort contained an orchid. When we met a Thai person, he or she greeted us with hands in prayer position, a slight forward bow and an angelic, breathy "Sa VA dee KAH."

The first years we went to Phuket, every other table on the sidewalks in town was a vendor hawking knock-off products. Stan purchased at least two "Rolexes." When examined closely, the name said "Roiex" watches. Coach bags, Guess shoes, Burberry scarves and enough perfumes to make an entire city dump smell good. I got a little LeSportsac wallet that says LESpORTSAC and has three zippered slots for folding money, credit cards or coins — perfect for two or more types of currency. That wonderful little wallet is still in my purse. When it falls apart, so will I.

Every year these knock off merchants became more scarce. Other than my little wallet, I never wanted any of that stuff anyway: I didn't understand why a person would buy a Coach bag at any price? That's not who I am, but Stan enjoyed buying his fancy watches. He would ask a street vendor and the guy would bend down and from under his skirted table he would pull out a box of Rolex watches. Over the years they became more expensive: $20.00 instead of $7.00 and the vendors tried to be far more covert.

Eventually, I got to know many of the directors and loved the time I spent with them. As the director of a small school, it's very hard to find peers with whom to interact. I had Stan and he had me, but unless we made friends with some of the teachers or parents of students, a bad idea in each case, it was hard to find people with whom to socialize. We were spoiled in Belarus because the embassy staff were so welcoming, not only the American embassy, but the other embassies as well. We were included in many social events — I suspect sometimes because we helped make more of a crowd at a party, but we didn't care. Also we got to know the two special couples who had no children in the school. They became and have remained true friends.

In the other countries where I lived during those years, there were fewer social events. But in Phuket, we could kind of let our hair down a bit — even though I still wanted to make a good impression with QSI management. The few women directors easily bonded at these meetings. Because of its patriarchal attitude, QSI didn't have many women directors so we knew who we were and counted on each other both in Phuket and back at our schools.

Another difficulty about going to Phuket was that we had to leave the school in someone else's hands. Depending on whom we chose to fill this temporary position, we might come back to chaos, a reborn military academy or rampant anarchy. One year a very sweet American woman was working on a song with the kids in music class to present at the holiday concert. The morning after I returned from my week in Phuket, I was catching up on email in my office when I heard the 5 to 10-year-olds — children from Nepal, Pakistan, Wales, Paraguay, Germany, Bosnia, Uganda, Mexico, India, and several other countries, including the United States, singing the Lee Greenwood song, "God Bless the USA" which if you're not familiar, has a line that says: "I'm proud to be an American 'cause at least I know I'm free." After practice I took her aside.

When I told her she could not proceed with that song, she was very disappointed and I am not sure she ever understood why it couldn't work.

On our first trip to Phuket, as we left the country, I saw Jim Gilson, the president of QSI, squeeze his 6'4" frame into a coach seat on the same flight we were on. I was impressed. If the directors had to travel coach, then so did he. Like any organization, QSI has its dysfunction, but I love its ideals.

## THE KIDS IN QSI (OR OTHER INTERNATIONAL SCHOOLS)

How lucky were the students in QSI (and other international) schools? They could make friends with kids from all over the world and learn about cultural differences. Mostly, though, they learned that human beings from planet earth are ultimately the same.

Imagine these students in leadership roles in the future. How accepting they will be of other cultures, how understanding of other languages, and how anywhere in the world they travel, they will likely know somebody.

## HOW I GOT MY PICTURE ON THE WALL AT QSI HEADQUARTERS

I worked in American schools for over 25 years. In all of that time, I never heard about accreditation. Did any of the schools I worked in have to go through accreditation? Maybe they did and I didn't know about it, but overseas, accreditation is a Big Deal.

In QSI, accreditation was pivotal and essential whether you were a teacher, a secretary, an administrator, or a custodian. In an international setting, it's easy to see how important it is for a school to be accredited. That stamp of approval means you're not teaching volleyball 5 hours a day, not requiring the kids to bring the teacher wine coolers in order to pass, or hiring teachers who show episodes of *The Big Bang Theory* to the kids because it's about science. These highly respected governing agencies are non-profit and associated with higher education. If a school gets accredited with one of the main agencies, it's a good sign that it's a well-run, financially sound, competent school with a rigorous curriculum.

If a school was going to go through the accreditation or re-accreditation process, (every 7 years) the year before the accreditation visit was to occur, the school had to form many committees and do a self-study. They used the topics for the study from the accrediting agency and got groups of teachers, other staff, parents and students to study each topic. The school was supposed to make an assessment of each area and set out a plan to improve any weaknesses while celebrating the strengths.

Accreditation is a long and exhaustive process that results in a detailed statistical report and a visit from a team of current educators who measure the written report the school created against what they observe in their three to four day stay. They talk to students, parents, teachers, staff and other stakeholders. They too make recommendations and at the end of their visit, they tell you if you have passed, passed with limitations, or not passed.

Not passing basically means your school is finished and as a director, your career is in jeopardy. Passing with limitations is also not good, but there is hope because you can work toward the topics that are unacceptable and then the team, or someone from the team, will return to make a final judgement. So, the only real option is to pass. The stress that causes, while different for everyone, for me was like sleeping with a bed full of elephants for about nine months.

For a re-accreditation, the school, seven years before, was supposed to have set one to three goals for the school to accomplish. The school would need data to support that they've been working on these goals and the data must have some numbers that demonstrate growth. For example, if one of the goals was to increase student reading levels, the school needed data to measure how well the kids were reading when the goal started and create an environment where reading is a huge focus with activities at every level in every discipline. The school then needed to measure the kids every year to monitor their improvement. Standardized assessments that are given anyway can be used, but there needs to be more: a multi-page action plan in spreadsheet format, graphs, documentation of committee meetings to talk about the goal, the progress on the goal and any changes that might need to be made on the goal or the methods used to achieve it. In fact, at the end of each school year, the school must send a report of all of this information to QSI headquarters. The director can't go home for the summer until this report is received.

All of this paperwork, the committee meetings, and data gathering was a steep learning curve for me in the beginning as I'd never had to do anything like it before. And, as any educator knows, trying to keep that kind of data on a transient population is not only difficult, it's hard to trust the results because your base group is always different. Not to mention a lot of the staff has also turned over. By the time I was in my last years of QSI, I was keeping good data and there were committees for each goal that met at least twice a year. However, when Stan and I took the jobs in Belarus, after we got there, we found out that this was the seventh year of the accreditation cycle so this was the year we would get visited. Did that have anything to do with why the previous director left? Hmm. So we poked around to get some data, (Mr. Sasha the wonderful math teacher had some on his computer), we filled in some of the missing numbers, (forgive us,) and got through the re-accreditation visit with flying colors.

In Brindisi the school was so new, it wasn't accredited yet. No previous report was there to reference, which was a negative, but there were no goals to find data on, so that was a positive. But the American parents with kids in high school were very hot to get the school accredited. So we set out to accomplish that during my second year as director. With only four American teachers in the whole school who were working like Lucille Ball on the candy factory line, it was hard to ask anyone to take the job of accreditation chair so the job fell to me. I always taught at least one class, but I wasn't as tied down as the teachers were. I worked with the QSI accreditation specialist and somehow got the job done. There were deadlines to meet, corrections to make, committees to form,

*One of many committee meetings.*

parents and students to talk to, and teachers, students and parents to survey. Some students and parents needed to fill out almost laughable questions for our many non-English speaking parents — "How can the Visiting Team assist the school in implementing the Plan for Growth and Improvement?" and one night I ate an entire bag of chocolate cookies to stay awake to finish part of the report. These were all part of the stress that is accreditation. I'm not sure I've ever worked that hard on anything in my life in that kind of time crunch, but it got done.

The team that visited us in Brindisi must have been fine, though I only remember the team leader. She wanted tuna on a plate for lunch which you better believe we provided, and at the all-school, all-parent, all-staff meeting when she said we passed, I started to cry.

Because I accomplished this task, my picture is on the wall at QSI headquarters in Ljubljana, Slovenia, or at least it once was because I saw it when I visited there.

A re-accreditation doesn't rate a photo on the wall at headquarters and it isn't quite as difficult as an initial accreditation, but it is hard and all encompassing. During my nine years at QSI I did a reaccreditation for Belarus, an accreditation for Brindisi and a reaccreditation for Armenia. If I'd stayed in one school, I'd have only had one or two, but since I moved around, I'm the lucky winner with three! There is a special place in accreditation heaven for me, I just know it! If they forget about the data we made up, that is.

And tell me, why in two schools to which I transferred, did I enter the same year that re-accreditation was happening? I admit I didn't ask whether either of the two schools was up for reaccreditation that year, so I guess you could put a tiny bit of blame on me but I also didn't walk away the year before it was due. That's where some of the blame needs to be assessed, and recorded and measured and written about and checked and rechecked and stayed up all night over, minus the chocolate cookies.

## A DIRECTOR'S LIFE

As director, my job was pretty all-encompassing. I was always balancing a hundred plates in the air while riding a unicycle in a circle. Plus, there was always a child sitting in my office awaiting his mother/father because, choose one:

- she has a crayon stuck in her ear

- he has had an "accident" and there are no clothes that will fit him, (eventually I learned to keep a stash at the end of the year from the unclaimed lost and found)

- she tossed her lunch all over the bathroom floor

- he has to poop and can't do it at school

- she hurt her head at lunch and now feels dizzy

- the music teacher just called in at noon to say that she can't make it to her 1:00 class because her neck hurts

- the whole computer lab is down and the tech guy is out with a really serious knee injury from the flag football game he played on Sunday and yes, he's young enough for that!

These are all examples of what was going on at the same time I was making sure I had just the right math assignment (because in a small school, the director also teaches at least one class a day) for the kids to master mode, range, and median (I took all of the kids outside and lined them up by age and they still didn't get it.) Plus, some of the parents want their kids to have an hour or two of homework each night while others want none at all. Not to mention, after school there might be an extra-curricular called "Scouts" to run. (Scouts was sort of a misrepresentation of girl and boy scouts but we didn't have enough kids to make it only boys or only girls) The kids will be learning about camping and one of the parts is about knot tying and I couldn't tell the difference between a clove hitch and a bowline, let alone demonstrate it to the kids. Let's hope that one of them will be able to show the others!

Oh, and your written reaccreditation report has to be perfect. All 120 pages of it.

# ARMENIA

Why did I decide to take the job in Armenia? Why didn't I retire after Brindisi? The main reason (get ready, because this is crazy) is because my younger daughter Melissa who had married in the summer of 2011 called me on Mother's day in 2012 with Laura on the line and told me to sit down. I did. She was pregnant. Joy to the world! I was crying, thrilled. I couldn't speak. She would call in a few weeks after she had seen the doctor.

I knew what day her appointment was. I sent her an email. "How did the doctor visit go?" She responded that she would call with the results. Well, how frustrating was that? The next day she called, again with Laura on the line. Was I sitting down? Yes.

It's twins! Oh, my God. Screaming, crying, laughing. How lucky could one grandmother be? Once you have a grand-child, you can never have an unhappy day for the rest of your life. Twins was a whole new category of euphoria. There should be a special word for a grandmother of twins. So this is what my sweet Melissa would be! How fitting!

However, no matter how happy I was, in my twisted thinking about this double blessing, I felt that I couldn't retire. My retirement would be an unhealthy jinx (I told you it was crazy) to the safe gestation and birth of these two babies. I had to continue working for at least one more year so that my total focus wasn't on the babies.

So, with Stan's blessing but warning that he wouldn't be there very much, I accepted the position as school director in Yerevan and off I went.

## ARMENIA

On my first ride through Yerevan, I recognized the Soviet style apartment buildings which looked just like the ones in Minsk, but they seemed older. Small porches on the outsides of the apartments looked as if they would tumble into powder if a saucer of milk was put out for the cat. But the city of Yerevan was full of life. The streets were busy with cafes, and happy looking people moving back and forth in the large, vibrant downtown. I didn't observe any of the Belarusian stoicism.

I was advised to hire Sarkis as a driver and forgo owning and driving a car. That sounded good to me as I patiently wait for self-driving cars. Sarkis was the procurement officer for the school: he bought things for the school on the local market. He asked for $100 per month to drive me wherever I wanted to go whenever I wanted to go there. I actually paid him $300 per month because he was so reliable. If I asked him to pick me up at 7:00 in the morning, I could look out my window at 6:45 and he was already there. Roads in Yerevan were full of potholes, odd speed bumps, some of which were just large pipes not buried deeply enough, or narrow spots in the road that were narrow because of a big rock. It was a great relief for me not to have to drive. Of course the best part about having Sarkis as a driver was Sarkis. He was a wonderfully kind man who patiently explained things about the school, Yerevan, and Armenia though I'm sure he had had to repeat himself many times to previous directors.

Sarkis

## ARMENIAN HISTORY
## (THE SHORT VERSION)

Formerly a part of the Soviet Union, Armenia's population is about 2,000,000. Sarkis said all of those 2,000,000 people are related! *Everybody,* according to him, *is your sister-in-law's uncle's father-in-law.* The language is Armenian which has its own alphabet, and almost all Armenian last names end with either ian or yan like Saroyan, Khachaturian, Kardashian, Yepremian. And every other man's first name is Armen. Armenia is landlocked and seems to be geographically divided into two zones: lush, green mountains which received lots of rain and brown, rolling grasslands (where Yerevan was) which didn't.

Supposedly Armenians descend from Hayk, a great-great grandson of Noah who was grounded on Mt. Ararat. We could see Mt. Ararat from Yerevan but could not visit because it's just over the border in Turkey, and Armenia and Turkey are not friends.

In the first century BC, Armenia stretched from Azerbaijan to Lebanon. It is thought to be the first Christian country. At one time, Muslims arrived and tried to convert Armenians to Islam but the Armenians wouldn't do it — many Armenians left. Over time Armenia got split and carved up. According to Lonely Planet, Armenians believe they share a history with each other because they all come from the same stock.

The only open borders are with Georgia to the north and Iran to the south. On the west is Turkey, which is considered an enemy, and on the east is Azerbaijan where a state of war still exists because each country claims the region called Nagorno Karabakh, currently in the hands of Azerbaijan. Every so often shots are fired between the two sides, but no progress has been made on this issue for a long time. No flights go from Armenia to Azerbaijan because of the fighting over Nagorno Karabakh. Sarkis said "We have no problem at all with Azerbaijan. We are ready to talk to them at any time about our ownership of Nagorno Karabakh. This is Armenian land. As soon as they are ready to give our land back, we will be happy to talk to them. We *want* to talk to them about it."

The fight with Turkey is a result of the genocide of approximately 1.5 million Armenians during and after WWI. The Armenians blame Turkey, and Turkey says that it is being accused of a crime it didn't commit. Some Ottoman Armenians sided with Russia in WWI and the Ottomans in control saw this as disloyal, so Armenians were rounded up and deported. Many were massacred, many were conscripted for forced labor which caused their deaths, and others were led on death marches in the Syrian desert without enough food and water. In the winter, going to school in the dark in Sarkis' car, we could look out and see the lights of a Turkish guard house. We were that close to the Turkish border, but no one could cross it.

In 1918 the Armenians suffered insurmountable obstacles like starving refugees and the Spanish flu. To preserve what was left of ancient Armenia, the Armenians surrendered to the Bolsheviks in 1921. The Soviets took Nagorno Karabakh and Azerbaijan. Many Armenians left and formed diaspora communities in other parts of the world. The largest one I knew about is in Glendale, California, but many others exist in Lebanon, Syria, and France. I once interviewed a person from Glendale for a job opening we had, thinking she was American. She had an Armenian accent!

Armenia prospered under Soviet control but voted for independence in 1991. A war over Nagorno Karabakh exploded then and the Armenian economy went into free fall. A new president got some wealthy diaspora Armenians to come back, and they became today's oligarchs. There was a massacre in 1999 in the national assembly of 8 parliament members. Between then and 2020 things in Armenia were calm for many years but oligarchs still ran things. In 2020 another war over Nagorno Karabakh broke out and was resolved with a cease fire and difficult capitulation by Armenia because they were outgunned by Azerbaijan who received money and arms from Turkey. It's complicated and it's not over!

The rest of the country is very poor. Some research said the average annual income for most Armenians is about $3,720. With only two open borders which are controlled by oligarchs, goods from the West come in at a high price while goods from Russia, though lesser quality, to my thinking, come in at much lower prices. Unfortunately, opening the other borders isn't something the oligarchs want because they like the profits and the control, so even if they could work out their differences with Turkey and Azerbaijan, I don't think the oligarchs would allow those borders to open.

## LIVING AND WORKING IN YEREVAN

QSI International School of Yerevan had been in existence for 17 years when I accepted the director position. The school population was approximately 135 students from ages 3–18 who came from all over the world. However, unlike Minsk or Brindisi, about 1/3 of the students came from Yerevan. The international students largely came from families of diplomats. The local students came from families who owned corporations

*The school with Mt. Ararat in the background.*

in Armenia. There were few private school choices in Yerevan and parents chose QSI because it was the only local option for an American style education. The building was only two years old and still had that new school smell. My office was at least two times larger than the little office I had in Brindisi, and the Minsk school didn't even have a director's office.

The school secretary was Zara, wonderful, efficient, professional, Zara. I still miss her. Ruzanna was the school's accountant. An accountant! What a boon! She helped with the budget and knew what we could and couldn't afford. The maintenance staff consisted of 4 men and the 24/7 security

*Zara and the yearly shipment of education supplies.*

team took care of who could come and go from the building. I felt like I was in the big leagues now.

My apartment was grand, the best I'd had overseas with heated marble floors, a large living area, two bedrooms and 1-1/2 baths. The elevator was strange, but not creaky. When we entered the building from the street level, we had to either go down or up 5 steps to catch the elevator. When Stan would visit, because of his declining mobility, he would use the elevator but first he had to go down some steps accompanied by some frustrated complaining. The building was built on the side of one of the gorges that divide Yerevan, so the view from the living room was dramatic. If I went out the back and down 3 flights of steps carved out of the rock, I could swim in the luxurious swimming pool, a godsend when I had to return to school in dry, hot, mid-August.

The apartment was in a pretty upscale neighborhood. The American ambassador's house was just down the street. Several teacher apartments were also nearby but those weren't as grand as mine. I liked being in the community rather than in a compound as local people could see that I'm just a normal person with family values and a strong work ethic. I liked to make friends with the neighbors.

My across-the-hall neighbors, the Bergums (from Wisconsin!), were the 3rd and 5th grade teachers in the school and just about my age. I broke all the rules by becoming friends with them, but I enjoyed them so much. Plus, Stan didn't come to visit until mid-November and then stayed only a month. He did the same thing in April. The Bergums used Sarkis as a driver, too and we all rode to school together in the mornings. Generally in the afternoon, I stayed at school much later than they did, and Sarkis would make two trips to get us all home. In all of my teaching career I subscribed to the theory that work should stay at work, so I often stayed late in order to not have to bring work home. To my delight, I found a great fitness instructor/personal trainer, beautiful Anush, who would come to the school at 5:00 and work with me three times a week for a very reasonable cost. The second year another teacher, Rachel, joined us. Every Friday Sarkis would take me, the Bergums and Rachel to a restaurant so that we could have a Friday night party (the kind people in their 60s have: dinner out, talk smart, go home and fall asleep on the couch.)

Because the school had existed for so long, my job was mainly to keep things running efficiently in this well-oiled machine and work on the accreditation goals. Of course, I learned *after* I had accepted the job that re-accreditation would have to be accomplished that year.

The first advisory board meeting showed me I was dealing with a different animal than the one in Brindisi. While I was thrilled to have a security team because in Brindisi we had an alarm on the windows and doors, security cameras and a monitoring agency that was off campus, the first question one of the Yerevan board members asked me was what I was planning to do to improve security. Improve? This was a Cadillac of a system. How could it be improved? I learned quickly to say in situations like these: "Let me have your suggestions on that."

The high school was great for a school with a total student body of 140 kids, but not the kind of experience an American teenager would get in a stateside school. The first year I was there, the junior class was 9 kids. That's a great teacher-student ratio in terms of one on one instruction, but for kids who want interaction with lots of friends and many co-curriculars, it was difficult. In one case the parents had been transferred to Yerevan and brought their teenagers only to send them home with mom after the first year because of the perceived lack of co-curriculars. On the other hand, for kids who would not have been the captain of the football team or a member of the debate squad, a school like QSI-Y provided an opportunity to be yearbook editor, student council president and first (and only) string members on the basketball team, playing their hearts out in every game.

Many of the host country nationals at the school had been there for years. Their kids had grown up together and the parents had strong opinions about what the school should be doing and how they should be doing it. So, just like in schools everywhere, being an administrator meant balancing the views of parents with what can be accomplished with budget restrictions, curriculum demands and the needs of students and staff.

Lots of the students traveled to school with drivers. The drivers, well known to our security staff and therefore allowed in the building, were touchingly caring with their little charges. They would park in the parking lot and carry the student's backpack while holding the child's hand and walk them to their classroom, helping them organize what needed to stay in the backpack and what needed to be given to the teacher. The younger kids treated their drivers like uncles and looked lovingly up at them while walking into and out of the building. One older girl was way too cool for this type of behavior and strutted ahead of her driver as he carried her backpack to her locker.

The previous technology manager for the school had been there for about ten years. He had married an Armenian woman and was a key figure in the school. Unfortunately, for the school, he got a job at QSI headquarters and had hired a new tech guy to replace himself. Other people were trying to fill in the gaps left by the previous tech manager, but since no one could do things as well as he could, many of those tasks fell to me to complete (not my strong suit) or pass to others. I was open-minded about the new tech guy for a few months, but eventually it was clear he was in over his head.

I had met a young Iranian man who looked like he could fit the bill as technology manager and I was surreptitiously ready with him if/when the tech guy would quit/get fired/get non renewed for the next year. In April, just days before the school was to begin its all-computerized academic achievement assessment, the tech guy quit. So I had to deploy the Iranian gentleman, Mr. Mostafa, who came in and I think pretty much slept at school for about a month. With the help of the tech manager from Tbilisi, Georgia (the country) he got everything going. In two weeks we started the computerized achievement assessment and he had almost everything else figured out soon after that. What a godsend! We're still friends. I love the way he pronounces the word, stuff. EHSTUFF. "We put this ehstuff over here."

## Interesting Facts/Observations about Armenia

- Apricots are a huge, extremely important crop in Armenia

- Lots of brandy is made in Armenia — the older the better (and more expensive.) Anyone can go to the factory, tour the operation, and have a tasting.

- Cars are converted to run on natural gas (it takes about 15 minutes to fill up the tank and everyone leaves the car in case of explosion — yes, really)

- If you suffer from arthritis, Armenia is a good place to be. My experience was that I felt no arthritis the whole time I was there. Was it the low humidity? The altitude?

- Dental tourism — Many people travel to Armenia to have all kinds of dental work done. It's 1/4 the price you would pay in America, and the results are perfect.

- Vernissage — This is a wonderful local art market — carpets, paintings, pottery, wood products, needlework, jewelry, flea market of Soviet artifacts.

- An orthodox Christian church service in Armenia can go on for a long time but it appears acceptable for people to move fluidly in and out. Beautiful, haunting chants are sung by the priests, but it's a stand-up service as there are no pews. Armenian priests have the option of marrying or not. (As a non-catholic, I can say, How sensible!) The unmarried priests wear a hood to differentiate themselves from the married ones.

- Example of oligarchs running everything — Carrefour, a French store similar to our Target, was planning to come into a local mall. We were all looking forward to this; however, one of the local oligarchs opened a similar store in the same mall and Carrefour had to change its plans and move to another mall far away, and its grand opening was delayed by many months.

- Couch surfing is a thing. A person can register as having space in their home or flat and travelers contact them to see if they can stay for a few nights (for free).

## WHAT TO SEE IN ARMENIA

Armenia is now considered to be a top travel destination. Here's why:

Armenia is the home of many centuries old sacred monasteries which demonstrate Armenia's historic support of Christian monks. Each site has its own charms and is within an hour or two of Yerevan. There is a restaurant next to a small river on the way to Dilijan which offers, instead of a large dining room, only little cabins in which to eat. A waitress comes to take your order and serves the food. Your table is the only one in the cabin. It feels like a very private indoor picnic but with fresh green salads, barbequed pork chops and many other irresistible dishes delivered by friendly waitresses.

Before entering the fourth century Geghard Monastery (a UNESCO World Heritage Site), visitors can purchase round loaves of home baked sweet breads with walnuts and cinnamon sold by vendors, each one with its own table and canopy. I've never tasted anything like it, so delicious. After walking through the beautiful Geghard Monastery visitors can walk outside to the surrounding area and see the tiny caves where monks lived. The caves are barely large enough for a human form. There is no door, no conveniences or comforts — only

*Geghard Monastery*

*Four-year-old Theodore in a Monk's cave.*

a rocky cavity. How strong their faith must have been to survive in such hardship.

About three hours from the city, very close to the Iranian border, the Wings of Tatev is a cable car ride across a deep gorge to a still active monastery. I once observed a woman who carried a live chicken in a tote bag on the ride to the monastery. On the ride back there was blood in the bag and the chicken's head was not where it was supposed to be. If you ever visit there, stay in the Mirhav Hotel in Goris. Its simple but beautifully rustic rooms are reminiscent of a caravansary and in my top ten list of best hotels in the world, not for its luxury but its simplicity.

Lake Sevan is a large inland lake more than one mile above sea level. It is 480 square miles in area and 45 miles long. Gorgeous. I thought I was back in Wisconsin.

The Temple of Garni from the first century AD is an example of Greco-Roman architecture celebrating the sun god, Mihr.

An unmarried priest.

Mirhav Hotel.

When visiting there I heard my first duduk music, (a double reed woodwind made of apricot wood) and knew that I would need to get some recordings so haunting was the sound. A picture of the Temple of Garni is featured on Armenian money.

The two story, Noravank Monastery of the 13th century is unique because of its cantilevered stairway on the outside of the building. Picture a New York city apartment fire escape with steps only about 12 inches wide affixed only to the wall of the building with no railing. Only the faithful make it to the second story and then back down again! Crafted out of the surrounding red cliffs, the monastery is full of carved relief sculptures inside and out.

### SKIING IN THE CAR

One time Sarkis had to take me downtown in the middle of the day in early December for school business. It had snowed that morning just enough to make the roads a little wet, and as Sarkis slowly inched down one of the steep gorges to get to the other side of town, he touched the brakes but the car kept moving. About 50 feet ahead, the road turned sharply left onto a bridge over the deep ravine, but Sarkis' car wasn't responding to the brakes, the steering wheel, or downshifting. We were only going about 15 mph but headed straight into a parked van which we would t-bone if we couldn't either stop or turn, then we'd be headed down into the gorge. Slowly, the car was sliding down that steep hill. Due to the slow speed, we weren't in terrible danger, unless we missed the bridge and went into the ravine, but it was going to be a messy accident right into the side of the big new van. Suddenly, about 10 feet from the van, our tires connected with the pavement that was no longer frozen and Sarkis was able to make the sharp turn onto the bridge over the steep ravine. Yikes! I trusted him with my life and that darling man came through.

*Noravank Monastery.*

## TAKING THE SUBWAY IN YEREVAN

As much as I enjoyed being taken places in Sarkis' car, I also loved my independence. I learned where the bakery, the out-door fresh market, and a nearby grocery store were, got a pull-behind shopping cart and was able to take care of my marketing independently. Not far from the market area was a subway stop. Lucky for me it was the last stop of the line (altogether I think there were two lines) so every time I used it I knew where to get off! Simultaneously, I also got on to an empty car so I always had a seat.

Downtown Yerevan was fun to visit. A large circle was the geographic center of the city and contained a Marriott Hotel (where an English speaking hair stylist, from Glendale(!) worked, thank you, Gina) and a person could get a pretty standard American type lunch if that's what he/she was craving. Many, many other restaurants downtown offered all manner of food styles. Actually it wasn't easy to find typical Armenian food! A nearby pedestrian mall was also fun to walk down. Lots of expensive shops, outdoor cafes, and foot traffic made for a vibrant city life. I always stopped in the Segafredo coffee shop just like the ones in Italy for a cappuccino decaffeinato. I had arranged with an Armenian woman to teach me to speak Armenian and I met her downtown on weekends. Thankfully she was a patient teacher because Armenian didn't come naturally to me. We had a good time anyway. Her husband was a priest.

The entrance to the subway was the biggest excitement of a downtown visit. Arriving at the platform we could see the turnstile and the head of the long escalator going down. The first step was the most exciting. The belt was so fast that I had to grab the black rubber railing with a good grip so that I wouldn't go airborne when the first step took its little upward bump. Then I went down, down, down, so quickly that I wished there could have been another hand railing (or a seat belt!) on the other side that I could reach. It was a cheap thrill that Disney could use in one of its theme parks! At the bottom I would have to step off quickly and look for my train. Once on the train the ride was much like any other subway, but the stops were all in Armenian in the Armenian alphabet. Instead of learning what the stop for downtown was, I simply counted the stops. Mine was number three. One time I was on the subway headed for downtown when Stan called. Imagine, me in the subway in

Armenia talking to Stan in Florida. He was calling to tell me some disappointing news. Then the phone cut out. Oh God. What disappointing news? My first thought was about the babies. I called him back. No connection. Again and again. By then I had lost count of my stops. I got off at the next stop. I had no idea where I was. I remembered my Armenian teacher telling me if I ever got lost, I could ask anyone where the opera, the most well known building in Yerevan, was. So I started to ask people, Opera? (Oh PAIR uh) Opera? People pointed and I'd walk. Meanwhile I tried to reconnect with Stan. Finally I did. He was disappointed because something he had ordered hadn't arrived. And it was a long weekend so he wouldn't get his order for another three days. AAARGH! Finally I found the Opera and continued on with my trip.

## GOOD OLD SOVIET LIFE

Before the dissolution of the USSR, Armenia, like Belarus, had been under Soviet rule for decades. People over 30 remembered the days of the Soviets and through the lens of history and reminisced fondly for that time. One of the Russian language teachers said, "There wasn't so much choice as there is now. If your mother told you to go get some bread, you went to get bread. There was only bread, one kind. The government gave you an apartment when you got married. You didn't have to pay for housing at all. Now apartments cost a lot of money." People had to line up for everything, but they enjoyed the sociability of standing in line. When our school secretary, Zara, talked about the years immediately after the Soviets left, a shadow crossed her face and she was back in her childhood when there was no electricity, no heat and little food: the Soviets had dismantled the electric plant and the central boiler as well as the vehicles and system that transported food into and around the city. Sarkis had small children at the time. He left Armenia for Moscow to work in a brandy factory where he was a chemist. He sent money home so that his children could eat. Every Armenian I talked to had similar feelings about those years right after 1991. The vacuum that the Soviets left took years to fill. The Armenians wouldn't go back to Soviet times if given the chance, but they are definitely not happy with what they have now in their oligarchy.

I once visited a zoo in Yerevan. A German woman was the director there and she described the conditions in the zoo when she got there a few years after the Soviets left. The animals that were still in the zoo were malnourished and sick. The cages were caked thick with excrement because no one had the authority/wherewithal/energy/money to take care of the animals. The German woman came in through an international grant to get the zoo functioning again and it looked as if she had been successful. They had some exotic animals there now that had been "donated" by local oligarchs. These oligarchs would build a beautiful new house and want to surround themselves with exotic pets. Eventually the pets got too hard to handle so they "donated" them to the zoo.

Armenians and Belarusians both talked positively about the educational system the Soviets had in place. It was strict and demanding, but many of the people had advanced degrees and were highly qualified for the jobs they held. Unfortunately those jobs no longer existed after the Soviets left. So, now, these highly educated people were no longer able to provide for their families.

## IT'S TWINS
Of course I kept in frequent communication with Melissa who was getting bigger by the day. The babies kept growing and had good weights according to the doctor. Fingers crossed, she would make it to her C-section delivery date, December 12, 2012. Yes, they chose it because it would be 12/12/12.

Finally December 12 came without any early labor, water breaking, or other complications. Melissa's husband Rick knew exactly how to contact me by phone because we had practiced several times. (I didn't want to repeat the experience I'd had with Jamie's surgery.) I walked around that day on twinkle toes and swallowed air that had lumps in it. I knew about all of the possible complications/catastrophes/fluke accidents that could happen but I remained optimistic. How I swam through that day, I do not remember. With the time difference, I knew I should expect a call sometime after 7:00 p.m. my time. About 7:20 the call came. Both babies, girls, were doing fine and mother was resting. I must have let out a hot air balloon worth of air before I cried and cried. Their weights were both around 5 pounds, great for twins, and there was already a picture posted on email. Oh, joyous, joy. The relief was immense and they were gorgeous. In 10 minutes I went from being a grandmother of 2 to a grandmother of 4. Just like the births of my daughters and my two grandsons, it would have been impossible to have a happier moment in my life.

*Adorable Emma and Maddie.*

## PATRIARCHY

When I arrived in Yerevan in 2012, the school had been open since 1995 and I was the first woman director. I'd heard from several sources that QSI Yerevan might not be ready for a woman director. After all, Armenia was a highly patriarchal culture and it was possible that the Armenian men were not quite ready to take direction from a woman. In fact, Sarkis, despite paying me complete and total respect, used to call women drivers, "A monkey with a bomb." I teased him about that and he quit saying it in my presence, while I'm pretty sure he still believed it, he treated me with the utmost respect. I enjoyed him and his friendship and knew that he would be there for me, no matter what.

So I wondered how I would do with the many Armenian men who were on staff at QSI Yerevan. The maintenance staff, several teachers, and the entire security staff were men. The male American teachers (all but one!) were used to dealing with women in leadership roles, so I wasn't concerned about them. I learned later that the male Armenian staff were also concerned that they wouldn't get along with a woman.

Contrary to what I'd been told, I enjoyed the Armenian men on the staff immensely. They seemed to look at me as their grandmother or mother and I tried to always treat them with respect, as I would with any colleague. At every meeting I had with the four men on the maintenance staff I asked them what they needed to make their jobs and the school easier/ better. They wanted a better way to keep people from slipping on the outside staircase when it snowed. They wanted better landscaping in the front of the building — a previous kitchen worker had started a garden that got straggly and unkempt looking after she left the school due to health concerns. They wanted the bad smell from the open sewer next to the school property to be fixed. They wanted a safer surface for the playground. One man wanted to plant four fruit trees along the property line so that the children could watch how the trees bud, flower and produce fruit. I worked with the regional supervisor to get all of these things accomplished. Over the first few months, my respect and admiration for those four hard-working, devoted men only grew larger and I was genuine in praise of their accomplishments. I was even invited to the home of one of these men who was celebrating a milestone birthday. When I left Armenia, it was those four men, Zara, plus my driver, Sarkis, that I was the saddest to leave.

I also had a soft spot in my heart for the security guards. Long ago they had hammered out a 24/7 schedule for themselves, with the help of a previous director, that worked efficiently. I told them that schedule worked well for me, too and I admired their self-sufficiency. I often worked on Saturdays and interacted with whomever was on duty. If I asked for anything — anything, they would try to provide it. One Monday they quietly reported to me that over the weekend one of them had seen a scorpion on the concrete patio next to the building in the back. The guard took a photo of the scorpion and then smashed it, but good with a shovel. The head of security showed me the photo and advised me not to tell anyone about this scorpion. These creatures are highly poisonous and, well, really, did we want everyone to know we had found one on our property? No, we didn't! That scorpion was a little secret between the security team and me.

I so liked those gentlemen and came to depend on them for many things. They were on top of everything that was happening in the school and out. If anything fishy happened, they always came to me to report it and see what they needed to do. Only one strange thing happened.

One of the security guards, named Armen, was kind of a weak link in this chain. He didn't like having to shovel snow, an unpopular but necessary task for the security team who were at the school in the wee hours of the morning when it was likely to snow and before our four maintenance guys could get there to clear the driveway, parking lot and sidewalks. This guard carried himself in a very self-important way and didn't quite fit in with the other security guards who were so low key and without ego.

One morning apparently the head of security spoke to this guard and told him in a pleasant but assertive way that he would need to shovel the front walk because it was snowing and the maintenance crew wouldn't be arriving for another half hour. Apparently Armen hauled off and punched the head of security in the cheek. Armen said he was through with shoveling snow, through with this job, and through with the head of security. He said, "Goodbye," got in his car and drove off. The poor head-of-security was a very gentle man who was stunned by this behavior, along with everyone else. No one could understand why Armen would behave in this way. He would be sorry because this was the best paying security job available in Yerevan and what nerve he had to punch the head of security. Later we learned that he already had another job, this time with the Marriott Hotel. I'm sure he used the fact that he was working for the international school to help him get the job, and would be starting on Monday. The pay was probably comparable, but the security team was happy to see the back of him and his bad attitude.

Mr. Armen, the math teacher had quite a reputation. I heard about him long before I met him. He tolerated no unfinished homework, no tardiness or coming to class without the textbook, but had endless patience to explain difficult concepts in algebra II, geometry and calculus. The kids had immense respect for him. I'm not sure he was ever really thrilled that he had a female supervisor, but he always treated me with dignity. I liked him, approached him with respect, asked for his advice and often implemented ideas he shared. He was kinder than my seventh grade math teacher who used to say, "The only way to kill time is to work it to death."

*The Bergums and Mr. Armen.*

## BASKETBALL TOURNAMENT

Even though our whole high school from 9th to 12th grades contained about 25 kids, our physical education teacher found a way to make a boys' basketball team. In good weather (and that was most of the time other than a few weeks during the winter) the boys were out playing basketball. Every. Single. Day.

Because the school was new, a regulation size, concrete basketball court lay right below the extended back "porch" of the school. The older kids had lunch a little later than the elementary kids so the whole court was available for them to play during lunch. The basketball games were fun to watch. The kids played hard but with excellent sportsmanship.

When we learned that there would be a basketball tournament in Tbilisi, Georgia (about a five-hour drive from Yerevan), I had no reservations about letting our beautiful team go play. This meant that the boys were practicing every possible moment and the coach scheduled extra practices. The team had to be ready because we had only six players. Only one person could be off the court at one time. So the whole team had to be ready to play their hearts out.

The entire school gathered for a Pep Rally complete with cheerleaders (where did they find those pom pons?) and we all shared our best wishes for them. I gave a really short speech in which I repeated what I had learned from the football coach at Appleton West so many years before: "If you lose, be quiet. If you win, be even more quiet."

I heard the tournament went well. They didn't win but they did play their hearts out and slept all the way home. We were all immensely proud.

### LIVING IN AN OLIGARCHY

If living in Belarus didn't teach me everything there was to learn about living in an oligarchy, an incident in Armenia re-convinced me that oligarchies are not a good place to live unless you are an oligarch.

In early June on a beautiful, warm Saturday night, my windows were open. I headed to bed around 11 p.m. Everything was fine until I woke up to some very loud noises on the street. Rock and roll music was pouring out of what had to be some concert hall grade speakers somewhere very near my apartment. I looked at the clock: midnight. I got up and looked out the bedroom window. Two houses down on the other side of the street, people were milling outside. I'm not usually bothered by noise, reasonable noise, during sleep. In fact, when I first go to sleep, I usually sleep so deeply that if I wake up, I'm quite disoriented. *Where am I? Why did I wake up? I don't need to go to the bathroom, do I? Yes.* Well, this time, after I went to the bathroom, I closed the bedroom window and tried to go back to sleep again. Another pillow on my head, a finger in my ear, nothing dulled the noise enough for me to go back to sleep.

After an hour or so, I decided that the noise wasn't going to stop. I was shocked that no one called the police to shut down this obnoxious party. Imagine a situation like this in a high end Wisconsin neighborhood. In 30 minutes the noise would stop and somebody might have been put into a police car. This rock concert level of noise had to have been affecting the other houses around. *When will somebody make it stop?* As a guest in a foreign country, not to mention the director of the international school, it wasn't my low-profile place to try to get the music stopped.

Finally, I grabbed my pillow and a light cover and headed to the living room which was on the other side of the apartment. I stayed there all night intermittently reading, watching TV, doing crossword puzzles and trying again and again to sleep. Picture me 50 feet from the stage of a rock concert. It didn't matter how I tried to insulate myself, I couldn't escape the thumping beat of the music.

About 7:30 in the morning, the music finally stopped. The sun was up and I headed back to bed, but I could still hear random noises from the party goers, not to mention even with my sleep mask, I couldn't block out the bright, bright daylight of the risen sun. Basically, I got up not happy that I had lost a night of sleep.

At school on Monday, I asked what had been going on. It seems that a very highly placed government official lived in that house and his daughter had gotten married that day. No ordinary citizen would have confronted anyone at the party and if anyone had called the police, they wouldn't have come.

Another oligarchy "problem" had to do with our school's location. The Yerevan school was set about 100 yards off of the main highway leading in and out of town. Only one road led directly from that highway to the school. Shortly before the school opened, the regional supervisor learned that the convenient road from the main highway to the school belonged not to the government as was thought, but instead to an oligarch who now demanded a huge sum of money for the school to be able to use "his" road. When the school refused to comply, the oligarch came in with heavy equipment and blocked the road with dirt, old vehicles, and large chunks of concrete. So the buses, parents, teachers and visitors to the school had to take one of two other routes to get to the school. One route was across some land, not the school's, that was so full of moguls and potholes, the ride felt like a bucking bronco and no one could do it without a 4-wheel-drive vehicle. The other route was a full 5 miles longer way out and around adding a good ten minutes to what should have been a two minute ride.

While I was there, I was told that the U.S. Embassy was working on this problem; it was making its way through the courts, and I wasn't to worry about it. I hope they have resolved this situation.

## THE GENOCIDE

I read about the genocide long before I set foot in Armenia.

This catastrophic event which killed over a million people affected every family in Armenia. It's important to remember that Armenians believe that they are all related and the people responsible for the genocide have neither admitted that it happened nor taken ownership of it. The Armenians want recognition not only by Turkey, but also the rest of the world; they want restitution; and they want an apology. April 24 is Remembrance Day in Armenia, a public holiday to commemorate the Armenians who died during the Genocide.

Over the last 100 years, 31 countries have recognized the Armenian Genocide: for example, Brazil, Canada, France, Germany, Italy and Russia but not the United States. Turkey, where I lived, as you remember, is not looking back with guilt at this incident that was committed by their ancestors. It seems as far as they are concerned, if this catastrophe occurred, it was perpetrated by someone else. My personal opinion is that Turkey will not change its mind in my grand-children's lifetimes. I'm glad the Armenians keep working on the recognition of the genocide.

## AZNIV'S (AAHZ NUH'S) WEDDING
The young Armenian woman who taught German at our school had had a long distance relationship with an Armenian man in Germany for years. During my stay in Armenia this relationship bloomed from afar and during the second year resulted in a wedding. Azniv was good friends with the Bergums and due to their large and beautiful apartment (like mine) Azniv asked the Bergums if she and her family could come to their apartment for the pre-wedding gathering and dressing in her long white American style wedding gown. Of course this was OK with the Bergums who served as a kind of surrogate family for Azniv. Her father had died many years ago. So that's where the wedding party started. Sarkis, who was also a friend of Azniv drove lots of us to the church where Azniv and her family took photos outside and at the appropriate time entered the church quite informally. Unlike many churches I had seen in Armenia, this church had pews

so we all sat while the priest said some words over the couple. Then it was over. More photos were taken and we all went to a large hall with about 20 tables each set with an array of bottles from sprite to vodka and some hors d'oeuvres, cold sliced meats, and fruit. Traditional Armenian music blasted from large speakers. Lots of people danced as more food came from the kitchen, typical khorovats (KHOR o vahts), grilled pork with potatoes.

Sarkis had brought his daughter Christina, and between dances with her made many toasts to the bride and groom, to the lovely spread of food and drink on the tables, to the beautiful family the bride came from, and to the wonderful friends who had gathered to give her a good send off to what would be her move to Germany. This is where I learned to appreciate a drink that Sarkis was enjoying. Because he was driving, he poured sparkling water on ice and squeezed half of a lemon into his glass. He did the same for me because I had to work later. It was delicious, refreshing, and so simple. I still love it. Everyone was so pleased for Azniv and her new husband who were positively glowing.

## SHOULD I STAY OR SHOULD I GO?
I truly loved living and working overseas, but my family was growing. I had always said that I would continue to work until Theodore was 3. Well, in 2014, he was almost 6. Once the twins were safely delivered, I knew that my time was running out. In some ways I was ready to leave Armenia at the end of the first year, but since the school had lived through the previous director's departure after one year, I didn't feel right leaving after one year too. So I stayed for a second year knowing it would be my last. Stan's health was also on a downward slant. The first time I saw the regional supervisor that second fall, I told him I would be leaving at the end of

that school year. I was comfortable with that decision and still feel it was the right thing to do. I like my life in retirement, but there's that little wheel spinning inside of me that thinks I would drop everything to go back! Then I think about re-accreditation and my adorable grandchildren and that wheel jerks to a stop!

# TWELVE YEARS OVERSEAS

My 12 years overseas were a journey outside of the world I had made for myself. These years gave me new ways to look at the larger world, taught me the truest sense of myself, and helped me see how I would move forward into the last chapters of my life. I met and formed relationships with people I cherish. I saw so much more of the world than I would have had I not taken this opportunity. I learned about other cultures and how other people view the world. What a gift.

I can lose myself in the words and letters of this story which surround and envelop me, a quilt of words flowing around me in waves of typeface. I am happy here, embraced by my memories. I was not perfect but parts of me are very good, and I was loved by a man who could see past my imperfections as I could see past his.

In an infinite universe, Stan grounded me. Like Marc Chagall's "The Promenade," the painting of a man holding the hand of a woman who is floating ever upward, Stan was the tether that kept me from careening through the atmosphere willy nilly, unhinged and loose. I am so grateful that he encouraged me and helped me step into this new way of being and seeing. I see everything differently now. *I am different now.*

# APPENDIX

—·»〉〈«·—

## ON RETURNING TO THE U.S.

*Noise*
Are we so bored or devoid of all thought that outside sources have to fill every moment of our lives with noise? Inescapable televisions in airports, canned music in elevators, music in grocery stores. Is there some unspoken rule in America that silence is unacceptable? I felt assaulted by the constant noise. Silence had to be searched for and treasured. Little TVs at the gas pumps?

*Kale*
Somewhere during the 12 years I was elsewhere, kale became the top food in America. Before I went, few people even knew what kale looked like nor how vile it tasted. Suddenly every recipe, every salad, every menu contained rubbery, tough, grainy kale. What next, hay?

*Public prayer*
Especially in the years immediately following 9/11, I noticed people openly, devoutly, fervently praying before meals in restaurants. I didn't remember as much of this behavior prior

to that horrible tragedy. Because I wasn't in America when 9/11 occurred, I didn't experience the shared horror of that day and the subsequent days and weeks of mutual caring and support. My experience was equally horrible but it was different.

### The Beauty of Barack

Barack Obama became President when I was in Italy. I was so happy on his Inauguration Day that I found the station that was airing the ceremony and turned up the volume to its max — the hell with the neighbors. Finally, after the humiliating years of George Bush, I was proud of my country again. To me Bush was the worst president since Nixon. He and his team disrupted the peace in the Middle East that is still unresolved. (Little did I know how 2016 would change my opinion that Bush was the worst president.) Returning to America I noticed that people of color seemed to have more confidence and assertiveness. Obama's becoming president still makes me happy.

### Nobody wants to hear about it

When I came back, I knew that the people who are my friends and who would become my friends, wouldn't be interested in the last 12 years of my life. I could share some of my experiences, but generally, the people I was living near hadn't done anything like what I had done and I knew that if I wanted friendships, and I did, I'd have to get interested in what they had been doing for the last 12 years. I hope I succeeded and in the years since, I've gained lots of shared experiences with so many wonderful people.

### Lucky Me

Two years after I returned to the U.S. I had another happiest day of my life when my daughter Melissa gave birth to

Benjamin. Five grandchildren! Truly they are my greatest gifts. This book is for them, their grandchildren's grandchildren and on and on. My message to them is: this is what your crazy ass Grama did with 12 years of her life! I love you!

*Peek-a-boo!*

## THINGS I'VE LEARNED ABOUT TRAVEL:

### Lounges

For a short time we had enough frequent flier miles to be able to use the Lufthansa special airport lounges. You could only use them if you were traveling that day on Lufthansa, but for someone who has endured the crowded gate areas of many airports, it was like being plucked from a Where's Waldo picture and put down under a palm tree at the beach with a cold beer in my hand. Quiet, coffee, pastries and comfy chairs were a glimpse of how the other 1% travels. I'm supposed to be excited about boarding first? I say, board last. *We're going to be on that plane for a long time, so stay away as long as we can.* Soon enough the guy in the seat ahead will slam his seat back into my nose and it will stay that way for the entire flight. Let's make the time we have to endure that as short as possible.

### Packing light

When traveling for less than a year, it's wise to go with the least possible amount of belongings. Here are my tips:

- Save small bottles to put cosmetics in. I compress the few that I take into the smallest possible containers.

- Take clothes that are in the "give away" pile and leave them in hotel rooms when they are dirty.

- All clothes need to be able to interchange with each other. Only solid colors.

- One or two pairs of long pants, depending on what the weather will be.

- One pair of capris if it's going to be warm enough.

- One pair of shorts if you're going somewhere that they are acceptable (surprisingly few places actually are).

- One long sleeved shirt,

- One short sleeved shirt.

- One fleece, jacket, or sweatshirt for cool weather or cool hotel rooms.

- One nightgown (or whatever you like to sleep in that doesn't take up much space or weight.)

- Lots of undies and socks. (4 to 5 pairs) Generally the longer I'm on a trip, the dirtier my clothes get, but I draw the line at undies and socks. Wash in the hotel sink or find a laundromat.

- Nothing I bring needs ironing.

- Personally I don't like those travel shirts that can be purchased at places like Travelsmith. No one in Europe wears those except tourists. Although I'm not worried about being looked at as a tourist (that's what I am) I try to mask it just a little.

- Nobody but you knows that you're wearing the same clothes every day, so get over yourself. You, plus anyone who has to carry your bag, will appreciate your economy in packing.

- Differentiate your luggage with something: duct tape, yellow yarn, words written in sharpie. Always take a photo of any luggage you check. For the first two years I lived in Brindisi, my luggage never arrived when I did. It always got there, but not at the right time. When Stan and I traveled together, one of us would wait at the baggage carousel and the other would get in the line for lost luggage. It helped to have a photo of the missing bag/s.

- On longer flights put your meds, a little make up kit, something to sleep in and clean underwear in your carry on. You'll be glad you did if you get stuck somewhere.

- Also, don't bring anything you can't afford to lose. (See Chapter 4 about the irreplaceable bracelet.)

If you're moving to a country, it's still a good idea to take the least possible amount of stuff with you. Yes, there are some things you can't get along without, but think small. Pack things in ziplock bags because when you get to your destination, the bags are helpful.

## HAPPY TV
Like most people who were raised during the 50s, I watched television in my childhood. My grandparents had a TV before we did, a wooden box bigger than a dorm sized refrigerator with a tiny 7x7" screen in black and white. At first I remember there being 2 channels, later 3: NBC, ABC and CBS. TV was more an event than a private pleasure. We all watched the same shows at the same time. That's all there was. During college I don't remember watching any TV. There was a TV in the dorm, but we had to compete with other kids, and life in college was infinitely more interesting than anything on TV.

Even into my adulthood, I still numbly watched all the popular TV shows (commercials and all) until the invention of the VCR. As soon as I could afford a VCR, I had one. What a boon! I could record my favorite shows, watch them later and fast-forward through the commercials. (Oh, God, I still have some of those tapes!) To save money, I would record several shows on one tape. The jumbled up way I had of organizing recorded shows is a window to my unorganized soul. The worst thing would be when my tape would finish before the program ended.

Going to Turkey, we didn't know what to expect regarding TV. Would there be any English speaking channels? It turns out that the TV in our apartment got the marvelous BBC Prime. What a wonderful change from American TV! Almost all shows were sit-coms-some hilariously funny and the dramas had clear beginnings and endings.

The other delight of the BBC shows is that there weren't any commercials. We could watch a whole sit-com for 30 minutes and not have one commercial. It was a new world!

In Kuwait there were a few channels in English but the shows were more like nature shows or instructional shows like how to fix a car. The only program I remember watching there was *Friends* which was good because I had never watched it in the U.S. and there were no commercials.

In Belarus I was busy with Rachmaninoff and the music Vadim had helped me download, but we had a television. I only remember watching two TV events there: the coverage of Hurricane Katrina and a documentary about the importance of laughter. An American woman had suffered terrible life events-the death of her husband, followed by the death of her mother and then being diagnosed with lung cancer all within a month. She decided that the only way to get through this disaster was to laugh. She went to the video store and rented comedies, every day more and more comedies. Six years later she was still cancer free and ascribed her recovery from all of those events to laughter. That show had an impact on me.

In Italy I had a cable channel called "Sky TV." These were shows in Italian, but almost every night they had a movie in English, most of which had Italian themes or Italian heritage actors like Robert DeNiro or Dean Martin. They played one of the Godfather movies every few weeks. What a treat. No commercials. Even when there were commercials, I couldn't understand the words so they just floated over my head while I worked on my puzzles.

The best part of that channel was that on Saturday nights they showed an episode from the week before of Jay Leno and the Tonight Show. That was a real treat. First because there were no commercials and second because there was no better way to keep up with American culture than a late night talk show.

In Armenia I had a TV, but it wasn't even hooked up so the only thing I could do with it was watch DVDs. I had bought a large collection of DVDs from a couple who were going digital and didn't want their big notebook full of whole series of things like Star Wars, Indiana Jones, Rocky, and I Love Lucy. When I wanted to watch TV, I just chose one of those and could watch as much or as little as I wanted. I had also downloaded Downton Abbey on my iPad and watched those early episodes with relish.

Since adulthood, I've always been interested in TV and movie entertainment I call "Happy TV." I don't want any sadness, shootings, husbands leaving their wives, kidnappings, dismemberments and so on. The way I see things is that there is enough reality out there. I don't want to be entertained (?) with it.

By the time I retired and moved back to America, I was pretty much weaned off of TV. At first I would try to sit and watch TV with Stan. That togetherness didn't last long. He could change channels faster than a middle schooler playing Nintendo and he didn't prescribe to the Happy TV doctrine. Anything with a *CSI* or *Law and Order* in the name was fair game for him and I started sewing doll clothes upstairs. Eventually we got two TVs and life was happy again. I learned how to use a DVR and paid the extra price to have one in each house. I could watch what I wanted and he could do the same. Now I record everything I want to watch. All Happy TV.

## MY COMMENTS AT MY LAST QSI ADMINISTRATORS' MEETING 2013

Here are my parting comments at my last administrators' conference in Phuket:

"This is my ninth and last year with QSI. I'll try retirement again. Hopefully the third time will be the charm! I can no longer be this far away for so long from my four grandchildren and other family members who need me.

Thank you, Mike, for hiring my husband and I after a job interview in a Perkins restaurant in Eau Claire, Wisconsin (I knew this was my kind of organization.)

Thank you, Tracie, for your encouragement and long hours on my three accreditation and re-accreditation efforts.

Thank you, Jim, Duane, Margery and Margaret for starting the organization and keeping it going.

Thank you to the regional supervisors I worked with:

- Scott for arm-wrestling with a few choice situations
- Merry for your strong leadership

- Steve for talking me down from the ledges during my first year in Brindisi

And thanks to all of you!

I won't be here next year, but I am really hoping that the vacancy I leave behind will be filled by a woman.

"Women continue to be significantly underrepresented in the most senior leadership positions in the U.S.," according to Deborah Gillis CEO of Catalyst, a global organization for promoting women in top leadership positions.

"Addressing complex challenges of the 21st century requires diversity of thought, experience and perspective." From Dean Lynn Gangone of Colorado Women's College.

How can we meet those challenges when 80% of the leaders have the same thought, experience and perspective?

Women have a strong emotional IQ. They are intuitive and are skillful in dealing with people. In QSI we have a huge pool of well-trained, intelligent, hard-working women who are mindful of how others perceive them.

May I use this bully pulpit to ask you (fellow administrators) to nurture and nourish the women with whom you work? Mentor and encourage them to understand that they have the skills to be good and even great leaders.

# The Brindisi Breeze

QSI International
School of Brindisi

*October 14, 2011*

It's been a busy week at QSI International School of Brindisi. A wall was built last weekend that created two classrooms instead of one in room 8. A huge thank you goes to Mr. Charles and his classes as they adjusted to a smaller space. Thanks to Mr. Cristiano for the efficient way the wall was built and completed over the weekend. This weekend the doors will be re-configured and in place by Monday morning. Ms. Gianna started teaching English lessons after school for some local students.

The 10-11 year old class presented a readers' theater of *Tonfucius* at the Monday morning. *Tonfucius* is a very old and wise narrator (at left) who weighs a ton and teaches us what the world would be like if people didn't behave according to the QSI Success Orientations.

*Brindisi Breeze October 14, 2011..*

# ACKNOWLEDGEMENTS

Thank you to the many people all over the world I have been lucky enough to call friends. You know who you are. Your gifts of friendship fill me with love and sustain me through the good times and bad.

Thank you Deb. W for giving me the title to the section on accreditation. Thank you Bernie Mitchell for giving me the "crazy ass Grandma" words to describe what I did.

Thank you, Mary Lange for helping me through my toughest chapter.

Thank you, Amy Phimister for reading this book as it was in progress. Your confidence in my work helped me move forward.

Thank you Pat Garrett for advice on publishing.

Thank you to Kristine Bennett, Dr. Steve Christensen and Dr. Bernie Mitchell for reading my work and making lovely and helpful comments. This book is better because of your help.

Without my friend Carol Ekkens Siporin, I might not have kept the dream alive to write a book. We two set up studios in our parents' basements and pursued our arts as junior high students. That Carol has been painting significant works of art most of her adult life has inspired me to achieve my dream. Here is my book, finally at 73! Thank you, my friend.

While I was overseas, my sister Judy Bialk, shouldered the responsibility of caring for our mother. Every time I asked Judy if it was time for me to come back and help out, she unequivocally told me, "Absolutely not, keep doing what you're doing," though it was at a great cost to her. Because of her, I was able to do this.

I couldn't be prouder of my two daughters and their lovely husbands. For several years I was far away and they managed without me. With their encouragement, technical and writing support, I have been able to accomplish this work.

Five of the world's most wonderful people have filled my life with joy. I adore them and they are all my favorite grandchildren. It's because of them and the children who will come after them that I have written this book. I love you all with everything I have: Theodore, Jamie, Maddie, Emma and Ben.

My editor, publisher, and friend Ann Heyse helped me know which of my writing projects to go for. She got intimately involved with this one and made it infinitely better. No words can adequately thank her for her help.

Stan, wherever you are, thank you for helping me get to live overseas. It was a peak experience full of love, happiness and growth. You helped make my dream come true.